THE RICH TIDE

THE RICH TIDE

TIDE

Men, Women, Ideas and
their Transatlantic Impact

DAVID FROST
and
MICHAEL SHEA

COLLINS
8 Grafton Street, London W1
1986

William Collins Sons & Co. Ltd
London · Glasgow · Sydney · Auckland
Toronto · Johannesburg

British Library Cataloguing in Publication Data

Frost, David
The rich tide: men, women, ideas and their
transatlantic impact.
1. Great Britain – Relations – United States
2. United States – Relations – Great Britain
I. Title   II. Shea, Michael
303.4'8241'073   E183.8.G7

ISBN 0-00-217427-8

Photoset in Linotron Meridien by
Rowland Phototypesetting Ltd
Bury St Edmunds, Suffolk
Made and printed in Great Britain by
William Collins Sons & Co. Ltd, Glasgow

To Carina & Mona

Contents

ACKNOWLEDGEMENTS

The authors would particularly like to thank all the people who so generously gave of their time and exclusive comments for our closing chapter, 'The Tide of the Future'. These special thanks go to President Reagan and Prime Minister Margaret Thatcher and to Vice-President George Bush, Secretary of Defense Caspar Weinberger, the Rt Hon James Callaghan, Dr and Mrs David Owen, former Ambassadors Lord Franks and Peter Jay, Lord Hanson, Sir Gordon White, James Reston, Alistair Cooke, David Hockney, Harold Evans, Clay Felker, Clive Barnes, Zandra Rhodes, Alan Coren, Andrew Lloyd Webber and Paul McCartney.

The research required for this book could well have kept a whole team of researchers gainfully employed. In our case we were fortunate enough to have an extraordinary one-man band in the shape of Ben Ramos, who did it all. The picture research was directed and organised with unstinting thoroughness by Sarah Waters and, as ever, the authors could not have functioned without the tireless enthusiasm of Tricia Pombo and Sarah Brennan.

Finally a word about our editor. The contributions of Stuart Proffitt throughout the past eighteen months have been, quite simply, indispensable.

DF and MS
London, June 1986

There is properly no history; only biography.

RALPH WALDO EMERSON

Introduction

At the time of the American Revolution, inhabitants of British stock comprised by far the largest element in the Thirteen Colonies. Even today, approximately thirty per cent of the entire population of the United States, just less than fifty million people, have British or Northern Irish ancestry. Yet because it is so much a part of the culture and history of North America, and since British immigrants became so quickly assimilated when they reached the United States, this fact, and in particular the contribution made by individual Britons, has often been taken for granted in contrast to the amount of attention paid to the place of other ethnic groups and people in that society. For the British link (memories of wartime colleagues-in-arms apart) is seen normally by Americans in terms of colonial history; post-independence immigration is largely ignored by historians for the simple fact that the British have never really been looked upon as immigrants. They spoke the same language, both in public life and in the home, followed similar customs and religious beliefs and had ways of living that were closest to those that were practised in the new America. They did not look or act like aliens; they were therefore, in Charlotte Erickson's definition, 'invisible immigrants'.

None the less, British immigrants were still newcomers, familiar, yet in an unfamiliar world, with many differences, including that of language, to discover and of which to beware, as even the contemporary British traveller discovers. Their influx was not the result of some great upheaval or persecution such as that which prompted the vast emigrations of the Irish or of the Jews from Eastern Europe. Admittedly, there were the Highland Clearances from Scotland but, tragic though these were in terms of human misery, that inflow to the United States was comparatively small.

Equally, the flow in the other direction has been much misunderstood and under-appreciated. The eastward movement of people and ideas has not been confined to the purveyors of Ford cars, hamburgers, jazz, westerns and *Dallas*-type soap operas. The history of the last two centuries is studded with the names of distinguished Americans who came, bearing talent, initiative and capital, to make their decisive influence on British lifestyles, thought and prosperity.

This book seeks to tell the story of that Rich Tide which has ebbed and flowed across the Atlantic over the last four hundred years. By such an expression, which gives this book its title, we mean the transatlantic movement of those people, who, with their backgrounds, training, skills, aptitudes and talents, have been the vehicles for the ideas and developments which have made the Anglo-American connection. For the resultant bond was and is of a special, perhaps unique, order of intimacy. Bismarck once suggested that the fact that North America spoke English was the single most important fact in modern history. But the link has not evolved just as a result of the much vaunted common language that, as some would have it, divides as much as unites us. Rather, it has emerged owing to a consonance of morals, ethics, culture (in a host of fields), inventiveness, even humour, as well as to the more obvious social, economic and political ties. All these similarities stem from a history that has always been tightly interlaced, even though, outwardly, this has often been camouflaged by well-perceived differences of style.

This is not to contend that, in some way, American civilization is a mere British clone, or, as some argue, that the reverse has become true in the second half of the twentieth century. Very obviously, because of the arrival of peoples from many other countries and ethnic backgrounds, coupled with the complex factors that stem from the geography of the vast American continent, the British heritage of attitudes and beliefs has been adapted to become entirely American.

Ideas are carried and developed by people. In the chapters that follow, the story is told of some key figures among the countless numbers, from all walks of life, who have made up the Rich Tide. When we began working on the subject we thought it would be relatively easy to confine ourselves to a handful of the best-known names. But as we advanced in our researches we found ourselves in danger of being overwhelmed by the multifarious-ness of the subject and by how many fascinating people, both British and American, could, with justice, be discussed. We have, none the less, had to confine ourselves to concentrating on a representative sample of individuals in each chapter – characters who best illustrate the depth as well as the width of the Rich Tide by their real and lasting influence. This has meant that large numbers of vital and prominent people have but brief mention here or have had to be left out of the text altogether. There are familiar names; there are some that are much less well known but whose contributions have been of major significance. While the chapters are arranged according to subject, just as some areas are difficult to separate, for example as between invention and enterprise, so also are there many people who could, with justice, appear repeatedly throughout the book. There were some figures such as the remarkable Benjamin Franklin who could have featured as politician, colonial agent, scientist, inventor, writer or educator; equally, we have concentrated on Robert Owen the social pioneer, though he might otherwise have been placed with the educationalists or the kings of the textile industry.

Again we had the dilemma of at what point an individual could be considered as part of the Rich Tide. Should it encompass those that made the journey as mere babes in arms? It is doubtless true that their lives were moulded by the cultural and educational backgrounds of their parents even when they reached their destination. In the end we have therefore been flexible in this regard depending on the proven degree of intellectual and other baggage that the individual brought with him, whichever way he or she travelled. We also discussed where else we drew the line. To take an extreme example: Shakespeare and George III are as much a part of the cultural and political history of the United States as they are of the United Kingdom. But they never made the crossing and are therefore excluded, as are Dwight Eisenhower and George Marshall, whose influence on Britain and her prosperity were immense but essentially in the context of a wider global condition.

We have found that those figures who were most compelling to write about, when brought together in sum, naturally reflected the fact that until the middle of the last century most of the tide flowed from Britain to the United States. Thereafter, this also revealed what we had been convinced of before we began — that it has since continued as a two-way process, even though the American effect on the United Kingdom almost always came at a later stage. Indeed, one of the fascinating aspects of the study has been to discover the period or decade in which that tide turned in each of the areas discussed, using individuals (as historians tend to use events and dates) to dramatize long-term trends.

When one asks why, after the first flush of settlement, the British emigrated, one finds that their reasons are certainly less sensational and violent than those that impelled other great emigrations, but they were, in their way, equally persuasive: the economic and social consequences of the first of the world's industrial revolutions; the pressures of an urban population explosion (Britain's population grew almost four times in the nineteenth century); rapid mechanization and a long agricultural depression. These negative factors were coupled with the positive attractions and challenges of a land where, according to the advertisements of the energetic recruiting agents for the new

States and railroads of North America, the streets were paved and the hills were rich with gold. These enticements meant that it was often the smartest, the fittest, the most articulate, the best educated, rather than the outcasts, that travelled (though, for a brief period, America, like Australia, was the recipient of both convicts and paupers).

Even the wealthy came, mainly farmers with finance and livestock. That did not always guarantee success, as the rich and prosperous men of Surrey discovered when they failed in their attempt to establish a colony, Albion, on the plains of Illinois in the second and third decades of the nineteenth century. But these and others always found their skills and education useful — especially those coming from Scotland which had universal elementary education long before its southern neighbour.

The consequent danger to the mother country, often remarked on with alarm in contemporary reports, was that it was not the ullage that left, but the best, an early brain drain of talent, initiative and resolve. It was, in sum, not want that drove the British, so much as the promise of better. That so many of them succeeded in America is where we begin. And, indeed, one must remember that for the would-be British emigrant, unlike most of those from the rest of Europe, there was the possibility, often with assisted passages, of the attractive optional goals of the greater British Empire — Australia, New Zealand, South Africa and also (after 1776) Canada. America was a positive choice.

The interaction of Britain and America on one another is most often discussed in terms of that ringing phrase, the 'Special Relationship'. Roosevelt and Churchill, Eisenhower and Macmillan, Reagan and Thatcher: there is a well-documented relationship between modern political leaders that has been branded as special. And so it is, though often (over the last two centuries just as much as in the more familiar post-war period) it lacks harmony and sometimes generates the reverse. It would be naïve not to note, just as well, the periods of British anti-Americanism and the other side of the coin, when Britain was, if not an enemy, far from being an ally. Indeed it can be argued that it was not until the 1940s that a full rapprochement was reached between Britain and the United States. But in general, after the transatlantic storms and strains, in Keynes's words, 'the seas come quiet again'.

An additional contemporary factor is that, even when American and British statesmen appear publicly to fall foul of each other, behind the scenes considerable harmony continues to prevail. Thus Suez, Vietnam, Grenada or something less sensational but equally serious such as high American interest rates, to take examples from the past few well-remembered decades, have not prevented the bilateral diplomatic, economic, defensive and political apparatus, the Establishments (and also the peoples) of both states from continuing to live and work together in close, and sometimes almost unspoken, unison. In other words, whatever the contemporary nature of the Special Relationship and whatever the noises of the public hustings, the scene behind is still usually one of deeply shared mutual understanding. *Time* magazine (3 May 1982) said it at the time of the Falklands crisis, under the heading 'The Firm, Old Alliance':

> There is no nation in the world that the American people value more highly than Britain; none to which they feel deeper personal and moral kinship; none for which they would sacrifice more, including their lives; and none on which they so depend for precisely the same attitude. Britain ought never to doubt where America's heart lies, especially in a crisis . . . If the American Government does not realise this, the people will soon remind it. The fate of Britain is their nation's own, and we would be worse than fools to think otherwise.

This said, an analysis of the contemporary political 'Special Relationship' is, quite specifically, *not* the purpose of this book. *The Rich Tide* seeks to discuss the relationship of people and ideas, not of governments and treaties, rooted in a conviction that the former have a more profound effect on our everyday lives than the latter. This is thus not intended as a history book, charting the intricacies of the development of economic, political and diplomatic relations between two countries. Nor is its purpose to cover current issues relating to the North Atlantic or Western Alliance – a subject well documented in current political literature. The theme of this book is specifically the Anglo-American or, more properly, the British-American relationship. (Our use of the term 'Anglo-American' should not be taken to refer to England alone. By convention it refers to the whole of the United Kingdom of Great Britain and Northern Ireland, just as, by contrast, 'American' tends to equate with the United States alone and includes neither Canada nor Mexico.) Nor does the book consider, except in passing, the important historic and contemporary links that both countries have with Canada. Until about two hundred years ago, it is difficult to divide North America for discussion in any precise way; but thereafter the Canadian connection is only discussed where there is a trilateral link, as for example in discussing the ubiquitous and peripatetic life and work of Alexander Graham Bell. In terms of the westward flow we are talking specifically of people of Scots, English, Welsh and Scots-Irish (or

Ulster) birth or descent, each of which have had a very different contribution to make. The role and place of Irish immigrants and their descendants is of a separate order and is not covered in this book.

It aims, equally, at British and American readers. While both the authors are British they have made the most stringent attempt not to try to make statements that in some way say 'we made you' or that 'we never left'. The relationship was and always has been a rich two-way flow, and our model is that of Henry James, who wished it to be impossible for anyone to say whether he was an American writing about Britain or a Briton writing about America.

CHAPTER ONE

The Spirit of Foundation

*England purchased for some of her subjects, who found
themselves uneasy at home, a great estate in a distant country.*
ADAM SMITH (Wealth of Nations, 1776)

The history of Britain and North America was, until about two
hundred years ago, to all intents and purposes the same history.
So too were their people. At the time of the first American census
in 1790, people of non-British stock amounted to less than eight
per cent of the total population. Inevitably, until independence,
the flow of individuals, with their thinking, their beliefs and their
talents, was, with a very few notable exceptions, largely in a
westerly direction. A selective glimpse at the earliest years includes the figures of Sir Walter Ralegh, Sir Francis Drake, the
Pilgrim Fathers, each of whom means something to every school-
child on both sides of the Atlantic. They were contributors to the
early process, part exploration, part settlement, part crusade, up
and down the eastern seaboard of the North American continent. The Bristol-based John Cabot, for example, encouraged by
Henry VII, reached Newfoundland in 1497, and again in 1498
when he also explored the coast of North America south to
Chesapeake Bay; but he was so uninspired by its prospects that
nearly a century elapsed before England was tempted to try to
plant settlements on the American continent.

The first of these settlements (setting aside earlier brief
attempts and rumours of such, by, for example, the legendary
twelfth-century Welsh prince Madoc) was that of Roanoke Island. In 1578 Sir Humphrey Gilbert received a patent from Queen
Elizabeth for discovery and colonization in north-west America.
He made two trips to the New World, but in September 1583 was
drowned when his ship went down returning from Newfoundland. The following spring Elizabeth renewed the patent – which
entitled the holder to explore, colonize and rule 'such remote,
heathen, and barbarous lands not actually possessed of any

An Indian chief's wife and daughter.
Drawing by John White

An Indian soothsayer.
Drawing by John White

Christian prince, nor inhabited by Christian people' – in the name of Gilbert's half-brother, and a member of his last voyage, Walter Ralegh.

Ralegh no doubt hoped that the patent would bring himself and his country wealth, prestige and power. Within weeks he sent out an expedition under Philip Amadus and Arthur Barlowe, who were to explore the north American coastline and to select a location for a future colony. Reaching the Albermarle region of present-day North Carolina in July 1584 they took possession of the land in the name of Queen Elizabeth. At Roanoke Island they were greeted with great hospitality by the Indians. After two months of fruitful exploration they returned safely to England with news of friendly natives, the endless supply of fish and game, and soil that was 'the most plentiful sweete, fruitfull and whole-some of all the worlde'. Pleased with their success Elizabeth knighted Ralegh, who named the discovery Virginia after his virgin queen.

In the summer of 1585 a colonizing expedition of about one hundred men, dispatched by Ralegh but under the command of Sir Richard Grenville and Ralph Lane, arrived at Roanoke, which they thought would be easy to defend, as much from Spanish as from Indian attack. This was no uncultured group. In it were scientists who carefully recorded what they found in the new world and the artist John White who made numerous drawings of the human, animal and plant life that the Europeans found there. This first attempt at settlement ended in failure. Instead of concentrating on fishing, agriculture and trade with the natives, the settlers were preoccupied with a fruitless quest for precious metals which provoked the hostility of the local tribes. When Francis Drake arrived at the colony from the Spanish West Indies he found a highly disillusioned group of men who, lacking the supplies that had been promised from England and harassed by the Indians and worried about Spanish raids, eagerly took up his offer of a passage back home. Shortly after their departure Gren-ville arrived at Roanoke with food and provisions only to find the deserted colony. 'Unwilling to loose possession of the country which Englishmen had so long held' he left fifteen men there equipped with enough supplies to last until a new expedition could be sent out.

When Ralegh's next expedition led by John White landed at Roanoke on 22 July 1587 they found only the bones of one of Grenville's men and the ruins of the fort and houses which Lane had built. White's expedition of 117 men, women and children incorporated as 'the Governour and Assistants of the Cittie of Ralegh in Virginia' was not intended to settle permanently at

John White's drawing of the Indian village of Secoton, in which he noted their domestic activities, their fields of corn at various stages of ripeness, and what he called 'A Ceremony in their prayers'.

Roanoke, but was to pick up Grenville's men and proceed to Chesapeake Bay where it was hoped they would find a more easily defended location. However, their pilot, who justifiably feared a Spanish attack, refused to take them any further. They had therefore to make do as well as they could in most difficult

'The Towne of Pomeiock and true forme of their houses, covered and enclosed some wth matts, and some wth barcks of trees. All compassed about wth smale poles stock thick together in stedd of a wall.' John White's drawing of the Indian settlement of Pomeioc.

circumstances. They had arrived too late to plant and harvest food crops that year and their supplies were limited. With the exception of the Indians from Croatoan Island, they were surrounded by hostile tribes, and the Spaniards, actively competing for the new lands all along the eastern seaboard, were a constant threat.

The colonists were understandably further alarmed when, only six days after landing, one George Howe, the first of many colonists to suffer the same fate, was killed by Indians while out fishing. On the other hand, in those superstitious times, they took as a good omen the fact that an Indian from Croatoan Island by the name of Manteo, who had already been to England with Drake (and may consequently be classed as the first recorded native North American transatlantic traveller), turned Christian and was baptised in August 1587. As a mark of this, the colonists quaintly but formally created him 'Lord of Roanoke', the first Protestant baptism and the first English title granted in the New World. A second event, considered of even greater significance, came on 18 August of the same year, with the birth of Virginia, daughter of Ananias and Ellinor Dare and grand-daughter of the Governor, John White, the first child born of British parents in the New World. These appeared to be happy symbols. Alas, they were not.

Shortly afterwards, Governor White was forced to return to England for much needed supplies. But his arrival home co-incided with the climax of hostilities with Spain and, with Ralegh, he was refused permission to return to America in March 1588, as all English ships were required by the Privy Council to remain to defend England against the Spanish Armada. Thus it was not until the summer of 1590 that White managed to return to Roanoke, which he found long deserted and overgrown. Of the settlers there was no sign and the fate of Ralegh's Lost Colony has baffled historians ever since, though it is generally assumed that they perished at the hands of the Indians. But, though this colony did not survive, it is none the less accepted as the spiritual beginning of an English America that was to become the United States. For it was there at Roanoke that on Sir Walter Ralegh's initiative the seed was planted that would later blossom at Jamestown. There for the first time men, women and children from the English-speaking world, with their beliefs, their aspirations and their resolve, came face to face with the harshness and promise of the New World.

After Roanoke, not until 1607 did a new group of settlers, financed by the London Company and whose members had been enticed by rumours of gold, found the first permanent village in America at Jamestown, named in honour of King James I (and VI of Scotland) who had granted them their charter. This colony, comprising three shiploads, carrying 144 men in all, landed in Virginia in April or May. It came under the impressive leadership of Captain John Smith (1580–1631), the son of a Lincolnshire farmer. He was a stern disciplinarian educated at Cambridge, who ruled following the grim biblical edict 'he that shall not work, neither shall he eat'. By his own admission, Smith's flamboyant past as pirate, Turkish slave and mercenary to a Transylvanian prince hardly matched his sober new responsibilities. But, despite much internal dissension – Jamestown was never a particularly placid place – he led the colony with style, masterminding the building of houses, a church and the crucial defences for the settlement. During the summer of 1608 he also found time to explore much of the Chesapeake Bay, mapping his findings en route. In later life too, when he had left the colony and returned to London, he spent his retirement encouraging further settle-ment of the new lands, by publishing remarkably accurate maps and pamphlets about them.

Short of food and other essentials, and unprepared for serious colonising, the settlers might not have survived but for Smith's

RIGHT: Captain John Smith, the steely leader of the Jamestown settlers, in an engraved portrait (detail from map opposite) in his *True Travels, Adventures, and Observations of Captaine John Smith*, (1630 edition).

OPPOSITE: A map of New England from Smith's *True Travels*. This remarkably accurate map, charted on Smith's 1614 exploration of the area, added greatly to the knowledge of the coastline of the New World and served as a valuable guide to new settlers, though he never returned to the colony itself after he left in 1609.

leadership and his expeditions to barter with the natives for food. Out of all the barren misery of Jamestown he was the one indispensable man who, by sheer force of character and courage, brought the necessary discipline to the colony to ensure that it remained in being.

Next to Smith the survival and growth of Jamestown, the first permanent English outpost in America, owed much to the contribution of John Rolfe (1585–1622), who came to Virginia in 1610. Finding that the local tobacco was deemed to be 'poor and weake, and of byting tast', he imported seeds from Trinidad and Venezuela and cultivated a tobacco leaf of superior quality which

immediately found favour in England. From this point both Rolfe and Virginia's economy prospered. Their economic good fortune solved the settlers' other major problem, which was to placate the local Indian tribes. This was achieved during the colony's crucial formative years thanks to a far-sighted treaty made with the Indians and to Rolfe's celebrated marriage with Pocahontas (*c*.1595–1617), the determined daughter of Powhattan, the supreme chief of all the tribes on that littoral, and a man who would undoubtedly have led the attacks that had wiped out the earlier settlements.

When Captain Smith was captured by Powhattan while on a

Smith's capture by the Indians: 'Their triumph about him' (above) and 'Bound to a tree to be shott to death' below, from Smith's *Historie of Virginia* (1624).

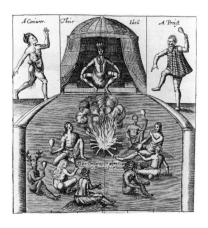

The Indians' 'conjuration about C. Smith 1607', the dire situation from which he was rescued by Pocohontas (opposite). From Smith's *Historic of Virginia*.

journey of exploration, Pocahontas, according to the Englishman, 'hazarded the beating out of her own brains to save mine; and not only that, but so prevailed with her father, that I was safely conducted to Jamestown'. There Smith found 'about eight and thirtie miserable poor and sick creatures to keep possession of all those large territories of Virginia; such was the weakness of this poor Commonwealth, as had the savages not fed us, we directly had starved. And this relief . . . was commonly brought us by this Lady Pocahontas.' When relations between the colonists and the natives again deteriorated Pocahontas risked her life by continuing to visit Jamestown, once warning the settlers of an impending raid by her father's tribe. 'Jamestown with her wild train she as freely frequented as her father's habitation; and during the time of two or three years, she next under God, was still the instrument to preserve this colony from death, famine and utter confusion; which if in those times [it] had once been dissolved, Virginia might have [lain] as it was at our first arrival to this day.'

Later she was taken as a prisoner by the colonists and used as a hostage to conclude successfully a peace treaty between the two sides. In Jamestown Rolfe fell deeply in love with Pocahontas and soon decided to marry her, despite his Calvinist fears that by doing so he would incur the wrath of God. He set out his thoughts on the matter in his famous letter to the colony's deputy Governor, Sir Thomas Dale, in 1613. Though it seems that Rolfe's desire to marry her arose from love (and indeed lust) he argues that their union would be of benefit to both Virginia and England.

> Lett therefore this my well advised protestacion, which here I make betweene God and my owne Conscience be a sufficient wyttnes . . . with the vnbridled desire of Carnall affection for the good of the Plantacion, the honour of our Countrye, for the glorye of God, for myne owne salvacion, and for the Convertinge to the true knowledge of God and Iesus Christ an vnbeleivinge Creature, namely Pohahuntas: To whome my hart and best thoughtes are and have byn a longe tyme soe intangled & inthralled . . .

'At last rejecting her barbarous condition', Pocahontas was converted to Christianity, christened Rebecca, and with her father's blessing she was eventually married to Rolfe – a happy occasion that was marked by an exchange of both gifts and prisoners by the two sides.

In 1616, attended by Indian servants, she went with Rolfe and their child to England, where, despite an initial reluctance to approve of this strange mixed marriage, she made much-heralded

Pocohontas at the age of twenty-one, attired in Jacobean dress for presentation at court, from an engraved portrait of 1616.

appearances at the King's Court, including one in attendance on the Queen at a Twelfth Night masque in 1617.

This much romanticized figure, whom Ben Jonson mentioned in his comedy, *The Staple of News* ('the blessed Pocahontas, as John Smith called her, and Great King's daughter of Virginia') has been dismissed by some as an apocryphal character. On the other hand, her rôle as a go-between can be seen as an important symbol in the development of the New World. She died in

Gravesend in 1617, as she was about to board a ship to return to the warmer climate of Virginia along with her husband and infant son. A statue was erected to her in St George's Church, where she is buried with the gentle epitaph, 'Rebecca Wrothe . . . wyff of Thomas Wroth, gent, – . . . a Virginia lady borne . . .'

Smith left Jamestown for England in 1609 never to return to the colony. The settlers missed his undoubted force of character, for his departure was followed by a period of extreme hardship known as the 'Starving Time' during which the population of the colony dropped from five hundred to around sixty. Only the arrival in 1610 of the first governor of the colony, Lord Delaware, who brought with him much-needed supplies, allowed Jamestown to survive. But from then on with John Rolfe's successful cultivation of tobacco the settlers achieved a growing prosperity. A natural step followed in July 1619 when, in the little church of Jamestown, the governor, six councillors and twenty burgesses, worthy men chosen by each 'plantation', 'hundred' or 'town', met as a general assembly to impose local laws and taxes. It was the first representative legislature in the New World. Five years later, when the Jamestown Company found it too difficult to run life in the new America from London and disbanded, the colony became largely self-administered under the Crown. Thus the first seeds of American democracy were sown, though still subject to the British monarch, and still acting in conformity with the laws and customs of the mother country.

The burgesses of Jamestown had therefore barely initiated civic life in America when in 1620 the group, who later became known as the Pilgrim Fathers, set out on their voyage in the *Mayflower* from Plymouth. They were a group of Puritans, otherwise known as Separatists, who in 1608 went from Scrooby in Nottinghamshire to Leyden in Holland to escape from the corrupting influences of the English world. Although in the Netherlands they were free from persecution and harassment, some of their congregation argued that they needed to find a more isolated place if they were to achieve their aim of establishing a pure Church of Christ. So between 1616 and 1619 their pastors, John Robinson and William Brewster, sent representatives to England to negotiate with the Virginia Company for the right to establish a colony on its American land. Thanks largely to the assistance of Sir Edwin Sandys they received a patent on 16 June 1619. Meanwhile two London merchants also obtained a patent from the Virginia Company and persuaded the Separatists to collaborate with them. In July 1620 about fifty members of the Leyden group sailed for England in the *Speedwell*, a vessel which was also planned to take them to the New World. When the ship proved unseaworthy the Separatists were forced to join the London merchants in the *Mayflower* which finally left Plymouth on 16 September. The majority of the passengers were not Pilgrims but indentured servants and hired artisans.

After a gruelling sixty-six-day voyage the *Mayflower* reached the American coastline but was prevented by rough seas and stormy weather from reaching the land they had been granted in Virginia. Instead they first landed on Cape Cod at present-day Provincetown, Massachusetts, before selecting the nearby site of Plymouth. The *Mayflower* remained anchored in port until the following April when it returned to England. On 21 November, prior to the landing at Plymouth, a document – which became known as the Mayflower Compact – was drawn up by forty-one male passengers which bound its signatories into a body politic for the purpose of establishing a preliminary government and pledged them to obey whatever laws and regulations its officers

'To be a Pilgrim . . .' Edward Winslow (1595–1655), one of the most important and dynamic of the Pilgrim Fathers. As an explorer and trader, and as the colony's agent, assistant governor and later, for three years, governor, he worked for over twenty-five years to ensure the birth, survival and growth of the Plymouth settlement. His *A Relation or Journal of the beginning and proceedings of the English Plantation settled at Plimouth in New England* (1622) and his *Good News . . . at the Plantation of Plimouth* were the first accounts of the colony to be published. This portrait by an unknown artist is the only known authentic contemporary depiction of one of the Pilgrim Fathers.

OPPOSITE: The Patent of the Plymouth Colony, issued in 1621 by the Council of New England.

would later create. It was not a constitution but an adaptation of the social compact idea found in contemporary Separatist Church covenants. The Compact was a consequence of the fear that some members of their group might abandon them and settle elsewhere. It was also a device for giving the colony a modicum of legitimacy until they received a patent from the Council of New England on whose land they were now squatting.

Among the signatories was the well-off Cambridge layman, William Brewster (1567–1644), who had helped organise the original exodus to Holland and was one of the moving spirits behind the emigration to the New World. As the Plymouth community's acting ruling elder he was to exert an immense influence on the colony. However, the leading figure among the Pilgrim Fathers was undoubtedly William Bradford (1590–1657), who by sheer determination was to hold the colony together for almost thirty years. A literate if not a learned man, he came of Yorkshire yeoman stock and joined the Separatists in 1606, in whose company, after a short term in an English prison for his beliefs, he went to Holland where he was one of the most energetic advocates of emigration. He later described his call to the New World in verse:

> From my years young in dayes of Youth,
> God did make known to me his Truth,
> And call'd me from my native place,
> For to enjoy the Means of Grace.
>
> In Wilderness he did me guide,
> And in strange lands for me provide.
> In Fears and Want, through Weal and Woe,
> As Pilgrims pass'd I to and fro . . .

When the first Governor of the colony, John Carver, died a few months after the Pilgrims' arrival in New England, Bradford was chosen as the natural successor and between 1622 and 1656 was constantly re-elected to this post (with the exception of five years when he chose not to stand). Bradford was a man who commanded respect for both his humanity and his practicality, and it was largely due to him and his skill in negotiating and trading with the Indians that the colony survived at all. From the outset, he noted in his diary – written up in his *History of Plymouth Plantation*, a unique record of the voyage and early years of the colony – the many difficult events during the first year that the Pilgrim Fathers spent in America. Plymouth Colony was, according to him, a small clearing surrounded by wilderness – the ocean on one side and dense forest on the other. It was a less desirable site than

William Bradford (1590–1656), the
leading figure among the Pilgrim
Fathers for almost thirty years.

Massachusetts Bay – but at least there they would not be attacked
by Indians since the ones that had occupied the site had been
wiped out by smallpox and other Indians did not approach for fear
of catching the disease. He also described how the *Mayflower*
herself remained anchored in the harbour while the Pilgrims
established themselves on land, putting up temporary huts made
from turf, branches and thatch. Then and later there were periods
when the inhabitants were close to starvation, particularly when
ill-prepared new arrivals came to share what limited food there
was in store. In the political life of the colony, Bradford gave the

lead in framing a constitution and a set of laws which were based on both 'God's Law' and the laws of England. He also helped set up a judicial court and a house of assembly.

The Plymouth Colony received a patent from the Council of New England in 1621, but this was little more than a vague land grant and licence to set up a local government. Plymouth's government was never endorsed by a charter or officially approved by the Crown. Eventually it became a mere part of the Massachusetts Bay regime. However, in the story of the Rich Tide the importance of William Bradford and the *Mayflower* Pilgrims is threefold: first, they survived; and second they established a compact which has been seen as the first written embodiment in the history of America of the notion of a fundamental law proceeding from the people; finally, their experience has become part of America's collective memory and a national symbol of the country's simple beginnings and original purity.

Thereafter, the process of colonization began in earnest with the foundation of a Puritan colony at Massachusetts Bay in 1630. Unlike its predecessors it was to prosper from the outset, and the original 2000 settlers – farmers and merchants in the main – increased to 16,000 by 1643.

From that time on, more and more groups, both large and small, set out on the arduous transatlantic journey to found settlements all along the Atlantic coastline from Maine to Georgia. They came to escape religious persecution, to find freedom of political expression or, more simply, to escape the poverty of the Old World, enticed by the promise of the new. All sorts and conditions of people arrived: religious fanatics, entrepreneurs, dreamers, criminals, in pursuit of what the poet Robert Frost called 'a fresh start for the human race'.

Among the most prominent leaders of the new land was the redoubtable John Winthrop, who was born in Suffolk in 1588. He was one of that élite, a Trinity College, Cambridge, man, to which he had been admitted at the ripe age of fourteen, as befitted the well-born son of the manor of Groton in Suffolk. He grew up to become known as 'The Moses of New England', an uncompromising introspective man, violently opposed to the sins of using tobacco and drink and the apparent epitome of the traditional Puritan (later defined by H. L. Mencken as a man with 'the haunting fear that someone, somewhere, may be happy'). He is said to have mellowed somewhat after acquiring a third wife (his first two died shortly after marriage), but judging from most contemporary reports there is little evidence of it. He believed that England was about to be damned by his vengeful God to 'some heavy affliction' as a penance for the liberal extravagance of the

John Winthrop (1588–1699) 'the Moses of New England'. A nineteenth-century copy portrait.

times of King Charles I, and he resolved to take his church and 'fly to the wilderness'. For, he believed, it would be a 'service to the Church of great consequence to carry the Gospel into those parts of the world, to helpe on the comings of the fullnesse of the Gentiles, and to raise a Bulworke against the kingdome of Antichrist wch the Jesuites labour to reare in thos parts'.

After Cambridge he was initially successful as a lawyer but in 1629 he faced financial difficulties. Concerned with the future of religion and morals in England, he became interested in the recently chartered Massachusetts Bay Company. Despite family opposition he decided to emigrate to New England. He became closely involved in the plans for the expedition and on 20 October

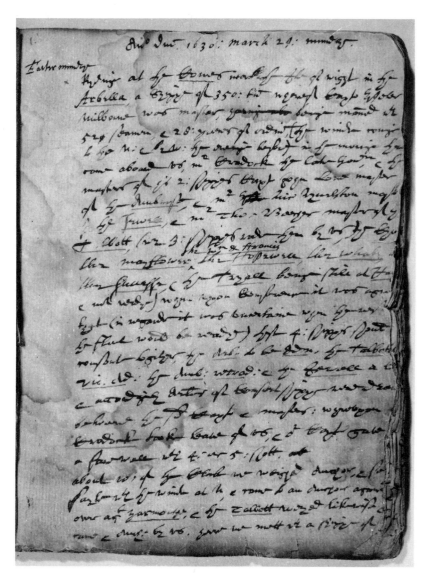

The first page of John Winthrop's Journal, written on Easter Monday (March 29th), 1630 describing his departure from the Solent for the New World. The Journal, which records the story of the Massachusetts Bay colony during its formative years, is often regarded as the most important and eloquently written document of early American history.

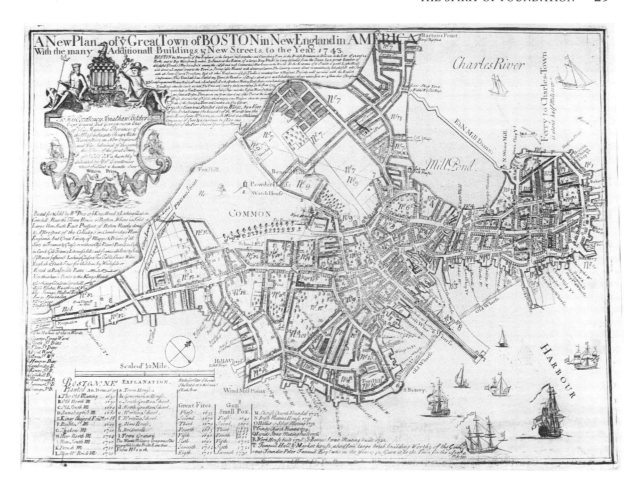

1629 was appointed Governor of the proposed colony. While waiting with his ships off Cowes on the Isle of Wight, he began writing his diaries which, more than almost any other source, provide the basis of much of the early history of the settlement. He eventually set out from there as leader of the largest of all the expeditions to the New World, sailing with four ships and some five hundred men, women and children. In a powerful sermon to his flock, delivered in the course of the voyage to America, he set out his creed:

> For we must consider that we shall be a citty upon a hill. The eyes of all people are upon us, so that if we shall deal falseley with our God in this work we have undertaken, and so cause Him to withdraw His present help from us, we shall be made a story and a byword through the world.

Joining those already in the area of what is now Boston, both as Governor and Deputy Governor Winthrop helped create what

A New Plan of Ye Great Town of Boston in New England, (Boston, William Rice, 1743), the earliest and most important map of colonial Boston, first engraved and printed by Francis Dewing in 1722, and reissued with new dates, statistics, streets and buildings as the town grew.

was virtually the first self-governing colony. A harsh place, made all the harsher by his arrival, it had vengeful laws and penalties including prison for drunkenness or the mere wearing of lace, and death for the great sin of adultery. As a result of his Old Testament rule and his support for a system where only members of his strict church had any rights whatsoever, Winthrop was subject to frequent challenge, doubly understandable given his belief that 'democracy is among most Civil nations accounted the meanest and worst of all forms of Government . . . and History does record that it hath always of least continuance and fullest of trouble'. But he easily survived such onslaughts by the simple expedient of fining or arresting those who opposed him, and his autocratic rule only ended with his death in 1649. Yet some of his attitudes were more enlightened, as suggested in a speech he made during a court case in 1645: 'I entreat you to consider that, when you choose magistrates, you take them from among yourselves, men subject to like passions as you are.' In addition, he helped found schools for all and it was during his tenure of office that Harvard College at Cambridge, Massachusetts, first came into being. To Winthrop also goes much of the credit for moving a step towards the birth of the American nation by confederating the four New England colonies of Massachusetts, Plymouth, Connecticut and New Haven in 1643.

There were, therefore, two colonized areas in mid-seventeenth-century America: bleak New England and Virginia, the second of which, to quote its Governor, Ralph Lane, was a happy paradise in every way. 'It is the godliest and most pleasing territorie of the world . . . if Virginia had but Horses and Kine in some reasonable proportion, I dare assure my self, being inhabited with English, no realme in Christendome were comparable to it.' Thereafter, a string of other settlements began to be founded along the coast in between, each precariously linked by a common language and by some common laws, and each born of British origins and conditions. (In order of founding they were New Hampshire, New York, Connecticut, Maryland, Rhode Island, Delaware, Pennsylvania, North Carolina, New Jersey, South Carolina and Georgia.)

One form of organized colonization that succeeded the chartering of trading companies as the main empire-building device was the Proprietary Grant. By this the British Crown would authorize a wealthy individual to establish a New World outpost as his private property. For example, the vast region that came to be known as New York, New Jersey and Delaware was granted by the King to the Duke of York in 1664, and it was not until 1688 that it became a Crown Colony. Later, Maryland was mandated to its 'Lord Proprietor', Lord Baltimore, in 1632, mainly as a refuge for English Catholics.

To the north of Maryland was, as yet, unsettled land which Charles II had given to William Penn in settlement of a debt of £16,000 owed to Penn's father. Thus, almost by chance, in 1682 Penn founded a settlement there, calling it, grandly, Pennsylvania. It was the last of the proprietary colonies; with Maryland it was the only one that had not converted to a Crown Colony by 1776. With the help of his fellow Quakers, a sect then also unpopular in conservative England, the colony prospered under Penn's leadership, owing particularly to their vigorous attitude to work and to Penn's intelligent and enlightened manner of dealing with the local Indians. This particular trait was shared by the really great names among the founding fathers – Smith, Bradford, Winthrop and Oglethorpe.

Georgia, named after George II, was founded last, with James Oglethorpe (1696–1785) as its founder. A tall, commanding man of unbounded energy and drive, who possessed a strong sense of right and wrong and of his own moral duty, he was born in the parish of St James's in London and studied at Corpus Christi College, Oxford, then served in the army and as a Member of Parliament for Haslemere. After the death of a close friend in a debtors' prison, he took up the cause of debtors and paupers who

One of the first students at Harvard was Winthrop's nephew, George Downing, who was to give his name to that most famous of London's streets. Sir George Downing (1623–84) was born in Dublin and emigrated to Salem, Massachusetts, in 1638 where, later, he became the second graduate of the new Harvard College. He returned to England in 1645 and was in turn a senior officer in Cromwell's army in Scotland, Member of Parliament for Edinburgh and British Agent in Holland. Despite his republican activities – he took the lead in offering the crown to Cromwell – he later turned Royalist and was knighted by Charles II in 1660. Downing actually blamed the fact that he had supported Cromwell on 'my training in New England, where I was brought up and sucked in principles that, since, my reason has made me see were erroneous'. (As a result of this and Downing's devious exploits, the *Dictionary of National Biography* quotes an unnamed American author as saying that a proverbial New England expression for a traitor was 'an arrant George Downing'.) Whatever his sins, he continued to serve the Restoration monarchy as Agent in Holland, acting vigorously in capturing his erstwhile regicidal colleagues – a good pliant character after whom to have named such a street.

Sir George Downing (1623–84)

ABOVE: Penn's treaty with the Indians, an idealised painting by Benjamin West (see Chapter 8), 1771. There is no solid evidence that the treaty, which guaranteed the Indians equal rights and freedoms in Pennsylvania, was ever signed. But West, a Quaker and a Pennsylvanian, was obviously keen to propagate the myth. As he lacked documentation for the scene his father and stepbrother appear in the picture.

OPPOSITE ABOVE: General James Oglethorpe (1696–1785), the founder of Georgia.

OPPOSITE BELOW: A view of Savannah, Georgia, as it stood on the 29th of March, 1734. An engraving after a drawing by Peter Gordon.

were at that time extremely severely dealt with under English law. In 1729, having brought the matter before Parliament, he became chairman of a committee on the issue which uncovered enormous corruption and cruelty in the English prison system. With a group of other wealthy philanthropists, Oglethorpe secured a charter to establish Georgia as a place of asylum for a number of carefully selected debtors, thereby embarking on the serviceable British practice whereby colonization, both forced and free, was used as a remedy for the political and social ills of the Old World. With the backing of the King, he brought a first group of 116 to Charleston and in the year 1733 founded Savannah. Realizing that there were dangers in only exporting this particular brand of settler, among whom there would inevitably be a leavening of the work-shy and of criminals, he instituted a compulsory system of military training to man a chain of defences against the Spanish. Parliament gave him a grant of £10,000 to this end since they saw the new colony not just as a means of resettling paupers, but also as a barrier against Spanish expansionism in the south.

Oglethorpe lived in and ruled Georgia for many relatively prosperous years, establishing good relations with the Indians, though frequently building up internal opposition to his rule mainly as a result of his ban on both rum and negro slavery. He was not always helped in his work by his choice of the revivalists John and Charles Wesley as the religious leaders of Georgia (with Charles for a time actually acting as Oglethorpe's secretary), since they were not infrequently at cross-purposes with him.

To the contemporary writer Hannah More, Oglethorpe was 'the finest figure you ever saw . . . He is quite a chevalier, heroic, romantic, and full of the old gallantry'. His actions in Georgia

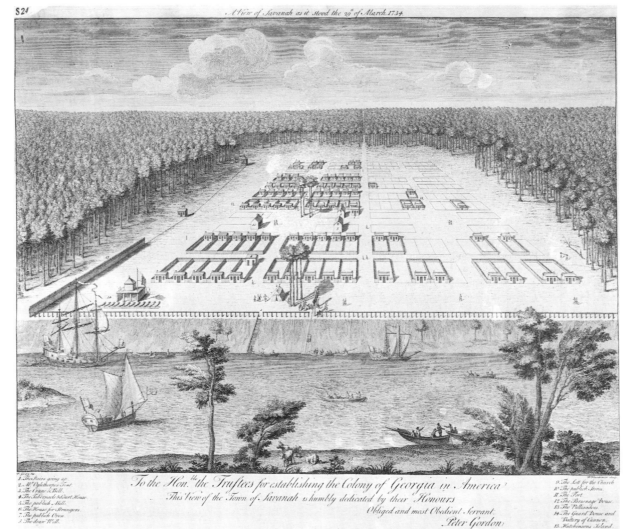

A View of Savanah as it stood the 29ᵗʰ of March 1734

To the Hon.ᵇˡᵉ the Trustees for establishing the Colony of Georgia in America This View of the Town of Savanah is humbly dedicated by their Honours Obliged and most Obedient Servant Peter Gordon

The Trustees' reception of the Tomochichi and the Yamacraws at the Georgia Office in London, 1734. Oglethorpe is featured in the centre, taking a message from a page.

were guided by a concern to strengthen the colony for both humanitarian and imperial reasons. His determination to achieve this at virtually any cost aroused the resentment of some of the settlers and the hostility of the Spanish, but ultimately he ensured Georgia's survival and development.

Oglethorpe's alliance with the Indians and his military resoluteness in containing the Spanish threat stood him in excellent stead over the years, otherwise the history of Georgia, indeed of the southern United States, might have been a very different one. Though his suspected Jacobite sympathies during the 1745 uprising led to his forced retirement from public life on his return to Britain, he is much remembered not only as a founding father but as one who made sure that the southern foundations were well and truly laid. George Bancroft eloquently summed up Oglethorpe's character and achievement.

> The gentleness of Oglethorpe's nature appeared in all his actions. He was merciful to the prisoner; a father to the emigrant; the unwavering friend of Wesley; honestly zealous for the conversion of the Indians; invoking for the Negro the panoply of the Gospel. He was, for a commercial age, the representative of that chivalry which knew neither fear nor reproach, and felt a stain on honor like a wound.
>
> (Bancroft's *History of the United States*)

The Process of Settlement and Recruitment

I always consider the settlement of America with reverence and wonder, as the opening of a grand scene and design in providence for the illumination of the ignorant and the emancipation of the slavish part of mankind all over the earth. JOHN ADAMS (1735–1826)

Despite all this apparent activity, throughout the seventeenth and eighteenth centuries the number of new arrivals was small. (At the time they were known as settlers – the word 'immigrant' did not come into general use until the late eighteenth century.) Even over the period of the great Puritan emigration to Massachusetts from 1628 to 1640, the number of arrivals probably amounted to no more than 20,000. The pace of emigration from Britain certainly quickened during the later part of the eighteenth century, but even then the total number arriving from the whole of Europe probably never rose above ten thousand in any single year. Indeed, the estimate for the whole century, from all countries, has been put at a mere 450,000. Besides English, Scots, Welsh and Irish, small numbers of Germans, Swedes, Dutch, French and Jews were beginning to arrive, most of whom headed for the central colonies, particularly Pennsylvania.

A highly active process of recruitment, as much as any particular economic, social, political and religious causes, appears to explain a large part of the exodus to the American colonies. In

1619, almost entirely as a result of vigorous recruiting methods, the Virginia Company induced 1,200 immigrants to come to their colony. Later, in response to the demand for labourers to grow the new cash crops of cotton and tobacco, recruiting methods became ever more businesslike and ruthless. The first negroes did not arrive in Jamestown until 1619 and, initially, the British authorities were solicited by the colonies themselves to provide a workforce by shipping the inmates of Britain's poorhouses and prisons to America. Then, once the tobacco plantations became profitable in Virginia and elsewhere, investors and planters were willing to put up capital to pay for the recruitment of volunteer workers or, more commonly, to entice indentured labourers who, in return for their passage, would promise to work for an employer for an agreed number of years.

In Virginia, an additional incentive was the 'headlight' system whereby fifty acres of land was given to every settler or to every person who imported a settler or servant into the colony. In Britain, the Virginia Company also used handbills, ballads and even the sermons of sympathetic ministers to persuade ordinary men and women to emigrate. Elsewhere, the majority of emigrants were probably recruited and shipped either by individuals or by small merchant partnerships who would use intermediaries such as carriers or packhorse men to spread the word of the benefits to be won in America throughout the towns and villages of Britain.

There is no doubt that the success of Winthrop and his kind owed much to their skills as recruiting agents, often arising from direct contacts they had with the Puritan gentry and clergy in East Anglia. William Penn was equally successful by using promotional tracts, exploiting his well-established links with leading British and Continental Quakers, in recruiting substantial numbers of immigrants to his new colony. Thus by a process of cajolery, bribery, compulsion, and ultimately by the promise of a better world the colonial leaders peopled their new land.

Mass Settlement

His echoing axe the settler swung
Amid the sea-like solitude,
And rushing, thundering, down were flung
The Titans of the wood. . . .

Humble the lot, yet his the race,
When Liberty sent forth her cry,
Who thronged in conflict's deadliest place,
To fight – to bleed – to die!
ALFRED B. STREET, 'The Settler'

In subsequent centuries the normal practice of new immigrants was to make for the colonies and townships already settled by people from their own backgrounds. But as the new America developed and took on its own character, the durability with which Welsh, English, Scots and Scots-Irish settlements provided pure microcosms of the British way of life was limited in comparison with other immigrant groups. This was because, for most, there were few cultural or social, and even fewer linguistic barriers to the quick and easy assimilation of the British into the American pattern. Thus British immigrants were regarded and regarded themselves as being of the same ethnic stock as the vast majority, sharing as they did a common language. This allowed them (excepting the Welsh- and Gaelic-speakers) to take part from the outset in all the social activities of the established population. Equally, because everything was to British, there was little need to defend particular British institutions, except new religions and creeds. Compare this with the experience of Italians, Germans, East Europeans and Jews who, from their arrival, had to congregate in order to defend themselves or to cope with the strangeness of their new environment, its language, its strange customs and ways. Successive waves of these immigrants found themselves often viciously segregated from the Anglo-Saxon society of the United States for at least a generation.

However, while the British immigrant experience was unique in comparison with that of other ethnic groups, it was (and is) often the case that many British arrivals did seek to retain particularly British habits and traditions for as long as they could. This was so particularly if they settled away from other major areas of population, where they could develop on an absolute pattern of their homeland, unsullied by any already purely 'American' habits and styles. (Gaelic- or Welsh-speaking immigrants, unless they were bilingual, tended to experience what nationals of other European countries did.)

Later, groups of British workers coming into urban areas would often arrive to find something of a 'closed shop', with either other ethnic groups already well established, or settlers from a particular part of Britain (e.g. textile-working Lancastrians at Fall River, Massachusetts) in the majority. These would not welcome outsiders, even from other parts of the United Kingdom,

KANSAS,

UNITED STATES OF AMERICA.

ITS RESOURCES, DEVELOPMENT, WEALTH, AND PRODUCTIVENESS.

VALUABLE INFORMATION

=FOR=

British Farmers

DESIRING TO EMIGRATE.

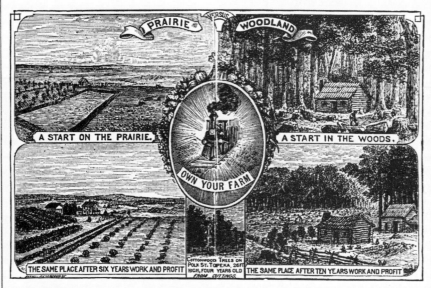

PRAIRIE versus WOODLAND

A START ON THE PRAIRIE.

OWN YOUR FARM

A START IN THE WOODS.

THE SAME PLACE AFTER SIX YEARS WORK AND PROFIT

COTTONWOOD TREES ON POLK ST. TOPEKA, 26 FT. HIGH, FOUR YEARS OLD *FROM CUTTINGS.*

THE SAME PLACE AFTER TEN YEARS WORK AND PROFIT

TWO MILLION ACRES Choice Farming, Fruit-Growing and Grazing **LANDS,** for sale by the **ATCHISON, TOPEKA AND SANTA FE R. R. CO.,** in the Richest Agricultural portion of the State, at prices varying from 12s. to 40s. per Acre, on six and eleven years' time. **One-third less for Cash.**

This Circular will be mailed <u>FREE</u> to any address. Read it through, and if further information is desired, write to or call on

CHAS. H. BRANSCOMBE, (Late U. S. Consul,)
Manager British Branch,

A. S. JOHNSON,
Land Commissioner,
TOPEKA, KANSAS, U. S. A.

Land Department A. T. & S. F. R. R. Co.,
Room 19, Victoria Building, Victoria St.,
MANCHESTER.

GUARDIAN Letterpress and Lithographic Works, Manchester

competing for work, accommodation and other benefits. Thus the Scots and others clubbed together to look after their own, additionally inspired by nostalgia and a wish to preserve their own cultural identity. But, even when British groups did band together in their own communities or societies, this, unlike similar moves by other ethnic groups, still did not cut them off from the greater American society in which they found themselves. Nevertheless, there were notable Scots, English, Welsh and Scots-Irish settlements in North America.

OPPOSITE: Cover of a leaflet advertising emigration to Kansas for British farmers.

The Scots

Of all immigrants to our country the Scotch are always the most welcome. They bring us muscle and brain and tried skill and trustworthiness in many of our great industries of which they are managers of the most successful ones.

NEAL DOW, American businessman and prohibitionist

Small, but mainly short-lived, Scottish colonies were established in New Jersey as early as 1683 and in South Carolina by 1684, though in the next century most Scots settled in the southeastern and Atlantic states, with some also in New England. As well as volunteer emigrants there were numbers of criminals and rebels, the losers in disputes with the Crown from the Cromwellian wars through to the Jacobite uprisings of 1715 and 1745. Following the destruction of the clan system, emigration from the Highlands was considerable, many going to the Carolinas and Georgia and to Upper New York State. The Scots were also among the first to move westwards and by the last quarter of the eighteenth century they had made settlements on the other side of the Ohio River.

In the next century, driven from their native lands by the notorious Highland clearances, there was a great exodus (mainly to or via Canada) with particularly substantial Scots settlements in Illinois, where native-born Scots were among the founding fathers of the city of Chicago. They had also settled in Texas by as early as 1820 and Scots were also among the first non-Spanish immigrants to California. Wherever they went, they set up their own societies either by town or place of origin, by clan, or through Caledonian or St Andrew's Societies. They would continue with their ancient traditions of Highland gatherings (the first was held in New York in 1836), ceilidhs, Common Ridings and other ceremonies with immigrants from the Borders.

Small Gaelic-speaking communities existed for several decades, though generally they were all assimilated by the 1860s.

Today, throughout the United States, Scottish organisations are strong and thriving, with Burns Clubs and a strong Scottish flavour to many events such as Hallowe'en, now widely adopted in the American way of life. The first recorded Burns supper was held in New York on 25 January 1820, only twenty-four years after the poet's death. To a lesser extent even Sir Walter Scott was celebrated: in 1871 Scottish-Americans marked the centenary of his birth and funds were raised for a statue of him in Central Park, New York.

The English

An Englishman never means the natives of the United States when he speaks of foreignors; he reserves that epithet for non-English speaking races.

JOHN FULLERTON MUIRHEAD, *The Land of Contrasts* (Boston, 1898)

Unlike most other national groups, the English seldom settled in purely English communities unless they had other religious or social motivations. The exceptions were in cases when an English workforce from a particular area or with a special trade deliberately encouraged a distinctive English institutional life for protectionist reasons. In textile towns such as Lowell, Lynn and Lawrence (all in Massachusetts), and Pawtucket (Rhode Island), they organized immigrant benefits, cultural and literary societies, meeting and drinking ale together in English-style taverns and playing cricket in their own clubs. More practically, they reproduced the self-help associations of the British working class: trade unions, friendly societies, co-operatives, and working-men's clubs, often to the detriment of new arrivals from other countries.

Elsewhere there were many examples of purely English settlement, from the far-sightedly humanitarian to the patently absurd. Morris Birkbeck (1765–1825), the scientific farmer and pioneer, was the leader of one that attempted the former and failed. Born in Settle, Yorkshire, he was brought up as a Quaker and became a prosperous farmer at Wanborough, Surrey, the first

OPPOSITE: 'Leaving Old England'. From *The Graphic*, December 1869.

M.W.R.

man to raise merino sheep in England. He emigrated to America in 1817 with, among others, the family of Benjamin Flower, a free-thinking pamphleteer. Birkbeck had found it increasingly difficult to accept being taxed by a government that denied him the vote and tithed by a church whose doctrines he opposed. Moreover, as a yeoman and tenant farmer he felt snubbed by Surrey county society.

Reaching Illinois he developed, with Flower, a tract of land as an English settlement, called Wanborough after his home town, and imported scores of humble fellow Englishmen to people it. He described the process thus:

> On any spot where a few settlers cluster together . . . some enterprising proprietor finds in his section what he deems a good site for a town; he has it surveyed and laid out in lots, which he sells or offers for sale by auction . . . The new town then assumes the name of its founder – a storekeeper builds a little frame store and sends for a few cases of goods and then a tavern starts up . . . as the boarding house of the weary traveller; soon follows a blacksmith; a school master, who is also a minister of religion, becomes an important accession to this rising community. Thus the town proceeds if it becomes the metropolis of the neighborhood. Hundreds of these speculations may have failed but hundreds prosper.

Birkbeck and Flower quaintly set themselves up as squires of this new community, the 'English Prairie' as it was commonly called, and tried to introduce and preserve the amenities and lifestyle of civilized English life, founding a public library, building Regency-style cottages and laying out lawns and formal gardens. More seriously, Birkbeck also attempted a number of scientific farming schemes. But his gradual estrangement from Flower and his tragi-comic death in a drowning accident, still clutching his very English green umbrella, brought about the end of the settlement.

There were many other bizarre experimental communities. A tradition in the nineteenth century was for the younger sons of landed families to be sent to seek their fortunes in the New World instead of going into the army or the church, which were their traditional refuge. It was hoped that the American frontier would make such remittance-men self-reliant and even wealthy, especially if, banded together in their own settlements, they might maintain some of the virtues of their class and country. Rugby, Tennessee, for example, was established by Thomas Hughes, the Christian socialist famous for his classic tale of English public-school life, *Tom Brown's Schooldays*. With the financial and moral

OPPOSITE: 'Between decks in an emigrant ship – feeding time.'

support of 'several English gentlemen', his company acquired a substantial tract of eastern Tennessee in 1880, laid out farms and a town site complete with a saw mill, a brick kiln and many of the amenities of a small English town including a hotel and a library. The colony failed within a few years since tennis, football, shooting and cricket, along with other gentlemanly pursuits, evidently proved to be more popular than farming to these aristocratic offshoots.

Then there was Le Mars, Iowa, which was founded in 1879 by three Cambridge oarsmen, the Close brothers, and attracted hundreds of young, upper-class Englishmen. Here, too, sport and refined living appeared to take precedence over work, though while polo was played and a Jockey Club formed, work was not totally neglected. Some achieved a modicum of success at stock-raising. But Le Mars, too, soon lost its aristocratic flavour as the majority of the gentlemen settlers sold out. Other communities of middle- and upper-class Englishmen were established at Decorah, Iowa, in the 1860s and at Fairmont, Minnesota, in the 1870s. There was another settlement at Runnymede, Kansas, founded 'for the sons of English gentlemen', fifty of whom acquired estates and established polo fields, a racecourse and tennis courts. Again, the enterprise soon floundered, since most of those involved had no experience of hard work or, worse still, money to pay others to do it for them.

Finally, there were of course the religious and social communities of English people that were often more successful. (We will look later at Mother Ann Lee's Shakers, Robert Owen's New Harmony and Fanny Wright's Nashoba Settlement, and briefly at the English Mormon communities that settled in Illinois and Utah between 1840 and 1890.) In the period after the Civil War, there were still a few purely English settlements being founded like the farming villages in Kansas peopled by Sussex emigrants, and the Somerset, Devon and Yorkshire farmers and artisans who settled eight townships in Clay County, Minnesota. But in the last decades of the century most of the rural mid-western counties where the English had once been prominent failed to attract any new emigrants from there and the communities themselves were inevitably eroded. From then on, most new English immigrants went either to the new mining, farming and cattle-raising areas west of the Mississippi, or to some of the nation's older mining and industrial areas in southern Massachusetts, Rhode Island, Pennsylvania, New Jersey and the Upper Ohio River Valley.

The Welsh

Utica at present is a very large and fine town and increasing in size very much every year. It has more than eight thousand inhabitants including many Welshmen. When I came here first about twenty-eight years ago there was not one religious meeting house but soon after I arrived the Welsh built one for use in their language and that was the first!!! Now there are fifteen houses of worship of different denominations and three of them belong to the Welsh. There are also more than forty Welsh preachers here. Many Welsh are coming over continually and almost all praise this country as soon as they know anything about it. . . . There are many new roads and canals being built in every corner of the country giving plenty of work for everyone. We would advise all our countrymen to come over.

Letter from a Welsh immigrant in Utica to his nephew in
Wales, February 1832

In comparison with the Irish, English and Scottish exodus, only a small proportion of the population of Wales went to America. But because of their separate language they retained their distinctive social and institutional life longer than the other British nationalities. Once that language barrier had failed, however, Welsh-Americans also quickly assimilated into the American way of life. And today, as Rowland Tappan Berthoff, the historian of the British immigrant in America, has commented, only in a few places which were either densely populated by them in the nineteenth century, like Scranton, Pennsylvania, or Pittsburgh, or have remained quite isolated, like Oak Hill, Ohio, has any great sense of a Welsh ethnic group persisted. In the colonial period there was some Welsh settlement, usually for religious reasons, the first organized emigration being made by a South Wales congregation of Baptists in 1667. They founded a settlement called Swansea on the Plymouth–Rhode Island border, and there were also some Welsh Quaker settlements in Pennsylvania.

Serious Welsh emigration, however, began in the late eighteenth century when economic deprivation at home led to sizeable numbers of Montgomeryshire hill farmers emigrating to frontier regions of the eastern seaboard states. After 1815, again as a result of economic depression, there was a new wave of emigrants, and settlements were established in Wisconsin, Minnesota and Iowa, while later in the century there were others to be found in Missouri and Tennessee. To the industrial and urban

A Welsh chapel, built in Radnor, Pennsylvania in 1717.

areas, skilled and unskilled Welsh iron, tin plate and coal miners also emigrated, attracted by higher wages. There were Welsh mining communities in many coalfields, often sited close to Welsh farming communities, with others in the iron and steel industries in Chicago and Cleveland.

As religious and social pressures drove the earliest Welsh settlers, so did it some of their successors. The radical republican and Baptist, Morgan John Rhys (1760–1804), founded a settlement at Beulah in Western Pennsylvania in 1796, and fifty years later the Reverend Samuel Roberts (1800–85) from Montgomeryshire, who had led an unsuccessful revolt in support of land reform, tried to found a 'pure' Welsh colony at Brynffynon in Eastern Tennessee which would develop away from 'alien', that is, English influences. Only a tiny number could be persuaded to follow when he went in 1856, and the exercise ended in failure.

The well-known Congregational minister, the Reverend Michael Jones, having emigrated to Cincinnati, decided, around the year 1849, that the American environment was sapping the moral fibre and religious faith of his fellow Welsh-Americans. It was he who in 1856 set off with three shiploads of his compatriots, for the distant Patagonia in South America, to found the famous Welsh colony there.

The nonconformist chapel, along with language, was the principal building block of Welsh America, where by 1839 there were some forty-six Baptist, Calvinist, Methodist and Congregationalist chapels. By 1890 there were more than ten times that number but, inevitably, the new generations soon lost their Welsh identity. Welsh itself was still spoken in the so-called 'Welsh Hills' of Ohio as late as 1890, some seventy-five years after the first settlement there. Through the remembered language, other items of culture were and are today maintained with Eisteddfods and other secular festivals in many places in the United States.

The Scots-Irish

That these Irish Presbyterians were a bold and hardy race is proved by their at once pushing past the settled regions, and plunging into the wilderness as the leaders of the white advance. They were the first and last set of immigrants to do this; all others have merely followed in the wake of their predecessors. But, indeed, they were fitted to be Americans from the very start; they were kinsfolk of the Covenanters; they deemed it a religious duty to interpret their own Bible, and held for a divine right the election of their own clergy. For generations their whole ecclesiastic and scholastic systems had been fundamentally democratic. In the hard life of the frontier they had lost much of their religion, and they had but scant opportunity to give their children the schooling in which they believed; but what few meeting places and schoolhouses there were on the border were theirs.

THEODORE ROOSEVELT, The Winning of the West (1904)

The contribution of the Scots-Irish, the Ulstermen, to American society, particularly in government, defence and education, has been very considerable. The first Ulster settlements in North America date from the 1680s, before William of Orange had won his victory at the Boyne. It was, for example, the initiative of Francis Makemie (*c*.1658–1708), an Ulster Presbyterian cleric who settled in Virginia in 1698, that led to the formation of the first presbytery in the New World – at a meeting in Philadephia in 1706.

Major emigration from Ulster began around 1717 and by independence there were an estimated quarter of a million Ulstermen in the American colonies, most of them Presbyterians of Scottish origin, emigrating, in the main, to escape the restrictions imposed on dissenting churches in Britain. But there were also economic motives at work: the poor land management and the high taxation imposed by the Irish landed class and the collapse of the linen trade on which the Ulster economy depended heavily. The Ulstermen who emigrated thus did so for the same reasons – crop failure, famine, high rents, social injustice –

that encouraged that other Irish emigration, by Catholics, in the next century.

The ordinary Ulster emigrants did as others and settled in groups of their own kind for protection and economic security. They were great pioneers and in the 1720s and 1730s there was a chain of Scots-Irish settlements stretching along the frontier from western Massachusetts right up to Maine. Even today, the place names Belfast, Bangor, Orange County and Londonderry testify to them. These Ulster people were not always popular with the existing settlers of New England, who found their uncompromising Calvinism hard to take. Unlike most new settlers the Scots-Irish did not arrive quietly, and their religious leaders were quick to denounce the laxity of the existing Anglican and other churches. They were also widely branded as a burden on the community and with justification: it is recorded that between 1729 and 1742 two-thirds of the occupants of Boston's gaols and almshouses were Scots-Irish.

From about that time on, almost all new Ulster immigrants went south to Pennsylvania, particularly to Philadelphia which had long had a healthy trade with the Six Counties; but they were always in the vanguard of the move westwards too – up the Delaware, beyond the Susquehanna and then after 1768 across the Allegheny Mountains. They were among the first to settle what was to become Pittsburgh, and were frontiersmen in western Maryland in the Shenandoah Valley and in the Carolinas.

While respecting their Scottish ancestry, the Scots-Irish in the New World at first tended to think of themselves as Irish rather than as Scots, and up until as late as the 1830s even allied themselves with the first waves of Irish Catholic immigrants in politics and in membership of benevolent organizations, including the Friendly Sons of St Patrick. They felt no affinity with St Andrew's or other Scottish societies. But after the huge Irish Catholic flood of 1840 caused by the Great Famine, the Scots-Irish, stimulated by events back home, moved into the vanguard of the anti-Catholic movement in the United States and all the age-old bitterness were borne again in the New World. Orangemen's orders, American Protestant Associations and others promoted anti-Catholic demonstrations which frequently led to violence, with notorious church-burning riots in Philadelphia in 1844.

In 1870 and 1871 in New York, Twelfth of July parades ended with fighting in which, in the first year, eight people were killed and in the second thirty-one civilians and two policemen died. (The last such sizeable parade in a city now noted for its annual St Patrick's Day Parade was in 1919.) Yet, for all their prejudices,

Ulstermen had little difficulty in assimilating themselves into American society, without forgetting their own particular heritage.

*   *   *

At the time of Independence, no part of American society failed to be dominated by the British, and predominantly the English. On the other hand, the *very existence* of the new America was of enormous, if not more, significance to the political, economic and social life of Britain. The economies of the two countries were especially closely linked by trade in tobacco, cotton, molasses, tea, furs, tar, pitch and slaves. Many might argue that the introduction of the humble potato and of tobacco from America in 1565 had as great an influence on European society as anything else that has ever come across the Atlantic in an easterly direction. There were, of course, many new, vigorously and purely American strands of thought and activity but they had arisen from conditions in America itself and owed little to any third country; neither Germany (except perhaps in Pennsylvania), Scandinavia, France, Spain, Italy nor the Jewish diaspora had yet made any substantial mark on the American way of life.

The signatories of the Declaration of Independence would give the most valid indication of the scale of British-born, or people of British origin, in the top ranks of the thirteen colonies and, as we shall see in Chapter 4, nearly all the signatories were of British descent.

In the period immediately before that great event, the political and social links across the Atlantic were, surprisingly, as strong as any in the history of British colonial rule. It has indeed been argued that the trouble which was to come was due, not so much to interference by Westminster in the laws or governance of the colonies – the image given by the couplet in celebration of the Boston Tea Party: 'We love our cup of tea full well, But love our freedom more' – but it was also the result of jealousies of trade and commerce, and the cry of 'no taxation without representation'. Whatever else, the bitterness that followed was heightened by the strong element of civil war in the events that led to Independence. What had been one country or empire was to become two. In the middle were the victims such as poor General Gage of Firle, near Lewes in Sussex, who had the misfortune to be Commander-in-Chief at the start of the Revolution. He found, like many colonial administrators after him, that, with his American wife at his side, he could please neither colonists nor the King. But in the long history of the Rich Tide, 1776 and all that was but a short and necessary stage in a relationship that was to become stronger and longer-lived as a result.

CHAPTER TWO

Language and Communication

We have room in this country for but one flag, the Stars and Stripes . . . We have room for but one loyalty, loyalty to the United States . . . We have room for but one language, the English language. FRANKLIN DELANO ROOSEVELT (1919)

At one stage during the Second World War, British and American soldiers were issued with a modest Anglo-American dictionary to avoid the danger that *The Times* foresaw in 1943, when it wrote: 'There is urgent need for surmounting what someone has called the almost insuperable barrier of a common language. It would never do for Great Britain and America to think they understand, yet miss, the point of each other's remarks just now. Both versions of the common language must be correctly understood by both peoples.' It is well known that our language sometimes divides us; there are many common words in one country that are uncommon in the other, words that have been known to trap the unwary traveller, either by the same word meaning different things or by different words being used to describe the same thing. Thus, from the first category we have words like 'homely' and 'to table' which have dangerously differing meanings on both sides of the Atlantic; and from the second – apartment/flat, pavement/sidewalk, car/automobile, coffin/casket and a host of others. Yet despite the commonplace of 'English being one of the hardest languages for an American to learn' the English language is the most fundamental of all the bonds that unite Britain and the United States and the most significant of all the legacies of their shared colonial past. Modern American speech has now of course been greatly enriched by words borrowed from Indian, Spanish, French, German, Italian and Yiddish, but, by and large, the vocabulary of power, justice, business, education and most other departments of society is common to both sides of the Atlantic.

So the anxiety expressed by *The Times* was small beer (trivial) when set against the great richness of the common English/American language. Coleridge could, half in jest, tell the story of

OPPOSITE: Alexander Graham Bell making a telephone call from New York to Chicago, 1890.

an American who 'by his boasting of the superiority of the Americans generally, but especially in their language, once provoked me to tell him that "On that head the least said the better", as the Americans presented the extraordinary anomaly of a people without a language.' That they had mistaken the English language for baggage (which is called plunder in America), and had stolen it.' But, in a serious vein, that common language, changed as it has been, ensures that in the main we know that the concepts and ideas, the ethics and mechanics of both societies are more likely to be understood by Britons and Americans alike than by any of the non-English-speaking nations. We do not have to translate truth or guilt, democracy or totalitarianism, even though we jointly recognize a longer history in the Greek, Roman or Germanic origins of these words. From words and language so much else of what is discussed in this book was derived. Without a common language it would not have happened.

Many of the words brought by the original settlers still remain in the American language with the original sixteenth- or seventeenth-century meaning even though that word or meaning has been lost in Britain. 'Fall' (for autumn), 'mad' (for angry), 'flap-jack', 'to approbate', 'to loan' (lend), 'to hustle' are a few common examples. They borrowed words such as 'maize', 'caucus', 'hickory' or 'canoe' from the Indians where such words were useful or where no English word existed for some new element, plant or activity, and they took up Spanish adaptations of other Indian words such as 'tobacco', 'tomato' and 'hammock'. As new immigrants arrived from other non-English-speaking lands they adopted some of their words or expressions too, where these provided a useful linguistic tool. They made the effort, not always successful, to have the newcomers adapt, at least within a generation, to the firmly entrenched language of the new America–English. Later on they firmly created or embraced new words that were particular to them – 'to endorse', 'presidential', 'to phone', 'editorial', 'OK', 'filing cabinet', 'to fall for' and a host of others.

The desire for linguistic conformity was not necessarily backed up by law (though laws did and do exist enforcing English as the language of the land) as much as by the requirement that to succeed it was necessary to speak English and to speak it well. The immigrant parents might continue to speak the old languages; the children might still speak with the parental tongues at home. But in the outside world good English was the first requirement. This rule did not just apply to language. It was also encouraged, if not enforced, as regards the very identity of the immigrants. Strange-sounding foreign forenames and surnames were anglicized or simply replaced by easily understood, easily written, clean-cut Anglo-Saxon substitutes, usually by hard-pressed immigration officials at ports of entry. And, in the new America, a Peter Smith was (to generalize, for the period up until the First World War) more likely to get a job and promotion than Petrovich Smolskevyeska. In essence, therefore, English conquered or submerged all other incoming languages, and, with the exception of a few ethnic-speaking communities (from Spanish, French, Latvian, Dutch through, increasingly, to Italian and Japanese) it still does today. (This does not ignore the fact – to which we will return in the final chapter – that there is much active contemporary debate on the whole question of English as the national language, and thus the validity, legality and worth of schools teaching in, for example, Spanish as first language.)

Noah Webster published his first American dictionary in 1828 'to cut free from the subservience to English English'. For his

Noah Webster (1758–1843), in a painting by James Herring, 1833.

belief was that 'America must be as independent in literature as she is in politics, as famous for arts as for arms'. He was perhaps only a little premature in prophesying that, 'In fifty years from this time, the American-English will be spoken by more people than all the other dialects of the language'. But he recognized that language, whatever its origins is the most important unifying force in any nation. (The great lexicographer is also renowned for the famous, and perhaps apocryphal, report of his being discovered by his wife *in flagrante* with the chambermaid. 'Noah,' she said, 'I am surprised.' 'No, my dear,' he responded. 'I am surprised. You are merely astonished.')

Language is not static and does not easily confine itself within geographical borders. It is continuously developing and expanding, and American English is no exception. Each element has fed off the other and the flow, as with other subject elements of this book, has, particularly in the last few generations, been as much, if not more, in an easterly direction. There is little evidence, for example, of new English words travelling to the United States over the last century and a half and plenty of evidence of the reverse. As Alistair Cooke (of whom more in a moment) has said, 'An Americanism is a word or phrase you recognize that came in during your sentient lifetime. In the nineteenth century there was a big movement to stop the word ''reliable'' coming into England – this dreadful Americanism, ''reliable''. And ''scientist'' was an American invention which was as offensive then as anything invented by *Time* magazine thirty years ago . . . I would say to my crew on ''America'', for instance, ''You know, you talk three or four hundred Americanisms a day but you don't know it, because they came in in say, 1860 or 1910.'' ' Or, to quote Harold Evans, 'It is very hard to think of an English word that is as good as ''gatecrasher'', ''go-getter'' or ''rubber-necker'' '.

All of which could suggest that the age of a society has an inverse correlation with the vigour of its vocabulary. That this earlier turning-point in language was the case is also partly as a result of the more dynamic nature of American society in expressing itself, as exemplified by the robust nature of its press, and partly because of the geographical size of that nation which has always demanded ever better methods of communication by physical means, wire, telephone, television and latterly by even more sophisticated methods of satellite communication. Webster's predictions have been more than fulfilled. Today in global terms, of the several hundred million people who speak English as a first language throughout the world, a very large percentage of them now live in the United States. This, helped by American forms of mass communication, must point the way in which linguistic influences are going to continue to flow in the future.

Dictators and enemies of democracy have, throughout history, hated, feared and banned, when they could, the uncensored, printed word. Freedom and freedom to print are, consequently, often held to be self-evidently synonymous. Such liberties – with a few well-documented exceptions – have been common to both Britain and the United States throughout the history of print, from unauthorized bibles and political tract-printing through to the investigative media reporting of the present day; this is probably as true for them as for any other two countries in the history of the world. Of course there have been unhappy historical episodes of book-burning and other forms of suppression in both countries, but these have been rare in comparison with what has happened even in what are now the other Western democracies.

The Printed Word

It is difficult to be an American because there is as yet no code, grammar, decalogue by which to orient oneself. Americans are still engaged in inventing what is to be an American. That is at once an exhilarating and a painful occupation.

THORNTON WILDER

Establishing who was first in history with anything is always fraught with danger, but Stephen Daye (1611–68) from London is credited with being the first printer in British America, arriving in Cambridge, Massachusetts, around 1638. He was encouraged to go there, taking his own printing press – the first in America – with him, by the Reverend Joseph Glover, the rector of Sutton in Surrey, who was trying to persuade others to join him in the settlement of Massachusetts. Paper, ink and typefaces were all he brought out on the same journey (during which Glover himself died) and the first product from the press at Cambridge, in the grounds of Harvard College, was a broadsheet entitled, *The Freeman's Oath*, with the first book ever printed in the American colonies, *The Book of Psalms*, published in 1640. While poor Daye had been given a grant of several hundred acres of land, he appears always to have been in debt, and, as his wages were low, he eventually fell on very hard times, ending up as a mere jobbing locksmith. None the less, in the history of printing in North America, his position with that of his son, Matthew, as the first stands unchallenged.

Among eighteenth-century publishers, one of the most influential was Thomas Fleet (1685–1758), who emigrated from London to Boston in 1712. With his son, John (1734–1806), he printed both religious and secular books and pamphlets and was also publisher of the *Boston Evening Post*, which was the leading New England newspaper of the time. The Fleets' importance lay not only in the quality, but also in the range of their work, making them among the first of the really professional American publishers.

It is only in the nineteenth century, with the development of more advanced methods of newspaper production, that an exceptional figure in the early history of American mass communications come on to the stage. In many ways he deserves to be considered equally as an innovator and an entrepreneur, but it was as editor and journalist that he had the largest role to play. James Gordon Bennett, Sr (1795–1872), born in Keith in Scotland, emigrated at the age of twenty-four first to Halifax, Nova Scotia, before moving to the United States. He apparently left Scotland on a whim, abandoning his potential calling as a Roman Catholic priest, after a chance meeting on the Aberdeen quayside with a friend who was about to emigrate. According to his own account he decided then and there to go and 'see the place where that wondrous man Ben Franklin was born'.

After spells working in Portland, Maine, Boston and New York, he was taken on by the Charleston *Courier* as a translator of foreign journals. In 1823 he returned to New York where he tried unsuccessfully to set up a commercial school. Then in 1825 he joined the staff of the New York *Courier* which he soon bought and almost instantly resold. Following a period on the *National Advocate* he spent two years writing for the New York *Enquirer*. As the paper's Washington correspondent he earned himself a reputation for his highly controversial and forthright style of reporting.

From then on his career blossomed. He became, in turn, Director of an amalgamated *New York Courier and Enquirer*, Chief Editor and Joint Proprietor of the Philadelphia *Pennsylvanian* and then, in 1835, much influenced by the growing popularity of the 'penny press', he founded a paper of his own – the four-page *New York Herald* which appeared daily at a mere one cent a copy. Combining an exciting, even salacious, reporting style and highly energetic newsgathering techniques (he was, as befitted a canny Scot, his own crime reporter, city correspondent and editorial writer), the *Herald* rapidly became the largest-selling newspaper

Kalendarium Pennsilvaniense, or
America's Messinger.
BEING AN
ALMANACK
For the Year of Grace, 1686.

Wherein is contained both the English & Forreign Account. the Motions of the Planets through the Signs, with the Luminaries, Conjunctions, Aspects, Eclipses; the rising, southing and setting of the Moon, with the time when she passeth by, or is with the most eminent fixed Stars : Sun rising and setting. and the time of High-Water at the City of *Philadelphia, &c.*

With Chronologies, and many other Notes, Rules, and Tables, very fitting for every man to know & have ; all which is accomodated to the Longitude of the Province of *Pennsilvania,* and Latitude of 40 Degr. north, with a Table of Houses for the same, which may indifferently serve *New-England, New York, East & West Jersey, Maryland,* and most parts of *Virginia.*

By *SAMUEL ATKINS.*
Student in the Mathamaticks and Astrology.

And the Stars in their Courses fought against Sesera, Jndg. 5. 29.

Printed and Sold by *William Bradford,* sold also by the Author and *H. Murrey* in *Philadelphia,* and *Philip Richards* in *New-York;* 1685.

Kalendarium Pennsilvaniense or America's Messinger, the first Pennsylvania imprint, by William Bradford (1663–1752), one of the great printers of the colonial era. Born in England, Bradford first came to America in 1685 and set up a press in Pennsylvania. He went back to England disillusioned four years later, but was persuaded to return later by the promise of greater support. In 1693 he was appointed printer to the Crown in New York. There, as well as printing numerous public documents he produced New York's first paper currency in 1709, the first American Book of Common Prayer, and in 1727 the first history of New York. He also issued New York's first newspaper, the *New York Gazette* in 1725.

in New York City. It eventually reached an exceptional circulation of 100,000 copies a day by 1864, by which time it was one of the best-known journals in the world.

To Bennett also goes the more dubious credit of introducing so-called 'yellow journalism' to the United States, through his encouragement of sensationalized reporting of political intrigue, violent crime and passionate, preferably illicit, love affairs among the great of the land. He was attacked, sometimes physically, and criticized as a result. When he accused James Watson Webb, the editor of the rival *Courier and Enquirer*, of touting certain stocks and bonds in the journal for corrupt Wall Street operators, Webb attacked him in the street and 'cut a slash in my head about one and half inches in length'. Bennett was unperturbed and afterwards said that: 'The fellow, no doubt, wanted to let out the never-failing supply of good humor and wit, which has created such a reputation for the *Herald*, and appropriate the contents to supply the emptiness of his own thick skull. He did not succeed, however, in rifling me of my ideas. . . . My ideas, in a few days, will flow as freshly as ever, and he will find it so to his cost.' Yet by going over the top, and unconcerned about making a caricature of himself (such as when he announced his marriage in the *Herald* – DECLARATION OF LOVE – CAUGHT AT LAST – GOING TO BE MARRIED – NEW MOMENT IN CIVILIZATION), he actually added to his sales. His many innovative techniques included the use of the most up-to-date printing machinery then available – and an additional reason for his runaway commercial success was his highly organized network of newsboys to guarantee the efficient distribution of his paper.

In 1838 Bennett returned to Britain and began signing up the best London-based foreign correspondents he could find to provide the *Herald* with a first-class European news service. He followed this up back in New York by instituting a system of chartering small boats that went out to meet the incoming ships from Europe so as to scoop his rivals by being first out with the news. He had another first in using the telegraph as a news-gathering device: when an important political speech was delivered in Lexington, Kentucky, in 1846 it was sent first by rail to Cincinnati and then telegraphed to New York to appear in full in the next morning's edition of the *Herald*. He also introduced the practice of on-the-scene interviews.

Despite what many saw as his moral dishonesty, Bennett's revolutionary determination to keep his paper free of party or partisan bias – and his success at exposing the corruption of politicians and financiers – earned him a unique if not always distinguished place in the history of American journalism. As one contemporary said, timid reserve was not one of Bennett's characteristics, and he himself, in his own memoirs, set out an excellent blueprint for many of today's tabloid editors: 'Since I knew myself, all the real approbation I sought for was my own. If my conscience was satisfied on the score of morals, and my

Cartoon of James Gordon Bennett Snr., 'the editorial Jim Crow' from 'Vanity Fair', April 1861.
Wheel about, and turn about,
An' do jis' so,
An' ebery time I turn my coat
I says I told you so.

James Gordon Bennett Snr.
(1795–1872)

ambition on the matter of talent, I always felt easy. On this principle I have acted from my youth up, and on this principle I mean to die. Nothing can disturb my equanimity. I know myself, so does the Almighty. Is not that enough?' In the words of Piers Brandon, 'Transfigured by power and vanity, he emerged as the first of a new breed of men: the press barons'.

His son, the super-rich, eccentric but influential James Gordon Bennett, Jr (1841–1918), who took over the *Herald* from his father, was no slouch either, whether at running newspapers, employing feature writers of the calibre of Mark Twain, or getting himself talked about. He was a great American jingoist: 'It is our

A carte-de-visite photograph of H. M. Stanley, captioned 'Mr. Stanley, in the dress he wore when he met Livingstone in Africa'.

manifest duty to head and rule all nations,' he wrote in the *New York Herald* in 1865. He owned papers in Europe as well, including the London and Paris *Herald*, and was, after all, the man who bought the famous restaurant 'Ciros' in Monte Carlo when he turned up one evening to find his favourite table occupied by someone else. He then told the diners at his table to leave, even though they were only halfway through their meal. When Bennett had finished his meal of mutton chops, he gave the waiter a generous tip – the restaurant.

The reputation of the Bennett family's paper was such that when, in October 1869, they commissioned, at the cost of ten thousand pounds, the journalist and explorer, Henry Morton Stanley (1841–1904), to set out on his famous expedition to Africa to find the missionary David Livingstone, Stanley's own achievement was to be criticized by the geographical establishment, particularly in London. Born in England in 1841, Stanley himself had emigrated at an early age to the United States where he had an unhappy time serving both as a Confederate, then as a Union soldier, and ending up almost destitute. But his highly graphic, journalistic style of reporting on his explorations appealed to the Bennetts and he began to thrive in their employment. His flamboyant journeys to report wars and other crises in far-flung parts of the world, coupled with his reputation for always getting his story back to New York first, were still derided because of the reputation of the *Herald*: thus the President of the Royal Geographical Society went so far as to suggest that the sensationalism of the Bennetts' style had actually camouflaged the truth that 'Livingstone had in fact found Stanley'. History shows that Stanley, though arrogant and impetuous, was fully justified in his heroic reputation: it was the nature of his employers in New York that gave rise to the doubts. It is interesting to note that in his later exploration of Africa, Stanley ensured that he was jointly sponsored both by the *Herald* and by the highly conservative *Daily Telegraph* in London, an example of transatlantic journalistic co-operation that seems imaginative even by the standards of today.

The other great figure in popular communication in the nineteenth century was the liberal journalist, Edwin Lawrence Godkin (1831–1902). Educated in England and at Queen's College, Belfast, he began his career as a war correspondent (1853–5) serving the London *Daily News* in Belfast. In November 1856, he emigrated to America where he was admitted to the Bar in New York but did not seek to practise. Instead he travelled round America continuing to write articles for the *Daily News*. In July 1865, Godkin became the editor, later owner, of a new paper,

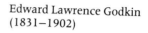

Edward Lawrence Godkin
(1831–1902)

The Nation, founded to support the interests of the abolitionist movement. The paper was the first of its kind in America; it was not solely concerned with the issue of slavery and much space was given in it to informed comment on other aspects of public affairs, as well as to literature, the arts and music, becoming, in the view of many contemporary commentators, the best weekly not only in America but also in the world. The paper's influence certainly went beyond its circulation figures, making a particular impression on the young intelligentsia of the age on both sides of the Atlantic.

In 1883 Godkin moved to become the editor-in-chief of the New York *Evening Post*, and soon won for himself a unique place in the history of American journalism, through his vigorous campaigns against corruption in New York City and his revealing biographies of the Tammany leaders which exposed their corrupt

Alfred Harmsworth, Lord
Northcliffe (1865–1922)

Ralph David Blumenfeld
(1864–1928)

practices. Above all he remained a prominent Anglo-American and had many influential British and American friends. As a leading figure in New York and Boston literary, artistic and professional circles, he was also recognized in Britain and in 1897 was awarded the degree of Doctorate of Law by Oxford University. Both he and the Bennetts demonstrated by their actions and achievements that the history of mass media is firmly embedded in a joint Anglo-American experience.

In the most recent period of that history press barons figure prominently as well as their journalist employees. The Beaverbrooks, the Northcliffes and the Astors had as many transatlantic links in their generations as the Atlantic Richfield Company or the Australian-American Rupert Murdoch has had in contemporary times. Indeed, in an unwitting acknowledgement of the future impact of the Rich Tide on the twentieth century, Joseph Pulitzer invited Northcliffe (then Alfred Harmsworth) to edit his New York paper, the *World*, for the first day of the new century. Harmsworth printed the *World* as a twelve-page tabloid, about half its normal size. On the front page he announced that his slogan, 'All the news in sixty seconds', was the right approach for 'the Twentieth or Time-Saving Century'. As late as 1929 Hearst was to tell his editors: 'We all thought it was a clever stunt, but few of us realized the vital importance of the principle.'

The example set by the press barons has led, inevitably, to their editors, journalists and other employees moving easily to work on one side of the Atlantic or the other because of the shared similarities of language and (with certain obvious exceptions) of journalistic marketing, ethics and style. This point could not be better illustrated than by looking at the career of the Wisconsin-born journalist, Ralph David Blumenfeld (1864–1948), who at the age of twenty-three first came to London to report on Queen Victoria's Jubilee. Three years later, James Gordon Bennett, Jr, having read an impressive eye-witness report by Blumenfeld of a New York fire, engaged him on the spot and sent him back to Britain to revive the ailing London daily and Sunday editions of his paper, the *Herald*. In a very short period of time Blumenfeld, known always as 'R.D.B.', both increased the circulation of the Sunday paper and even brought in a small profit. Impressed though he was, Bennett was still unhappy about the newspaper's profitability and ordered Blumenfeld to close down the Sunday edition. Despite this, Blumenfeld stayed on as London correspondent of the New York *Herald* until he was appointed superintendent of the paper in New York in 1893.

In 1894, parting company with Bennett after a heated dispute, he moved back to England and set up a business of his own selling linotype printing machines. From the Empire Typesetting Company in New York he secured manufacturing rights and opened a factory in Yorkshire. While the enterprise was a success, after a few years Blumenfeld decided to return to journalism, accepting in 1900 an offer from Alfred Harmsworth, the first Lord Northcliffe, whom he met by chance in a barber's shop in Fleet Street, to become the news editor of the *Daily Mail*. Two years later he was recruited on to the staff of Cyril Arthur Pearson's *Daily Express*, newly founded to challenge the *Mail*'s supremacy in popular journalism. In 1904 he became editor-in-chief and four years after that was made a director of the company. (Not the least of his achievements was that, as a director of the company, he brought the Canadian, Max Aitken, the future Lord Beaverbrook, into journalism.)

This American, who took out British nationality in 1907, was to hold the editor's post for some twenty-eight years, before he was promoted to the chairmanship of the board. During that period he helped lay the foundations of modern popular journalism in Britain, in particular developing the urgency and zest of the tabloid-style format, which had already been pioneered in America. He was the first editor to use another American innovation, the banner headline, and to force news on to the front page of his papers – until then exclusively used for advertising – and, though no sportsman, he also recognized the importance and selling power of the sports sections of popular papers.

A devoted supporter of the Conservative Party (indeed he was the first journalist to be elected to the Carlton Club, that bastion of Toryism), Blumenfeld was on intimate terms with several leading Tories including Stanley Baldwin. In early December 1916, soon after the new War Cabinet was formed, he suggested to the Chancellor of the Exchequer, Bonar Law, that Baldwin would be an ideal choice as his Parliamentary private secretary. On 15 December, Baldwin got the appointment and so began his climb to the top of the political tree. Years later Baldwin wrote to Blumenfeld: '. . . I admire your courage in backing a rank outsider, it doesn't often come off . . . your kind letter carried me back many long years when I was innocent of office and frequented the Carlton Club and was inclined to think Cabinet Ministers great men.'

The best-known and most influential American commentator in Britain on the Second World War, Edward R. Murrow, was born in Greensboro, North Carolina, as Egbert Roscoe on 25 April 1908. A keen scholar, he became the president of the National Student Federation in 1930. After working as the assistant director of the Institute of International Education, he joined CBS as the director of Talks and Education. Two years later in 1937 he was sent to London to head the network's European Bureau. (He was their only correspondent.) He was to undertake the fairly routine task of arranging and finding speakers for cultural programmes. However, events in Europe soon transformed his role. While on the way to Poland in 1938 to set up children's broadcasts for CBS's 'School of the Air', the Germans entered Austria. Murrow quickly chartered a small plane to Vienna and arrived in time to describe on the radio the German march into the capital. Back in London he reported on the vital pre-war events from Munich to the invasion of Czechoslovakia. 'I averaged two hours' sleep per day, I imagine,' he later said, 'and I didn't dare risk any more. You just had to be up and about almost every minute because events moved so rapidly it would be impossible to catch up if you allowed yourself the luxury of eight hours' sleep.'

During the war Murrow gave regular broadcasts from his London office. His opening words 'This is London' became his catchphrase, known to millions in the United States. He covered most of the vital episodes in the war – from the Battle of Britain, the campaign in North Africa, the Normandy landings, to VE Day. He shared the fears, hopes and terror of British people during the Blitz, providing American listeners with graphic and emotional, but always objective and accurate, descriptions of the bombings: 'Five times I've fallen flat on the pavement,' he said in one of his broadcasts. 'The individual's reaction to the sound of falling bombs cannot be described. That moan of stark terror and suspense cannot be encompassed by words.'

Twice the CBS studios were bombed and on one occasion the BBC studios were attacked as Murrow was broadcasting from the building. Of this he said: 'I can tell you from personal experience that it's not pleasant to sit in a studio filled with the odor of iodine and antiseptics and talk to you at home while good friends are being carried on stretchers along the corridor outside the studio door.' In 1941 in a preface to *Bloody but Unbowed*, a pictorial record of England during the Blitz, he wrote: 'This book is too small. In order to convey an adequate impression of the courage, determination and good humour that sustain the people of this island, it should be the size of two telephone directories wired for sound.'

After the war Murrow returned to America where he was now a household name. He had made his reputation from his vivid descriptions of the sufferings and resilience of the British people, for whom he kept a special fondness. They in turn owed him a considerable debt for the way in which his broadcasts helped to influence American opinion towards greater support for the Allies.

Ed Murrow, broadcasting in 1954.

In the modern history of Anglo-American journalistic communication there are a multitude of other memorable figures like James (Scotty) Reston, from Scotland, who through the brilliance of his writing ('America started the Sixties thinking it could save the world and ended them wondering if it could save face') rose to become Executive Editor of *The New York Times*. There are many Americans in the top ranks of publishing and journalism in Britain and many other Britons in senior media positions in the United States. In terms of electronic media journalism, the greatest single Anglo-American in post-war communications must be Alistair Cooke, whose letters, broadcasts and writings to the British about America, have influenced a generation and made a unique contribution to contemporary understanding between our two peoples. He is the man whom Harold Nicolson called 'the best broadcaster on five continents', who, with his urbanity and understanding, has made Britain and America

better informed about each other. This journalist, essayist and broadcaster was born in Manchester in 1908 and educated at Cambridge, Yale and Harvard. He has worked for newspapers and broadcasting organizations on both sides of the Atlantic, but his main contribution to the Rich Tide has been by his percipient and humane interpretation of one nation to another, and, indeed, with his television series (and his book) on the making of America, a nation to itself as well.

Take, for example, his profile of President Theodore Roosevelt, in which, in a few words, he can encapsulate a character, his perception and his achievement: 'Theodore Roosevelt is affectionately recalled today as a half-heroic half-comic figure, a bespectacled barrel of a man, choking with teeth and jingoism.' But 'he was the first influential man of his time to see clearly that the United States was no longer a rural nation but an industrial giant running amok.' Or, again, some of his glimpses of the America that he has reported on over the years: 'America, it may be news to the learned, is a part of the human condition and within its borders there is still vast variety of interest, amusement, goodness, evil, humor, absurdity, and all the other human attributes.' And then: 'How comparatively rare with Americans is an orderly set of hobbies; and how even rarer is the quality from which hobbies spring – namely, eccentricity.'

*   *   *

By communication we mean not only printing, publishing, newspapers and journalism, but also the means whereby ideas, along with news and, thereby, understanding, is transferred from one country to another. First of all people had to get across physically, and for the first centuries news had to be brought by individuals who had taken passage in sailing ships as and when they could. Gradually, however, regular sailings were introduced with steamboats first used in the transatlantic trade from 1838. With the introduction of the telegraph and the telephone, however, Britain and America could pass messages and then speak to each other with much increased accuracy and speed. No longer was it necessary to wait until men or mails crossed the Atlantic, for information or understanding to be transmitted. (As it happens, the Briton, Rowland Hill, the founder of the British 'penny postal' system, inspired the movement for cheaper postal services in the United States.) One of those largely instrumental in the laying of the first transatlantic cables of 1858 and 1866 was William Thomson (1828–1907), later Baron Kelvin, the Belfast-born scientist and inventor. It was over this cable that, by virtue of Samuel Morse's invention of the Morse code and of submarine

OPPOSITE: Alistair Cooke, photographed in his New York apartment in 1968.

The first transatlantic telegraph cable being laid from the stern of HMS *Agamemnon*, 1857–8.

cable telegraphy, Queen Victoria and President Buchanan were able to exchange a message on 17 August 1858: 'Europe and America are united by telegraph. Glory to God in the Highest.'

Alexander Graham Bell (1847–1922) pre-eminently exemplified the rich tide of talent that left Britain in the second half of the nineteenth century to seek prosperity in the United States. Born in Scotland and educated in both Scotland and London, Bell, a teacher and scientist, moved first to Canada in 1870 and then on to Boston where he took American citizenship and as Professor of Vocal Physiology and the Mechanics of Speech, devoted his energies to helping the deaf to speak. It was in 1876, when he was only twenty-nine, that he developed his invention that was granted the American patent covering 'the means of, and apparatus for, transmitting vocal or other sounds telegraphically . . .', the telephone. The first prosaic words spoken on the telephone were delivered in Boston on 10 March 1876: 'Mr Watson, come here: I want you.'

While Bell is most famous for this single invention, he developed many other different processes both scientific and medical, including the transmission of sound on a beam of light and the graphophone – the earliest method of sound recording. In his lifetime his greatest humanitarian work for communicating with the deaf brought him honours and awards – perhaps his most famous protégé was the child Helen Keller. In 1898 this bold and generous man succeeded his father as President of the National Geographical Society in Washington and with his future son-in-law, the famous Gilbert Hovey Grosvenor, believing in the need to communicate some of the world's marvels to a wider audience, transformed a modest pamphlet into the unique journal of geographical education that the *National Geographic Magazine* is today.

He did not stop with these considerable achievements – he was much involved in the early development of flying machines and held five American patents for 'aerial vehicles'. He was also a pioneer of sonar detection systems and designed a hydrofoil craft that as early as 1919 achieved a speed record of 70 m.p.h. The genius of Alexander Graham Bell therefore encompassed a huge spectrum of activity in that most important of all fields – communication between peoples in the widest of all possible meanings of the word.

*   *   *

In his *Table Talk*, published in 1833, a visionary Samuel Taylor Coleridge wrote: 'The possible destiny of the United States of America as a nation of a hundred millions of freemen – stretching from the Atlantic to the Pacific, living the laws of Alfred, and speaking the language of Shakespeare and Milton, is an august conception. Why should we not wish to see it realized? America would then be England viewed through a solar microscope; Great Britain in a state of glorious magnification!'

Coleridge's grand premonition related to all aspects of the Rich Tide with the flow mainly in a westerly direction. He was not to know that there would be a great sea change and that, of all the areas of activity covered by this book, the sea change in language and communication would begin rather earlier than anywhere else. Without a common language and an ever improving means of communication across the Atlantic – the written word, the spoken word on to the marvels of modern satellite communication – the rest would not have been possible.

CHAPTER THREE

By Creed and Conscience

America is the only nation in the world that is founded on a creed. That creed is set forth with dogmatic and even theological lucidity in the Declaration of Independence; perhaps the only piece of practical politics that is also theoretical politics and also great literature.
G. K. CHESTERTON

The strong cross-flow of influences between Britain and America in the three fields of law and justice, spiritual belief, and humanitarian and utopian endeavour was founded on the common ethics of the two countries, origins of fundamental importance to the Rich Tide as a whole, because, in many respects, they constitute the bedrock over which that Rich Tide flows. Let us look first at law, constitution and justice, remembering as we do that while the United States has a Constitution and a Bill of Rights upon which its law and government depend, Britain for the moment does not, and bases the administration and enforcement of its laws largely on precedent and convention, a point which the American Secretary of State George Shultz stressed when he said: 'We have a written constitution; yours is unwritten. But the only principle of constitutionalism is the same: Government limited by the rule of law to protect the freedom of the individual against arbitrary power.'

On 15 December 1791, the first ten amendments to the United States Constitution – known unofficially but universally as the Bill of Rights – received their ratification. These amendments specify the basic rights of the individual in the United States and ensure their protection against the arbitrary action of the government. For example, the First Amendment guarantees the freedom of religion, speech, press, assembly and petition, just as the Sixth Amendment ensures the right to trial by jury in criminal cases. Taken together, the ten amendments form the 'core of American civil liberty' and provide the basis for the judicial protection of the individual.

Roger Williams (c. 1603–82), the founder of Rhode Island, holding his 'Bloody Tenet'. There is no contemporary likeness of Williams: this one was engraved in 1847.

Although the authors of the Federal Bill of Rights modelled these amendments on the 1776 Virginia Declaration of Rights (which was the first to proclaim that the rights of man must constitute part of the fundamental law of the land and be protected by it) the document is ultimately derived from English sources – namely, the rights and freedoms established by the common law of England or defined in the three great charters of English liberty: Magna Carta, the 1628 Petition of Right, and the 1689 Bill of Rights. For example, by a mixture of deliberate intent and custom, 'due process of law', the vital clause of the American Fifth Amendment was directly derived from clause 39 of the Magna Carta which includes the guarantee that 'no free man shall be captured or imprisoned . . . except by the law of the land'.

Equally, the section in the 1689 Bill of rights providing that 'excessive bail ought not to be required, nor excessive punishments inflicted' is the direct ancestor of the Eighth Amendment.

Taken together, the three great documents of English liberty established the important principle that there were fundamental rights belonging to the individual which even the sovereign must not violate. This principle was strengthened, in American minds, by the tendency of the colonial charters and enactments to contain such explicit written statements of individual rights.

The primary guarantee mentioned in the First Amendment of the Constitution, the right to freedom of religion, was, by contrast, not based on English constitutional precedent. Its inclusion in the 1791 document and its emergence as one of the key characteristics of American liberty owes more to one man, the English-born religious leader and founder of Rhode Island, Roger Williams (c.1603–1682). His creed was stark and simple.

> No one tenet that either London, England, or the world doth harbor is so heretical, blasphemous, seditious, and dangerous to the corporal, to the spiritual, to the present, to the eternal good of all men, as the bloody tenet (however washed and whited) I say, as is the bloody tenet of persecution for the cause of conscience.

Williams was born in London, the son of a merchant tailor. In his early teens he was employed as the stenographer to the great English lawyer, Sir Edward Coke, through whose influence he was sent to Sutton's Hospital (later Charterhouse) from where he won a scholarship to Pembroke College, Cambridge. At this stage he was destined for a career in law, but after receiving his BA in 1627 he began reading for an MA in theology. Never a conformist, he left Cambridge prematurely, almost certainly because he could not subjugate his developing Separatist convictions to the rigid practices and policies of the Anglican church.

Some time before February 1629 he became the chaplain to the family of the militant Puritan Sir William Masham and, through this connection, Williams was put in touch with a group of Puritans who were planning to start a colony in New England. Whether or not they persuaded Williams to join them is not known, but as the alternative was harassment or even imprisonment at the hands of Archbishop Laud he decided to leave England. By contrast, the New World offered him asylum and (in an age of missionary zeal) an opportunity, as he saw it, to convert the heathen Indians to Christianity. So in 1630 he sailed for Massachusetts. On his arrival, he was disappointed to discover that, in his view, the Boston church was not truly Separatist in

A romanticised 1866 engraving of the landing of Roger Williams.

that it had not severed all its links with the Anglican church. He rebelled, and in 1635 was called before the General Court for espousing 'new and dangerous opinions' against the authority of the magistrates of the Bay Colony, since he had repeatedly expressed the view that governments had no right whatsoever in matters of conscience. 'It is unnecessary, unlawful, dishonourable, ungodly, unchristian in most cases in the world [to persecute people for their faith], for there is a possibility of keeping sweet peace in most cases, and if it be possible, it is the express command of God that peace be kept.' To make matters worse, he had further incensed the Bay Colony magistrates by arguing that the Massachusetts Charter was invalid because it took no note of Indian rights. 'Boast not proud English of thy birth and blood. Thy brother Indian is by birth as good. Of one blood God made him, and thee and all, as wise, as fair, as strong, as personal,' he argued in a sermon in Plymouth in 1633. A year later he went further:

The attack on a Pequot fort, 1637, one of the first major punitive expeditions by the colonists against an Indian tribe. This attack led to the virtual annihilation of the Pequots, despite Williams' efforts to persuade the colonial councils to show mercy to the Indians. Williams was almost the first English colonist to respect Indian rights as first occupants and take an interest in their culture. Barber wood engravings, 1830.

'We have not our land by patent from the King, but that the natives are the true owners of it, and that we ought to repent of such a receiving it by patent.' Taken together, Williams's views challenged all the principles upon which the Massachusetts theocracy was founded. Not surprisingly the verdict of the court was severe and Williams was banished.

Pushed into the wilderness — 'in a bitter winter season, not knowing what bread or bed did mean' — he eventually made his way, after many adventures, to what is now Rhode Island. There he bought land from the Indians that he had befriended (he lived with them 'in their filthy smoky holes . . . to gain their tongue'), and founded a settlement as a haven for his fellow victims of religious persecution. 'Having a sense of God's merciful providence unto me in my distress, [I] called the place Providence.' From its earliest days the colony did the unthinkable and accepted not only Separatists, Baptists and Seekers, but also, at a later stage, Jews and Quakers (even though williams believed they were blasphemous), who came there to practise their beliefs in peace, for, as he said, 'conscience is found in all mankind, more or less, in Jews, Turks, Papists, Protestants, pagans, etc.'

Surrounded by his opponents in the New England Confederation and beset by growing arguments within his own circle, Williams was forced to go to England in 1643 to obtain more authority by a charter for the Providence Plantations. It was there that he threw down his most famous challenge to the Massachusetts theocracy with his *Bloody Tenet of Persecution*, published in 1644, in which he pleaded for complete political and religious liberty. After various quarrels back in the colony and a further trip to England, during which he became friends with and gained the support of both Milton and Cromwell, Williams eventually triumphed and was elected President of the colony in 1654. Though he became embittered in later life, he maintained to the end his democratic, 'Leveller' principles, both in civil and religious matters.

Williams, a pugnacious and lively man, not merely propagated the idea of complete liberty of conscience but successfully incorporated that idea in the new 1663 Rhode Island Charter, the fundamental law of the colony he had founded. For, as he wrote with more than a little cynicism, 'the blood of so many hundred thousand souls of Protestants and Papists, spilt in the wars of present and former ages for their respective consciences, is not required by Jesus Christ the Prince of Peace'. He was also a practical man, and in a handbook for settlers and traders, *A Key into the Language of America* (1643), he provided both a description of the language and ways of life of the Indians and a further

ROGER WILLIAMS' DEPARTURE FROM SALEM.

Roger Williams' departure from Salem.

statement of his own attitudes towards liberty of conscience. It was his advocacy of toleration in all its respects that was Williams's mark on history.

*　　*　　*

While in seventeenth-century America there was great flexibility and inconsistency in administering justice, due partly to the lack of trained lawyers and of legal texts and judgements, by the eighteenth century, with an increase in the size and expertise of a largely English-educated legal profession, English law was being universally practised throughout the colonies. Thus it was only natural that at Independence most colonies adopted some part of the pre-revolution law of England along with their own colonial enactments. From then on, through the late eighteenth and early nineteenth centuries, the American legal profession's main role was shaping inherited English law to suit American conditions. Even as the United States moved west, English common law and practice were generally accepted in the new states (with the exception of Louisiana which was influenced by French civil law, and Texas, where, for a period, Spanish/Mexican legal practices prevailed).

Although there was no uniform growth, the historical basis of most American law is the common law of England as developed down to the eighteenth century. And, while American lawyers no longer cite English authorities, they are still conditioned by the English ideas imported into American law two centuries ago. In particular, there is the concept of the supremacy of law as well as the English tradition of precedent, by which decisions are based on earlier cases. Additionally, there is the shared belief that a trial

Sir Edward Coke (1552–1634), an oil painting by Paul van Somer.

OPPOSITE: Map of Virginia by John White. (see page 10)

is a contentious proceeding, usually before a jury, in which adversary parties take the initiative and in which the judge is an umpire, not an inquisitor. American law also remains close to English law in such fields as torts, contracts, trusts, sale of goods, real property and conflict of laws.

It is not easy to discuss English influence on American law without mentioning the contribution of the two great English common lawyers – Sir Edward Coke and William Blackstone, even though they never actually reached America themselves: Coke, Roger Williams's mentor, has been seen as the juristic progenitor of the American Revolution. His writings and arguments, for example that 'Common law is above Parliament and King', were employed by the colonists to prove the invalidity of the Acts of the British Parliament which sought to restrict their rights. Coke achieved further popularity in the colonies after 1616 when King James I actually dismissed him from the post of Chief Justice for upholding common law against Royal Prerogative, this despite his earlier notoriety as a result of brow-beating Ralegh at his trial.

Blackstone, too, exerted a far-reaching influence on law and legal thinking on both sides of the Atlantic through his *Commentaries* (published 1765–9). He argued, for example, that 'The most universal and effectual way of discovering the true meaning of law, when the words are dubious, is by considering the reason and spirit of it; or the cause which moved the legislator to enact it. For when this reason ceases, the law itself ought likewise to cease with it.' Again, 'To make a particular custom good, the following are necessary requisites: that it has been used so long that the memory of man runneth not to the contrary'. Such views formed the basis of American common law and shaped the course of American and, indeed, English legal education. After the Declaration of Independence, Thomas Jefferson argued that it would be improper to continue to cite British legal precedent and was concerned to 'uncanonise' Blackstone. But until 1826–30 and the publication of James Kent's *Commentaries on American Law*, itself heavily influenced by Blackstone, Blackstone's was the only major text available to American lawyers.

These basic links in constitutional and civil law were re-inforced by the fact that most of those primarily involved in the drafting of the Constitution and its amendments, and codifying the laws of the new America, were of British stock. Where they perceived weaknesses in the parent model, they adapted according to local circumstances, convictions and religious beliefs. Nothing one says about America holds for all America: with law (and morality) this is particularly true, and when one gets away from the law as it is enshrined in the Constitution the enforcement of it varied greatly and still does between, for example, New England, the (often still) Wild West and the (at times, very) deep South.

*　　*　　*

Sir William Blackstone (1723–80), an oil painting attributed to Sir Joshua Reynolds.

OPPOSITE: *James Gordon Bennett Junior* Cartoon by Nemo from 'Vanity Fair', 15th November 1884 (*see page 55*).

> *When an American walks down the street of an English city,*
> *he will be reminded of home as he passes Anglican (Protestant*
> *Episcopal), Presbyterian, Congregational, Baptist, Methodist*
> *and Roman Catholic churches. He may be handed a*
> *Plymouth Brethren tract, encounter a Salvation Army lassie,*
> *or find a Quaker meetinghouse or Jewish synagogue half*
> *hidden in a side street. Travelling north of the Tweed, he will*
> *discover that many of the Presbyterian divisions at home had*
> *their origin in divisions which took place in Scotland.*
> WINTHROP S. HUDSON (Religion in America, 1981)

The impact of British immigrants in the purely religious as opposed to the socio-religious life in the United States was no less profound. From the days of the Pilgrim Fathers, religious beliefs and people's dedication to them were prime reasons for the passage to America. The first preachers (Spanish and French missionaries on the West Coast and in the French possessions apart) were all British, not just from the established church, but often more importantly from the Quakers, Puritans, Roman Catholics and others seeking a freedom denied them in their home country. The first people and the Christian ethic, in a variety of forms, came in a very English guise. But in the eighteenth and nineteenth centuries, as we shall see, the religious traffic became anything but one-way.

One of the most interesting figures to arrive in America with religious ideas and beliefs that eventually had an effect well beyond the confines of the movement she created, was Mother Ann Lee. In May 1774 she and her group of shaking Quakers set sail from England bound for America. Like a number of other British nonconformist sects they had a messianic vision that the opening of the gospel would occur in the New World. They were also attracted to America because they hoped that it would offer them an asylum from persecution and a testing-ground for experimentation in religious communal living. Ann Lee herself (1736–84) was born in Manchester, one of eight children of a blacksmith. Before the age of ten she went to work in a textile mill and never received a formal education. In her early twenties she joined a religious sect led by two former Quakers, James and Jane Wardley, who had broken away from the Society of Friends under the influence of the French Prophets (or Camisards). The members of the sect became known as Shakers because of their highly eccentric manner of worship which consisted of 'trembling, whirling, dancing in rings, and speaking in strange tongues'. They believed that the second coming of Christ was close at hand, but otherwise had no specific creed.

Shakers at a meeting, 1870: the religious dance.

In 1762 Ann reluctantly married Abraham Standerin, a black-smith at her father's shop. Following the tragic death of all four of their children in infancy she had a serious physical and mental breakdown, and became convinced that her sufferings were the result of sexual desire. On the brink of death she was, she said, born again to God. After recovering her health and composure she returned to the Wardleys and soon rose to the leadership of the small sect. The other members began to regard her as their prophet and messiah. Taking to the streets of Manchester, she was attacked and stoned by an angry mob, who accused her of being a witch, and imprisoned on at least two occasions for 'violation of the Sabbath'. While in prison she claimed she had a series of visions, in one of which she received 'a divine commission to complete Christ's work', and in another a command to go to America.

She took with her a small group of loyal followers, and after two years of struggle in the New World these Shakers established themselves on a small tract of land in Niskeyuna, near Albany in New York State. In its early days, disillusioned Baptists and others flocked to Niskeyuna after hearing about Mother Ann Lee or 'Ann the Word' as she was known, and several of them converted to Shakerism. Following a number of campaigns, led by her almost singlehandedly, on which she was sometimes greeted as if she herself were the Second Coming, other settlements were founded elsewhere in New England. After four years of almost

The spare and distinctive lines of Shaker furniture: a Sister's sewing chair and 'round stand' both in cherry wood. From New Lebanon, New York, c. 1815.

non-stop proselytizing, and weakened by a series of often vicious attacks by mobs who accused her of being everything from a witch to a Loyalist spy, she died in 1784. Three days before her death she told a fellow Shaker, 'I shall soon be taken out of this body; but the gospel will never be taken away from you, if you are faithful. Be not discouraged, nor cast down: for God will not leave his people without a leader.'

When Charles Dickens visited the United States in 1842, he went to a Shaker meeting house where 'we walked into a grim room, where several grim hats were hanging on grim pegs, and the time was grimly told by a grim clock which uttered every tick with a kind of struggle, as if it broke the grim silence reluctantly, and under protest. Ranged against the wall were six or eight stiff high-backed chairs, and they partook so strongly of the general grimness that one would much rather have sat on the floor than incurred the smallest obligation to any of them.' A successor to Ann Lee was in residence, whose 'rule is understood to be absolute, though she has the assistance of a council of elders. She lives, it is said, in strict seclusion, in certain rooms above the chapel, and is never shown to profane eyes. If she at all resembles the lady who presided over the store [whom Dickens had earlier met], it is a great charity to keep her as close as possible, and I cannot too strongly express my perfect concurrence in this benevolent proceeding.'

His commentary on their ways of living and beliefs was that they 'eat and drink together, after the Spartan model, at a great public table. There is no union of the sexes, and every Shaker, male and female, is devoted to a life of celibacy. Rumour has been busy upon this theme, but here again I must refer to the lady of the store, and say, that if many of the sister Shakers resemble her, I treat all such slander as bearing on its face the strongest marks of wild improbability.'

But the Shaker communities she had inspired continued, believers adhering to a unique lifestyle founded upon celibacy and equal rights for women. Ann Lee had believed that carnal lust was the source of all evil and suffering in the world, and that those who could resist it and thus rise above the 'Adamic Plane' of existence would enjoy equal privileges whatever their sex, race or means. Americans who did not share Ann Lee's religious beliefs were none the less influenced by important aspects of the Shaker settlements' social structure, not to mention their fine furniture. For example, the advocacy and provision of equal rights for women by them was a source of much encouragement to the American feminist movement, quite apart from the inspiration it gave to others to try out new and unconventional lifestyles. The settlement reached the peak of its development between 1830 and 1850, one of the most successful experiments in communal living in America, though of course the ever-present emphasis on celibacy was not perhaps the best way to ensure the movement's long-term future.

The Evangelical Revival

The Great Awakening, which was to exert a decisive and far-reaching influence upon the development of American religious life, was but one manifestation of a general spiritual quickening during the eighteenth century . . . this surging tide of evangelical religion supplied the dynamic which emboldened the Protestant churches of America to undertake the enormous task of Christianizing a continent, nerved those of the British Isles to assume a similar responsibility for an expanding population at home and overseas, and led both the British and the American churches to join forces in a vast mission to the entire non-Christian world.

WINTHROP S. HUDSON, *Religion in America*

The Evangelical Revival, or Protestant Counter-Reformation as it is sometimes called, was in every sense an Anglo-American movement. In this field perhaps more than in any other, ideas flowed eastwards and westwards almost simultaneously. While the Revival originated in the first half of the eighteenth century with the ministries of the two great English Methodist pioneers John Wesley and George Whitefield, its growth owed much to Jonathan Edwards and the 'Great Awakening' which he helped to inspire in his native Connecticut. In the 1730s John Wesley came to Georgia to act as a spiritual adviser to Governor Oglethorpe and to set up a mission for the conversion of the Indians. The mission was not a success, but by attracting Whitefield to America in 1737 it was indirectly responsible for bringing the American and the British roots of the Revival together. For, in the New World, Whitefield's brand of Calvinist Methodism crystallized under Edwards's influence and his extensive preaching tours, from Georgia to Massachusetts, helped carry the Great Awakening to the backwoods of America where it is not unusual still to find it in a remarkably unchanged form.

In the nineteenth century the cross-flow of influence between

Jonathan Edwards (1703–58), the champion of the Great Awakening. Oil painting by Joseph Badger.

The hypnotic preacher George Whitefield. Oil painting by John Wollaston, *c.* 1742.

the British and American strands of the movement increased, with American evangelicals much taken by the writings of William Wilberforce and others. In return, the techniques of the so-called 'camp meetings' and urban crusades were imported into Britain by fiery American preachers such as Lorenzo Dow and Charles Finney. In 1806 Dow, whose denunciation of orthodox Calvinism was summed up in the rhyme

> You can and you can't
> You shall and you shan't;
> You will and you won't
> You'll be damned if you do,
> And you'll be damned if you don't . . .

prompted William Clowes and Hugh Bourne of the Wesleyan Connexion to found the Primitive Methodists. In 1844, Finney inspired the London shop worker George Williams to form the Young Men's Christian Association, an organization which was soon introduced to America. It was at the Chicago YMCA that Dwight Lyman Moody and Ira D. Sankey first rose to prominence. In turn these two famous evangelists did more than anyone else to re-inject vigour into the Revival in both countries.

Moody (1837–99) was born in Massachusetts but while still a teenager he moved to Chicago where he embarked on a successful business career, spending his spare time teaching at a Sunday school. In 1858 he established the North Market Sabbath School, in conjunction with which he introduced a programme of evangelical services, prayer meetings, welfare and relief work, and social recreation. Gradually these activities took up more of his time, and in 1860, after much painful contemplation, he resigned from business to become a full-time city missionary. It was a big step to take: he was sacrificing his business career for a vocation which had no salary or assured support.

Dwight Lyman Moody (1837–99), photographed in 1875 by Robert Thrupp of Birmingham.

In 1866, after serving as secretary, he became the President of the Chicago YMCA, and in the following year and again in 1872 Moody visited Britain to meet and study the techniques of evangelicals there. On the first trip, which lasted four months, he established several informal contacts with leading British evangelicals like Robert Morgan and Charles Spurgeon. By the time of his second trip he was well advanced in his plans for a major evangelistic crusade in Britain.

In the summer of 1873, at the invitation of his British friends, he was back in Britain, this time to conduct a preaching tour of the country's towns and cities. He was accompanied by Ira D. Sankey (1840–1908), an organist and gospel singer, who was also a leading member of the Chicago YMCA.

During Moody's 1872 visit, Cuthbert Bambridge, a wealthy Newcastle layman, and William Pennefather, a well-known London evangelist, had promised him financial support for any revival work he might take on in Britain. Alas, when Moody arrived in England he discovered that both of his potential benefactors had died. Disappointed but determined, Moody and Sankey headed for York where Moody had sometime before received an invitation to speak to the city's YMCA. After a slow beginning there, and in Sunderland, their meetings eventually created such enthusiasm that in late November 1873 their tour was extended to Scotland.

Ira David Sankey (1840–1908). photographed in 1875.

In Edinburgh the public's response was astonishing. At their first meeting hundreds were turned away at the door, and soon

'Mr. Moody Preaching in the Opera House, Haymarket, London.'

they became overwhelmed with nationwide demands for them to speak. To solve the problem they rented the city's largest hall, the Corn Exchange, and still had no difficulty in regularly filling its 6,000 seats. Their stay, which was prolonged for two months, was an overwhelming success, and reports of the meetings were given much coverage in the public and religious press. It was even noted that the traditional Scottish antipathy to the use of instrumental music in worship was conquered by Sankey's organ-playing. At Glasgow and in several other Scottish towns and cities their meetings generated a similar response. In the autumn of 1874 they moved to Belfast and then on to Dublin, while the winter months were spent in the North and Midlands of England. Their visit ended with a mammoth and exhausting four-month mission in London, at which they conducted 285 services, attended by an estimated 2½ million people.

In August 1875 they returned triumphant to America, their visit having caused the biggest upsurge in religious feeling in Britain since the days of Wesley and Whitefield. Capitalizing on the publicity generated by the trip Moody and Sankey began, in 1875–6, the first of a series of highly successful crusades in their home country, which took them from Boston to San Francisco. Moody had left the United States virtually unknown, but less than three years later he had become a famous figure ready to sweep America as he had done Britain.

In the autumn of 1881 Moody and Sankey embarked on a second extensive tour of Britain. By this time they were national institutions in both Britain and the United States. On their arrival in England they were inundated with requests to conduct meetings, but, perhaps inevitably, the trip was not as successful as their earlier visit. Nevertheless, on this three-year crusade they were still to pack auditoriums up and down the country. In Moody's last years he supplemented his campaigns with other evangelical activities. In 1879 he had established a Seminary for Girls, and in 1881 the Mount Hermon School for Boys. In 1889 the Moody Bible Institute was established by him in Chicago, and his evangelical work only ceased with his death on 22 December 1899.

Moody died a layman, having never sought ordination. His knowledge of theology was limited. Indeed when a woman told him that she did not believe in his theology, Moody replied, 'My theology! I didn't know I had any.' His great achievement in both Britain and America was to introduce the revivalist message in the new industrial towns. It was mass revivalism, but, especially in his later years, mass revivalism with a strong personal touch and emphasis on the individual. He was successful because of what he said and the way he said it. Speaking directly and earnestly, he optimistically stressed the gospel of love – that God was willing to save anyone who decided freely to accept the gift of grace. Though his sermons were lively and moving, he did not, like several other American religious crusaders, drive his audiences into hysterical displays of religious emotion.

Moody's first Sunday-school class in Chicago.

Inevitably Moody had plenty of opponents in Britain and America both inside and outside the churches. To Walt Whitman he was a target for ridicule:

Having heard Moody I am satisfied
But I shall not come to him to be saved
He is not my idea of a Saviour.
I do not believe in him.
Nor his God
Nor his method of sinners nor his stories which sound like
    lies.
I, Walt, tell him he is an ignorant charlatan, a mistaken
    enthusiast,
and that Boston will ere long desire to *git*.

Others must have been put off by the practical businessman-like image that he seemed to cultivate, which characterized his type of American nineteenth-century crusade. Indeed, as a historian of American religion has recently commented, Moody 'not only was a businessman, he looked like a businessman, talked like a businessman, took things in hand like a businessman'. But he also had a sense of humour, as with his brisk termination of a priest's long and tedious prayer: 'While our brother is finishing his prayer we will sing number 75.' And he had a telling way of encapsulating ideas to make them stick, as with 'Character is what you are in the dark.'

Sankey's singing and organ-playing were a vital ingredient of their success. 'A preacher through music', he heightened and added extra colour to Moody's sermons. The success of Moody

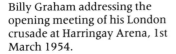

Billy Graham addressing the opening meeting of his London crusade at Harringay Arena, 1st March 1954.

'May the Lord bless you real good.'
The magnetic Billy Graham.

and Sankey further illustrates the fact that the evangelicals were a truly transatlantic community, neither completely British nor completely American, who crossed the Atlantic and were accepted and always welcomed as brothers 'under God's name'.

The cross-flow or, rather, the cross-fertilization of religious revivalism initiated by Wesley, Whitefield and Edwards, boosted by Moody and Sankey, continues today with the tours of Billy Graham, whose crusades in the 1950s and 1960s and again in the 1980s rivalled those of his eighteenth- and nineteenth-century forebears in the amount of religious enthusiasm they generated, and in their effect on the churches' agenda by re-asserting more biblical or 'fundamentalist' themes.

The Abolitionists

*Go on, in the Name of God and in the power of His might, till
even American slavery, the vilest that ever saw the sun, shall
vanish away before you.*

JOHN WESLEY (writing to Wilberforce on his deathbed)

Opposition to slavery emerged in Britain and America at approximately the same time – in the late eighteenth century – and its total abolition was to a considerable extent the achievement of co-operation between movements in both countries. Given the importance of the slave trade to the Atlantic economy and the strong connections between evangelicals in Britain and in the United States, it was inevitable that the abolition movement would have such a strong Anglo-American flavour. In 1807, thanks largely to the campaign mounted by William Wilberforce and other evangelicals, the slave trade was abolished in the British Empire. Twenty-six years later, after a long and skilful campaign to mobilize public and political support, slavery in the West Indies was finally and totally abolished. The agitation now turned to America where most anti-slavers favoured a moderate policy of gradual emancipation rather than immediate abolition. The British victory, however, inspired American campaigners to adopt a more radical approach and to copy the techniques and organization of the British campaign. Thus in Philadelphia an American Anti-Slavery Society, closely modelled on the British Anti-Slavery Society, was founded.

In the 1830s and 1840s the abolition campaign took on an even more Anglo-American character as British anti-slavers lent their material and moral support to the American cause. In 1839 the British and Foreign Anti-Slavery Society was founded, and in 1840 the first World Anti-Slavery Convention was held in London, attended by leading American abolitionists. Many British campaigners and supporters – Sturge, Stuart, Martineau – visited America to support the cause and there was a huge outpouring of British anti-slavery literature, pamphlets, letters and money, which had a considerable impact on the eventual outcome.

During the course of the campaign many personal friendships were made between abolitionists of both countries, which were a source of strength to the movement and the key to its success. They were also, in a sense, microcosms of the wider Anglo-American relationship in the field of humanitarian endeavour. Among the deepest and most important friendships was that

The Anti-Slavery Convention, 1840.
Oil painting by Benjamin Robert
Haydon.

1. Thomas Clarkson
2. William Allen
3. Samuel Gurney
4. George Stacey
5. Josiah Forster
6. William Forster
7. G. W. Alexander
8. J. H. Tredgold
9. Mrs Mary Clarkson
10. Master T. Clarkson
11. James Birney
12. John Beaumont
13. George Bradburn
14. Sir Thomas Buxton
15. Dr S. Lushington
16. Sir E. E. Wilmot
17. Daniel O'Connell
18. Robert Greville
19. William Dawes
20. Samuel Bowly
32. William Crewdson
33. J. Cropper junior
34. Rev Thomas Scales
35. William Morgan
36. Henry Beckford
37. John Scoble
38. Rev William Knibb
39. Rev John Burnet
40. Rev William Bevan
41. Rev Joseph Ketley
42. George Thompson
43. Samuel Prescod
44. Henry Stanton
45. M. L'Instant
46. Robert Forster

William Lloyd Garrison (1805–1879).

George Thompson (1804–1878)
Sketch by Harry Furniss.

between the Massachusetts-born abolitionist William Lloyd Garrison (1805–79) and the English agitator George Thompson. Garrison emerged in the late 1820s as the first major American anti-slaver to support the total and immediate abolition of slavery rather than its gradual extinction. In 1830 he launched his famous anti-slavery journal, the *Liberator*, and the following year he helped found the New England Anti-Slavery Society.

In the first issue of the *Liberator* he wrote: 'I will be as harsh as truth, and as uncompromising as justice. On this subject, I do not wish to think, or speak, or write, with moderation. No! No! Tell a man whose house is on fire, to give a moderate alarm; tell him to moderately rescue his wife from the hands of the ravisher; tell the mother to gradually extricate her babe from the fire into which it has fallen; – but urge me not to use moderation in a cause like the present. I am in earnest – I will not equivocate – I will not excuse – I will not retreat a single inch – AND I WILL BE HEARD.'

As that Society's salaried emissary, he came to Britain in May 1833 to enlist the moral energies of her philanthropists for the American cause. In London he met the British leaders of the emancipation movement, who were on the verge of their famous victory, and among others he befriended was the masterly and flamboyant English agitator, George Thompson. After hearing him speak, Garrison was struck by Thompson's oratorical powers and the sincerity of his message: 'His person was tall and graceful; his social manners captivating; his voice of great compass, and very pleasant in its lower tones; his action natural – at times vehement – yet generally governed by oratorical rules; his elocution beautiful, spontaneous, irresistible . . . He had the faculty of "thinking on his legs" faster than any other speaker I had ever heard. But it was not his quickness of perception, nor his fluency of speech, nor his brilliancy of retort, upon which he placed reliance. He felt the cause which he espoused was invincible, inasmuch as it was based upon the rock of TRUTH, supported by the pillars of JUSTICE and MERCY, and patronized by GOD. He was strong in faith – that faith which is as an anchor to the soul, both sure and steadfast – that faith which has so often overcome the world.'

These qualities were equally applicable to Garrison, who found in Thompson a kindred spirit. Both were zealously dedicated to the worldwide abolition of slavery and its related evils, through the power of moral principle. Both were irrepressible high-minded idealists. Both believed that 'our country is the world – out countrymen are all mankind', and were well aware of the pitfalls. At one dinner in his honour in London, Garrison was presented with a gold watch. Thanking his hosts he remarked, 'If this had been a rotten egg, I would have known what to do with it. As it is a gold watch, I am at a loss for words.'

While in London, Garrison invited Thompson to go to America to stir up support for the cause. Thompson accepted and came to America in 1834. The extremely delicate nature of the whole issue in America at that time prompted the more moderate British anti-slavers, such as Sturge, to doubt the wisdom of Thompson's trip. One of them, Thomas Buxton, Wilberforce's successor in Parliament, suggested to Garrison that, as an Englishman, Thompson would excite the prejudice of the American people: 'Would not the slaveholders, especially, and their violent adherents, endeavour to inflame the jealousy of the nation, and misrepresent the real object of his mission?' Garrison knew that Thompson 'would undoubtedly stir up the bile of all those who were opposed to the abolition of slavery; and that he might expect to encounter severe ridicule and bitter denunciation', but he believed that the Englishman would be safe (at least in New England) and would 'disarm prejudice, extort admiration, and multiply converts to our cause; and that he would finally remove every obstacle in his path, arising from his transatlantic origin'. But, as Garrison later admitted, he did not then imagine that 'such was the ferocious spirit which slavery had generated among the sons of the pilgrims, Mr Thompson would soon be compelled to secrete himself from the daggers of a people, boasting continually of LIBERTY and EQUALITY, and proudly living within sight of Bunker Hill, for simply inculcating "the self-evident truths" contained in their own Declaration of Independence'.

From the start of his visit Thompson provoked the antagonism of a large section of the American people. Branded a 'foreign incendiary' who had come to 'sow the seeds of discord and disunion', he was derided, threatened, physically attacked and condemned by state legislation, by Congress and even by the President in his State of the Union address.

In Boston on 21 October 1835 an ugly mob assembled at an anti-slavery meeting in the city's Faneuil Hall ready to tar-and-feather Thompson. But when he did not appear the crowd grabbed Garrison and dragged him through the streets with a rope tied around his neck. He was only saved by the timely intervention of the Mayor. Two months later Thompson's American visit came to an abrupt end when he had to escape from the Boston mob in an open boat, to join an English ship bound for New Brunswick.

In some respects Thompson's trip was counter-productive. With Garrison, he stirred up the enmity of the South against the Northern interferences and at the same time fuelled American anglophobia. However, to popular supporters of the abolition cause, the two men gave the movement its heroes – and, potentially, its martyrs. Moreover, during the fourteen months he spent in the north-eastern states, Thompson made about five hundred speeches, usually before large audiences, which generated support for the prodigious growth of hundreds of local anti-slavery societies. Garrison, writing in 1836, had no doubts about the success of the visit, 'which had been followed by the most brilliant results in favour of the immediate abolition of slavery'.

Although Garrison remained at the forefront of the anti-slavery movement, and served 22 terms as the President of the American Anti-Slavery Society, his extremism and abrasiveness alienated or antagonized the more conservative supporters of the abolition cause. However, the Resolution adopted by the Massachusetts Anti-Slavery Society in January 1843 shows that the power if not the effect of his arguments remained vitally undiminished. 'Resolved: That the compact which exists between the North and the South is a covenant with death and an agreement with hell, involving both parties in atrocious criminality, and should be immediately annulled.'

Sixteen years later he was still thundering: 'Was John Brown justified in his attempt? Yes, if Washington was in his, if Warren and Hancock were in theirs. If men are justified in striking a blow for freedom when the question is one of a three penny tax on tea, then, I say they are a thousand times more justified when it is to save fathers, mothers, wives and children from the slave-coffle and the auction block, and to restore them their God-given rights.' In all, Garrison's main achievement was – with Thompson's help – to give the abolitionist cause its initial impetus at a time when it was at its most unpopular. But they did not let things lie; the two men remained close friends, and when the Civil War ended in April 1865 they celebrated the event together in Charleston, South Carolina.

When Thompson first came to America through Garrison's agency in 1834, he had been denounced by Congress and the White House. Thirty years later, a public reception was held in his honour by the House of Representatives, a function attended by Lincoln and his cabinet.

Freed slaves such as Redmond and Douglass were brought to Britain, lectured extensively and were exhibited as 'noble savages' in stately drawing rooms up and down the country. And whether the reasons were to do with a British interest in the anti-slavery campaign or, simply, a more well-developed habit of buying good literature it is a surprising fact that Harriet Beecher

Frederick Douglass (1817–95), from the frontispiece of his autobiography, *My Bondage and My Freedom* (1855).

Harriet Beecher Stowe

The versatile English author, Harriet Martineau (1802–76), who became an active abolitionist while visiting America in 1834–6, also had plenty of first-hand tales to write about pro-slavery mobs burning, tarring and feathering. She was also an active campaigner for women's rights. Believing that 'the United States had been useful in proving things before held impossible', she would argue: 'Is it to be understood that the Principles of the Declaration of Independence bear no relation to half the human race?'

Harriet Martineau, a chalk drawing by George Richmond.

Stowe's *Uncle Tom's Cabin*, published in 1852, sold around a million copies in its first year of publication in the United Kingdom, but a mere hundred and fifty thousand in the United States. When praised for it she said, 'I did not write it. God wrote it. I merely did his dictation.' By public demand, Mrs Stowe, whom Lincoln had called 'the little lady who wrote the book that made the big war', came back to Britain on three separate occasions during the 1850s where she was even received in audience by Queen Victoria herself. As Sinclair Lewis said of her, 'Harriet Beecher Stowe's *Uncle Tom's Cabin* was the first evidence to

'Haley packs up Uncle Tom for the
"Down South" market', an
illustration from *Uncle Tom's Cabin*.

America that no hurricane can be so disastrous to a country as a ruthless humanitarian woman'.

In the search for a better form of society, an outstanding venture in utopian living was established by Robert Owen (1771–1858), who had already made a considerable name for himself by creating a model community at New Lanark in Scotland. With Welsh drive he moved to the United States in 1824, determined, with his Benthamite belief in the social benefits rather than harms that could come from industrialization and the example of the Shakers before him, to create a new Utopia by the Wabash in Indiana. This would, he believed, be achieved, above all, by education and by socializing the means of production. Co-operative activity in his view was the answer to men's ills. He said:

> What ideas individuals may attach to the term Millennium I know not; but I know that society may be formed so as to exist without crime, without poverty, with health greatly improved, with little, if any, misery, and with intelligence and happiness increased a hundredfold; and no obstacle whatsoever intervenes at this moment, except ignorance, to prevent such a state of society from becoming universal.

Owen alienated many through his lack of religious beliefs and his socialism – which he illustrated with the story of asking one twelve-year-old boy who had just emerged from a coal-black mine if he knew God, to which the boy replied: 'No. He must work in some other mine.' He persevered with New Harmony where property was commonly held and co-operation was the order of the day, but though he was a great thinker he was not a great leader, and his settlement soon broke up into various factions largely as a result of the disparate intellectuals, idealists and spongers that had been attracted to it. None the less, Owen's life and example were, without doubt, fundamental in providing a core for early American social awareness. New Harmony was also to give a lead to Owen's son, Robert Dale Owen (1801–77), the Congressman who drafted the Bill that created the Smithsonian Institution, in his own campaign for social reforms. Overall, New Harmony became the focus of Anglo-American concern for social reform, and its followers, Owen himself, his sons and those inspired by him, were among the true forefathers of trade unionism and the labour movement.

Owen's partner, the wealthy Scot, William Maclure (1763 –1840), was also closely involved, for example, particularly in terms of New Harmony's educational experiment. Born in Ayr, he

The effects of good and bad circumstances, woodcuts from Robert Owen's *Essays on the Formation of Human Character* (1834 edition).

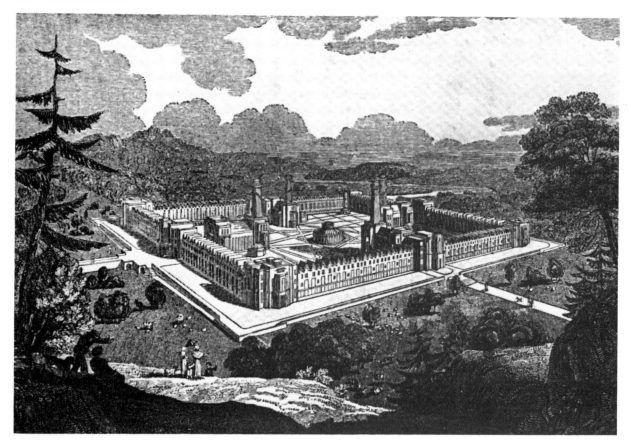

A model of New Harmony, Robert Owen's proposed community; from the *Cooperative Magazine*, 1828.

settled in the United States around 1796 and became a successful importer as well as indulging in his hobby as President of the American Geological Society, and compiler of one of the earliest geological maps of the United States. He also introduced the Pestalozzi system of education there, as well as endowing libraries throughout Indiana.

Among others inspired by the New Harmony experiment and by Owen's ideas was the Scottish-born radical, Frances (Fanny) Wright (1795–1852). Born in Dundee to wealthy parents but orphaned by the age of three, she was influenced in her teenage years by the pro-republican and utilitarian views of her great-uncle James Mylne and his like-minded group of Glasgow intellectuals.

Fascinated by America from an early age, she made her first visit there in 1818. After trying unsuccessfully to establish herself as a playwright in New York City, she toured the north-eastern states and recorded her impressions of the country in *Views of Society and Manners in America*. The book's favourable impression of the new republic won her the admiration of, among others, the Marquis de Lafayette, and after returning to Europe she developed a close and scandalous relationship with the famous French general. She later claimed that Lafayette was like a father to her. But, although he once proposed to adopt her as his legal daughter, there is evidence to suggest that they were lovers. A frequent visitor to his estate in France, Fanny became involved in his often clandestine schemes on behalf of European revolutionary movements. When these activities threatened to lead to a prosecution, the Frenchman wisely took up an invitation to visit the United States in 1824.

Fanny soon followed. With her sister, Camilla, she accompanied him, and not always discreetly, on his triumphal tour, the highlight of which for Fanny was perhaps a stay with Jefferson at his Monticello estate. But when Lafayette returned to France in 1825 Fanny decided to remain in America. While touring the southern states she had been horrified by the slavery system, which she saw as 'odious beyond all that imagination can conceive', and became interested in schemes for its gradual abolition. She did not think that immediate emancipation was the answer to the problem as she believed the freed negro would find it impossible to adjust to life in a free society. First he needed to be educated and taught to fend for himself. This could best be achieved, she argued, in isolated communities where negroes, bought from their owners, would learn a vocation while working for their freedom or re-colonization abroad.

Determined to put her ideas into practice, she used her inheritance to establish the commune of Nashoba in western Tennessee, by the Wolf River, about fifteen miles from Memphis. Here, as well as negroes, others would live co-operatively on an Owenite model. The project, which Fanny ran almost single-handedly, was never a success. Set in the wilderness and in a hostile climate, Nashoba was beset with problems from the very start. Frances Trollope, a friend of Fanny, visited and described the settlement in her *Domestic Manners of the Americans*:

> One glance sufficed to convince me that every idea I had formed of the place was as far as possible from the truth. Desolation was the only feeling – the only word that presented itself. . . . Each building consisted of two large rooms furnished in the most simple manner; nor had they as yet collected round them any of those minor comforts which ordinary minds class among the necessaries of life.

By the time of Frances Trollope's visit in January 1828, Fanny Wright had already reorganized the settlement by laying more stress on the New Harmony mode of co-operative communitarianism, which she hoped would act as a model for the social

and moral regeneration of American society. But by the end of
April all her companions, including her sister, had left Nashoba.
Keeping her pledge to her negroes she personally resettled them
in Haiti before going on to join the New Harmony community.
Her experiment was a failure but her dedication and commitment
to make it a success could not be faulted. As Frances Trollope
observed, 'I have never heard or read enthusiasm approaching

Fanny Wright (1795–1852)

hers, except in some few instances, in ages past, of religious fanaticism'.

The disappointment of Nashoba persuaded Fanny that the regeneration of society must take place in the towns and cities, not in isolated communities. She thus became involved in wider social and religious issues, provocatively challenging, on public platforms, many of the moral taboos of the pious majority of America by advocating free love (especially between whites and blacks), contraception, liberal divorce laws in order to achieve equal status for women (which she defined as when 'the two persons of human kind – man and woman – shall exert equal influences in a state of equal independence'). She also attacked organized religion and positively promoted utilitarian education ideas, even going as far as to suggest that the latter should be 'free from the undesirable influence of parents'. She later moved to New York where she helped Robert Dale Owen edit the *Free Enquirer* and joined with him the Workingmen's Party (dubbed the 'Fanny Wright' party by opposition press), an early socialist movement. She was widely attacked in the American papers as a 'bold blasphemer and voluptuous preacher of licentiousness' and this led to internal conflicts for and against her within the party and its subsequent rapid collapse.

The settlement at Nashoba, from Fanny Trollope's *Domestic Manners of the Americans* (1832).

Frances Trollope described how Fanny took on a striking appearance when taking up the cause of 'insulted reason and outraged humanity' before a public audience. 'Her tall and majestic figure, the deep and almost solemn expression of her eyes, the simple contour of her finely formed head, unadorned, excepting by its own natural ringlets; her garment of plain white muslin, which hung around her in folds that recalled the drapery of a Grecian statue all contributed to produce an effect, unlike anything I had ever seen before, or ever expect to see again.'

Fanny Wright's highly progressive ideas and her willingness to espouse them before mixed audiences (in 1828 she became the first woman to address a large secular audience) shocked the public in a country where, in Frances Trollope's words, 'women are guarded by a sevenfold shield of habitual insignificance' and earned her other sobriquets as 'the Great Red Harlot of Infidelity' and the 'whore of Babylon'; and 'Fanny Wrightism' became a pejorative term employed against women who held feminist or morally suspect views.

By the time of her death in Cincinnati in 1852, her reputation had been severely impaired. She had not achieved any of her aims, but during her long and controversial time in America she had identified a number of social and moral questions that have since agitated the national conscience on both sides of the Atlantic. As her recent biographer, Celia Eckhardt, has written: 'She was important because she dared to take Thomas Jefferson seriously when he wrote, "All men are created equal", and to assume that "men" meant "women" as well. She was important because she made her life a determined search for a place where she could help forge the institutions that would allow that principle to govern society. She was important because she had the integrity and courage to renounce the upper middle class world in which she was born – a world whose prizes and comforts were hers for the taking – and to risk her health, her fortune, and her good name to realize, in the United States of America, the ideals on which it was founded.'

*   *   *

Churchill said in 1941, when America was edging towards coming into the war in support of Britain, that 'the United States have written a new Magna Carta which not only has regard to the rights and laws upon which a healthy and advancing civilization can alone be erected, but also proclaims by precept and example the duty of free men and free nations, wherever they may be, to share the responsibility and burden of enforcing them'. Because they are so close, Britain and the United States have fed and will continue to feed off each other in many moral, idealistic and religious ways. But, because of this very fact, they will, as they have always done, continue to be highly critical of each other's peceived lapses, be it in Northern Ireland or in Vietnam. They are each other's mentors, inspirers, watchdogs and ombudsmen, and no harm in that.

CHAPTER FOUR

Towards the Rights of Man

The real basis of their political alliance . . . depends on one matter only: the rather slippery and rarely mentioned principle of the rights of the individual. Both countries have violated that principle too often in the past, but the principle prevails. Add the rights of property, free speech, freedom of religion, and a few other advantages that Britain and America have developed over the years, and you will have the central reasons that if these two nations continue to blunder through history, at least they will do so together. TIME (May 1982)

It is a little surprising to find that, during the heady days of the Philadelphia Convention of 1787, compliments were still being paid to those valuable ideas inherited from the British Constitution. Alexander Hamilton, one of the towering figures of the new United States, himself said in a speech on that occasion, 'I believe the British government forms the best model the world ever produced . . . This government has for its object public strength and individual security.' But, given the very different social, political and geographical conditions in the United States, the Founding Fathers, equally, were intent to avoid copying what they saw as the inbuilt injustices and difficulties of the British system when they defined their own. What they did take in particular, or believed they took, was the British system of separation of powers between the various branches of government – legislature, executive and judiciary – and also that system of checks and balances which each could use on the other to guard against misuse.

None of this is surprising, given that the people involved in setting up the political institutions of the new America were almost entirely of British origin. While only six or seven of the 56 signatories of the Declaration of Independence (John Wither-spoon, James Smith, James Wilson, Button Gwinnett, Robert

Morris and Francis Lewis) were actually born in what is the present-day United Kingdom, nearly all the other signatories, except three or four with Irish origins and one who was said to be of Italian blood, were of British descent. Of the sixty-five members of the first House of Representatives, thirty-nine had sat in a State or Colonial legislature, all of which had been modelled, to a certain degree, on the British Parliament. It was therefore natural for them to try to bring with them the best inherited practices from their individual colonies.

Anglo-Saxon influence after Independence may be seen merely by looking at a list of American presidents, showing that seventeen have been of English stock, four of Scottish and five of Scots-Irish background, a total of twenty-six out of forty.

	AMERICAN PRESIDENTS OF BRITISH STOCK	
1st	George Washington	Scotland/England (Washington, Co. Durham)
2nd	John Adams	Somerset, England
3rd	Thomas Jefferson	Suffolk, England
4th	James Madison	Gloucester, England
5th	James Monroe	Family of Munro of Foulis, Scotland
6th	John Quincy Adams	Somerset, England (son of John Adams)
7th	Andrew Jackson	Scots-Irish descent (Carrickfergus, Co. Antrim)
9th	William Henry Harrison	England (exact place unknown)
10th	John Tyler	Shropshire, England
11th	James Knox Polk	Scots-Irish (Coleraine, Co. Derry)
12th	Zachary Taylor	Carlisle, England
14th	Franklin Pierce	England
15th	James Buchanan	Scots-Irish, family branch of Buchanan of that Ilk, Scotland
16th	Abraham Lincoln	Norfolk, England
18th	Ulysses S. Grant	Yorkshire, England
19th	Rutherford Birchard Hayes	Scotland
20th	James Abram Garfield	England (exact place not known)
21st	Chester Alan Arthur	Scots-Irish (Ballymena, Co. Antrim)
22nd & 24th	(Stephen) Grover Cleveland	Yorkshire, England
23rd	Benjamin Harrison	England (grandson of William Henry Harrison, the 9th President)
25th	William McKinley	Scots-Irish
27th	William Howard Taft	England
28th	(Thomas) Woodrow Wilson	Scotland
29th	Warren Gamaliel Harding	England
30th	(John) Calvin Coolidge	Cambridgeshire, England
36th	Lyndon Baines Johnson	Scotland (probably)

Mr. Thomas Paine.
Author of the Rights of Man.

Tom Paine

The right of voting for representatives is the primary right by which other rights are protected. To take away this right is to reduce a man to slavery.   THOMAS PAINE

There was, however, one man who, more than any other, was to contribute to the political attitudes and organizations of the new United States, and then, with equal success, to have his thinking re-exported to the land of his birth. The son of a humble corset-maker from Norfolk, England, Thomas Paine was born in the market town of Thetford on 29 January 1737 to Joseph Paine, a Quaker, and Frances Cocke Paine, the Anglican daughter of a well-to-do local lawyer. After a grammar-school education, Paine began working for his father, but, eager of adventure, he ran away to sea, and despite opposition from his father, signed on as a crewman in the privateer *King of Prussia*.

Following his brief and unsuccessful service at sea, Paine went to London and returned to the humdrum profession of making women's corsets. He alleviated the tedium of this work by developing a keen interest in science, which was to become a lifelong obsession and, at the same time, he began training for the excise service. He could not have chosen a more unpopular occupation: excise officers were responsible for stopping the widespread and popular practice of smuggling, thereby incurring the displeasure of the public at large, who hated the Excise Acts. Risking their lives at the hands of cut-throat bands of smugglers, they received, none the less, only a pittance for this hazardous work. Not surprisingly this led to corruption, from which Paine was apparently not exempt, since in 1765 he was dismissed from the service for the not uncommon practice of 'stamping' – making entries for examinations that had not been made. Later he was reinstated and in 1768 he obtained a post in the excise service in Lewes, Sussex, a town rife with smugglers. But it was also a place with an active radical tradition, and here he became acquainted with leading local radicals, including his future biographer, Thomas 'Clio' Rickman.

Joining a social club, Paine soon acquired a reputation as a skilful and irrepressible debater, and in 1770/1, he published his first pamphlet, an outline of the grievances of his fellow excise-men. His enthusiasm for this early 'union' cause did not endear

OPPOSITE: 'Mr. Thomas Paine, author of the Rights of Man', a contemporary engraving.

him to his superiors, and in spring 1774 he was once again dismissed from the service. Paine left Lewes for London where he met Benjamin Franklin, who was then serving as a colonial agent. When Paine told Franklin that he would like to try his luck in America, the latter gave him warm letters of introduction to some relations, particularly his son-in-law in Philadelphia. One part of this conversation was said to have been:

FRANKLIN: Ubi libertas, ibi patria. Where there is liberty, there is my country.
PAINE: Where liberty is not, there is mine.

Paine emigrated in the hope that the New World would provide him with a better life after his professional and marital failure in the Old. (He had had two wives; one died and the other he divorced.) Although there may have been ideological reasons behind his decision to leave his native country, he was not yet, unlike later radicals and free-thinkers, a political exile. Using Franklin's introduction Paine began assisting Robert Aitken to start a new journal – the *Pennsylvania Magazine*. So impressed was Aitken with Paine's dynamic contribution to the first issue that he offered him the position of editor, and from then on Paine wrote many articles on Anglo-American political and humanitarian issues such as slavery, which he violently condemned.

Paine had arrived in America at a time when passions were building up against the British government. But despite the fighting that had spread across the colonies in 1775 many Americans continued to press for reconciliation and the redress of grievances with the mother country, rather than for complete separation. Even the majority of American resistance leaders till justified their actions by claiming that they were merely demanding the natural rights of Englishmen rather than aiming for independence. From early in his editorial career Paine firmly allied himself with those who called for more extreme action against Britain. In an article of October 1775, he made what has been seen as the first plea for complete independence to be published in America, and in January 1776 he produced his sensational forty-page pamphlet, *Common Sense*, in which he called for a declaration of independence, imploring the American people to take up the sword against 'the hardened, sullen-tempered Pharaoh of England'.

The pamphlet had an immediate and far-reaching effect in the colonies. It was estimated that more than 100,000 copies were sold in under two months, and it went through twenty-five editions in its first twelve months, though Paine himself did not gain financially, as he donated all the profits to the revolutionary cause. In it he wrote: 'O! ye that love mankind! Ye that dare oppose not only the tyranny but the tyrant, stand forth! Every spot of the Old World is overrun with oppression. Freedom hath been hunted round the globe. Asia and Africa have long expelled her. Europe regards her as a stranger and England hath given her warning to depart. O! receive the fugitive and prepare in time an asylum for mankind.' He went on: ' 'Tis repugnant to reason, to the universal order of things, to all examples from former ages, to suppose that this continent (America) can long remain subject to any external power.'

While *Common Sense* cannot be said to have caused the movement or the decision for independence, its polemic convinced many hesitant or indifferent colonists that there were no benefits to be gained from maintaining the connection with the so-called parent country. Yet, while most of the arguments he employed had already been expressed by others (such as John Adams), what was new about Paine's contribution was that it presented a single comprehensive statement in support of the cause. In his pamphlet he ruthlessly destroyed all the arguments in favour of reconciliation, and stated that Britain was only protecting America in its own interests and not for those of the American people. Additionally, he said, dependence on Britain only involved the colonies in corrupt European wars and had, consequently, a bad effect on American trading interests.

Paine did not merely call for independence, but advocated that the whole 'corrupt system' be replaced with a representative, republican form of government. While most radicals in Britain and America still believed that the balanced British constitution, though often undermined by corruption, was still the best system of government in the world, Paine, on the other hand, challenged such ideas, and maintained that no system based on the 'evils of hereditary monarchy' could ever be perfect. He further wrote, in a letter to a newspaper: 'Reconciliation is thought of now by none but knaves, fools, and madmen; and we cannot offer terms of peace to Great Britain until, as other nations have before us, we agree to call ourselves by some name. I shall rejoice to hear the title of the UNITED STATES OF AMERICA, in order that we may be on a proper footing to negotiate a peace.'

Paine was not responsible for America's adoption of a republican government; the main ideological influences on American republican thought were Greek, Roman and Renaissance theories as transmitted to the colonies via the writings of seventeenth-century English classical republicans. But what he did do was effectively to advance the view that *republicanism* – until then a pejorative term – was respectable, effective and not, as Loyalist propaganda would have it, prone to anarchy. Of course even the framers of the American constitutional system had reservations about adopting a fully fledged republican democracy, since they did not share Paine's optimistic view of human nature, which they believed was all too susceptible to corruption and self-interest. For this reason, democracy – or 'mobocracy' as it was sometimes dubbed – was considered both inexpedient and undesirable.

Influenced by John Locke's *Two Treatises of Government* (1690) they declared that while government could only be legitimate with the consent of the governed and that a government's sole purpose was to allow the individual to pursue his rights to life, liberty and happiness, the safest way of exercising authority was by a fair system of representation and by having checks on the abuse of executive power. American republican and constitutional ideas, therefore, were heavily influenced by several different though sometimes overlapping strands of British political thought and practice – by seventeenth-century classical republicans, by Locke, by eighteenth-century Whig radicals, and by what Americans thought the British constitution was like or ought to be, as well as by the revolutionary writings of Thomas Paine himself.

After the Declaration of Independence, Paine gave up his editorial post and joined the revolutionary forces. While serving in the Continental Army he wrote a series of sixteen propaganda pamphlets, *The American Crisis*, which were designed to boost the morale of the revolutionary troops, (and did, since Washington ordered them read out). The language was stirring. 'These are the times that try men's souls. The summer soldier and the sunshine patriot, will, in this crisis, shrink from the service of his country; but he that stands it now deserves the love and thanks of man and woman. Tyranny, like hell, is not easily conquered; yet we have this consolation with us, that the harder the conflict, the more glorious the triumph.' In 1777 he was appointed Secretary to the Congressional Committee on Foreign Affairs and later travelled extensively in France and Britain urging support for the world revolutionary cause.

The tide had turned. Based on his experience in the United States, in 1791–2 Paine published the most famous of all his works, *Rights of Man*, in which he argued that 'Governments arise either out of the people or over the people'. The book, partly a defence of the French Revolution against Edmund Burke's attacks, and partly an enunciation of the general principles of Republican government, had a stunning effect on radical thinking in Britain. By the end of 1793, 200,000 copies had been sold or

OPPOSITE: *Robert Owen*
Oil painting by William Henry Brooke, 1834 *(see page 90)*.

distributed free in Britain and Ireland, making it easily the most popular and widely read political pamphlet in British history. While it did not in itself create the radical movement, it helped inspire the establishment of hundreds of radical clubs and societies which had a far broader social base than the organizations previously involved in the movement for Parliamentary reform.

In 1792 Paine fled to France after being tried and convicted of treason as a result of these activities. There he was made a Citizen of the Republic and elected to the Legislative Assembly. But when the moderate republicans that he supported lost power during the Terror of 1793 his citizenship was revoked and, though outlawed in his native country, ironically he was arrested by Robespierre's regime as an English enemy and spy. In gaol he wrote his great deistic work, *The Age of Reason* (1794–5), before being released at the specific request of the then American Minister in Paris, James Monroe, later the fifth President of the United States.

Paine remained in France for seven more years before returning to America. During his time in Europe he had certainly not been forgotten in the United States, but initially, while his *Rights of Man* had been well received by Americans of all political persuasions, following the execution of Louis XVI, the Terror, and the outbreak of war with Europe, the French Revolution became as much a partisan issue in the New World as it was in the Old. Jefferson's Republicans had continued to praise the French Revolution while the opposition Federalists felt that it demonstrated all too clearly the dangers of excessive democracy. Thus *Rights of Man* came to be eulogized by some and reviled by others. After the publication of *The Age of Reason* in 1795, however, Paine was branded with preaching deism and atheism as well, and as Jefferson and his followers relied on Methodists, Presbyterians and Baptists for much of their support it became increasingly dangerous for them to continue to identify with Paine. In kindlier light G. K. Chesterton has written that 'Tom Paine invented the name of the Age of Reason and he was one of those sincere but curiously simple men who really did think that the age of reason was beginning at about the time when it was really ending'.

Whatever one's view, by the time Paine actually arrived in America he had become something of an embarrassment and a liability to his former friends, as well as a continuing object of ridicule and hatred for his enemies. He was thus variously attacked by the Federalist press as atheist, coward, traitor and drunkard, and almost totally ignored by the Republicans. In 1809, after years of isolation, poverty and ill-health he died. He was buried at his farm at New Rochelle, New York, which had earlier

OPPOSITE: *Thomas Paine*
Detail of oil painting of Paine, *c.* 1793 (after Romney)

'Mad Tom's first Practical Essay on the Rights of Man', a caricature of Paine, Sheridan and Whitbread as conspirators setting fire to the House of Commons, by Cruikshank, 1792.

Mad Tom's first Practical Essay on the Rights of MAN

'Sedition, Levelling and Plundering; or the Pretended Friends of the People in Council', 1792. 'Sedition, Levelling and Plundering' was adapted from an alternative version of 'God Save the King'. One verse ran:

> Tom Paine and Priestley are
> More base and desp'rate far
> Than vile Jack Cade.
> He for reform did cry
> They for equality
> W'd stain true liberty
> With British blood.

SEDITION, LEVELLING, and PLUNDERING;
Or, The PRETENDED FRIENDS of the People in Council.

been given to him by a then grateful American people. Later, the British reformer William Cobbett had his bones brought back to Britain with the intention of building some memorial to him, but when Cobbett died the monument was never built and Paine's mortal remains were lost for ever. Of this event Lord Byron wrote:

> In digging up your bones, Tom Paine
> Will Cobbett has done well;
> You visit him on earth again
> He'll visit you in Hell.

Paine, a quintessential example of the Rich Tide, took his intellectual baggage with him wherever he went, and he left a considerable mark not only on American politics, but also on British political society. Above all, his most lasting contribution on both sides of the Atlantic was that he made politics *accessible* to the middle and lower classes through a new style of political writing which avoided the flowery legalistic jargon of the then political establishment. For they understood phrases like 'the summer soldier and the sunshine patriot', or 'He that would make his own liberty secure must guard even his enemy from oppression'. He also helped to present British radicals with an appealing image of America as a 'beacon of freedom' and as a living example of the viability and desirability of democracy and republican institutions. In consequence, in the late eighteenth and early nineteenth centuries, the American Revolution and the American democratic experience were great stimuli to British liberal movements. The comparison has been made that America, until the 1880s, represented for British radicals exactly what the Soviet Union represented for British left-wing politicians until the beginning of the Second World War – the apparent realization of a utopian idea. In the years 1830–2, for instance, the working men's associations, fighting for the extension of the franchise, passed resolutions praising the American Republic. Later, Radicals and Chartists alluded favourably to America in their campaigns for universal suffrage, free and secular education, land reform and other social goals.

In general, these radicals believed that America possessed most of the desired liberal virtues such as free institutions, the rule of law, the constitutional protection of the individual and religious toleration. Conservatives argued, on the other hand, that America exhibited all the dangers of a new democracy, with its tendency to produce insipid governments, subject to the dictates of mob rule. Thus it has been argued that, until the late nineteenth century, whether one supported or opposed the 'Americanization' of British political institutions was a symbol of where one stood on the fundamental issues of the age. That and the heightening of mutual political involvement by the United Kingdom and the United States was to no small extent Paine's legacy.

*   *   *

Of the many leading radicals who, in Paine's wake, praised, even idolized, the American Republic, there were two men, Richard Cobden and John Bright, who were so captivated that they became known or derided in the House of Commons as 'the

Richard Cobden (1804–65) in 1860.

honourable members for the United States'. Richard Cobden was born in the Sussex village of Heyshott in 1804. After a poor and miserable childhood, he started working in the London cloth trade and in 1828, having been both clerk and travelling salesman, ended up in the calico printing business in Manchester. When his business started thriving, Cobden found time to turn to politics and the social problems of the age. In 1835 he fulfilled a long-standing ambition to visit the United States, from where he returned, unlike so many of his contemporaries, highly impressed (apart from the slavery issue) by the country and by its vigorous political and social institutions. Near the end of his visit he wrote:

'I predicted when leaving England for this continent, that I should not find it sufficiently to my taste to relish a sojourn here for life. My feelings in this respect are quite altered. I know of no reasonable grounds for an aversion to this country, and none but unreasonable minds could fail to be as happy here as in England.'

Entering public life, he unsuccessfully tried to win a Parliamentary seat. Undismayed by failure, he threw his energies behind the social and economic reform movements of the time, and helped orchestrate the national agitation for the total repeal of the Corn Laws. After his eventual election to the House of Commons in 1841, he emerged as the leader of the Anti-Corn Law League, whose victory in 1846 ushered in the era of free trade.

Now famous, Cobden became involved in several other campaigns, most notably for a national system of non-sectarian elementary education and for world peace. In both these moves he was much influenced by American theory and practice. On his American visit he had been impressed by the pioneering Massachusetts system of elementary education, and in the British campaign he contributed to the close dialogue between educationalists on both sides of the Atlantic. Equally, in the field of peace and international relations, he wanted Britain to follow America's policies of non-intervention and minimal military expediture. Such policies, he argued, explained America's remarkable growth as a commercial rival, because it had enabled her to devote more money and energy towards business and domestic reform.

In 1859, following the loss of his Parliamentary seat, Cobden returned to America, primarily to investigate the state of an investment he had made in the Illinois Central Railroad, but also to see how much the country had changed since his last visit. During this tour he was once again struck by the 'vitality, force and velocity of progress' of the American people and by 'their inborn aptitude for self-government'.

Returning to Britain once again, he discovered to his surprise that, in his absence, he had been re-elected to Parliament. Despite refusing a place in Palmerston's Cabinet (he has been called the greatest statesman of the nineteenth century never to have taken office), he masterminded the Anglo-French Commercial Treaty of 1860 which resulted in the removal of tariff barriers all over Europe, the second major triumph for the advocates of free trade. He hoped that this would mark the beginning of a new era of national prosperity and international peace. Then, during the American Civil War, Cobden helped to preserve the United Kingdom's neutrality despite widespread British sympathy for the rebel South, and through his American friends, in particular Charles Sumner, the influential chairman of the American Foreign Relations Committee, his views on the state of British opinion were channelled to President Lincoln.

Throughout, Cobden never missed an opportunity to lecture his fellow countrymen on the fundamental importance of America to Britain. He told Gladstone in December 1861: 'If we force a war on the 20 millions of the Free States in this their great agony – and there can be no war unless we force it – it will be remembered against us to all future generations. – In the life time of my youngest child, I doubt not those Free States will contain 100 millions of prosperous people. – Perhaps it is only one who, like myself, has visited, twice, that region, at an interval of 20 years, that can fully appreciate its solid and rapid progress.'

Cobden died in April 1865, just before the end of the war. Of

The famous radical English journalist, agitator and author of *Rural Rides*, William Cobbett (*c.*1763–1835), made two journeys to the United States. In 1792, after failing to substantiate his allegations of fraud by the British army while serving as a soldier in Nova Scotia and New Brunswick, he came to the United States to escape punishment. There he stirred up great controversy with his literary attacks on the Republican supporters of France. When he was convicted of libelling Dr Benjamin Rush he wisely returned to England where his Tory stance was replaced by a more radical, anti-establishment attitude. In 1817 he made a second visit to America to escape the infamous 'Gagging Bills', and settled on a farm in Long Island. Always seeking a controversy, Cobbett accused Morris Birkbeck of being in the pay of land speculators. Disillusioned with America he came back to England in 1819, where he was to devote much of his time to agitation for Parliamentary reform.

John Bright (1811–89), a drawing by Harry Furniss.

Cobden's friend and fellow liberal, the Rochdale-born radical, John Bright (1811–89), though he never reached its shores, was an equally vociferous supporter of the United States. The Civil War came both as a surprise and a grave shock to Bright and his beliefs, since he had expected the slavery question to be resolved in other ways. He was torn by fears that the system of government which he so admired was in danger of falling apart and realized, more importantly, that the chances of electoral reform in Britain considerably depended upon the outcome of the struggle. If the Union side was defeated, his opponents would cite the United States as an example of the dangers of democracy; if Lincoln won, democracy would be vindicated. Bright helped Cobden in his campaign to ensure that, while the British government remained neutral, it put its moral support behind the North. His greatest single achievement was to persuade the working people of Lancashire to support Lincoln's cause, despite great hardship in the domestic cotton industry caused by the Union's blockade of Confederate ports, and at a time when most of Britain sympathized with the South. A statue of Lincoln, commemorating this, still stands at Platt Field, Manchester.

Bright's analysis of the implications of the war on the reform issue was sound: two years after the cessation of hostilities in America, the second Reform Bill was passed by Parliament. Of course no one could argue that the franchise was extended because of the North's victory, but it was appreciated both by Bright's supporters and by his opponents that the outcome had certainly helped.

him, Benjamin Disraeli said he was 'the greatest political character the pure middle class of this country has yet produced'. During his lifetime, he did much to improve Anglo-American relations, even in times of discord between the two countries helping to organize pro-American sentiment. At the same time America was the single most important influence on his pacifism, his anti-colonialism, his support of free trade and his ideas on educational reform.

Less spectacularly than a Tom Paine or a Richard Cobden, diplomats, that much-maligned race, have always provided the necessary machinery to keep international relations well oiled; this has nowhere been more true than between Washington and London. The Foreign Office and the State Department and their subsidiaries in, latterly, Massachusetts Avenue and Grosvenor Square, have provided an essential channel of communication as much in times of harmony as in periods of tension. Ambassadors and their staffs are largely there to influence the thinking and events in the country to which they are accredited. They are therefore, by definition, the 'official' Rich Tide.

The first fully fledged American Ambassador to the Court of St James (all before this held the rank of Minister) was Thomas Francis Bayard (1828–98), who fell into the professional trap of so many diplomats by becoming more attached, in the eyes of those at home base, to the ideals and interests of the country to which he was accredited than to his own country. From his appointment in 1893, his activities in promoting Anglo-American friendship and his popularity in London were undisputed, but in a speech made in Edinburgh in 1896 he went too far in criticizing American tariff policy, and was promptly censored by Congress for his pains.

The author of *American Commonwealth* was a diplomat whose influence in the country of his accreditation was outstanding. James (later Viscount) Bryce (1838–1922), jurist, historian and politician, became British Ambassador to America in 1907. Born in Belfast, the son of a Presbyterian schoolteacher, he had moved with his family to Glasgow where he was educated at university and at Oxford. His career included being Oxford Regius Professor of Civil Law, 1870–93, Liberal MP, 1880–1906, Chancellor of the Duchy of Lancaster, 1892–4, President of the Board of Trade, 1894–5, and Chief Secretary for Ireland, 1905–6. Bryce, who admitted that to him 'America excites an admiration which must be felt on the spot to be understood,' paid a number of extensive visits to America before he took up his ambassadorial duties in Washington. He is best known for his book *American Commonwealth*, first published in 1888 but still a highly valued study. The aim of the book was, in his own words, to portray from an outsider's viewpoint 'the whole political system of the country in its practice as well as its theory', and to explain 'not only the National Government, but the State Governments, not only the constitution, but the party system, not only the party system but the ideas, temper, habits of the sovereign'.

The book, which with a British eye looked with detached frankness at the problems of corruption in local government, became one of the most important accounts of the American political system and was used as a textbook in American schools for over thirty years. His analysis of that country, with its classlessness and widespread property-owning democratic structure, was precise: 'America is a Commonwealth of commonwealths, a Republic of republics, a State which, while one, is nevertheless composed of other States even more essential to its existence than it is to theirs.' Such was Bryce's reputation that when he reported, in 1915, on German atrocities in Belgium he was central to

James Bryce with 'Uncle Sam'. This drawing, by James Boardman, was captioned: 'Uncle Sam to James Bryce – I shall be sorry to say Goodbye.'

bringing many Americans over to the Allied point of view. Though a diplomat, a representative of one nation to the other, his was more than just an official postbox role, for he, like Adams before him, took his thoughts and skills with him to the end of helping Americans better understand themselves, and their rights as men.

'Like Adams before him . . .' The history of the remarkable Adams family alone makes phrases like 'bilateral diplomacy' spring into unaccustomed life, a whole American political dynasty with not only its roots in Britain but one whose members, during their lifetimes, spent much of their careers dealing with the bilateral relationship, three generations serving as American Minister in London. The family, which came originally from Somerset, became prominent in the decade before the Revolution in the shape of John Adams (1735–1826), the small, fiery and rotund future second President, leader of the Massachusetts Whigs, and one of the drafters of the Declaration of Independence. It was he who is said to have first uttered the fateful words: 'No taxation without representation.' On 3 July 1776, he wrote to his wife, Abigail, 'Yesterday the greatest question was decided which ever was debated in America; and a greater perhaps never was, nor will be, decided among men. A resolution was passed without one dissenting colony, that these United Colonies are, and of right ought to be, free and independent States.'

As one who, with Franklin and Jay, signed the Treaty of Paris in 1783, he was a logical choice to move on to become American Minister to the Court of St James, a post which he held over the years 1785–8. After he had presented his credentials, George III is said to have told him: 'I was the last to consent to the separation, but the separation having been made and having become inevitable, I have always said that I would be the first to meet the friendship of the United States as an independent power.' As Gore Vidal has remarked, John Adams, with his son and grandson, were, in a sense, made by England, since each was to do his job well at a time of crisis. John lived a highly social life in a house in Grosvenor Square where the American Embassy is now sited. He had a shrewd common sense as he again showed in a letter to his wife: 'I must study politics and war, that my sons may have liberty to study mathematics and philosophy, geography, natural history and naval architecture, navigation, commerce, and agriculture, in order to give their children a right to study painting, poetry, music, architecture, statuary, tapestry, and porcelain.'

For a founding father the British found it odd that he should later argue that democracy was 'the most ignoble and detestable form of government'. His belief instead was in government by the

John Quincy Adams (1767–1848).
Oil painting by John Singleton
Copley (see chapter 8). Courtesy the
Museum of Fine Arts, Boston. Gift of
Mrs Charles Francis Adams.

meritocracy, 'the rich, the well-born and the able', views which
he consolidated during his time in London. When combined with
his own testy vanity, such arguments never made him an entirely
popular figure, but his belief in government by law made him
respected. Thomas Jefferson summed him up: 'He is vain, irrit-
able, and a bad calculator of the force and probable effect of the
motives which govern men. This is all the ill which can possibly be
said of him.'

Adams, like Paine in his very different way, took his intellectual baggage with him as he went back and forth across the
Atlantic. When he went to Britain he brought and left there a
greater understanding about what the new America was all
about. That he did it with authority to an authority, rather than in
the public hustings, made it no less effective. His beliefs, tempered
by his experience of the establishment and environment of

Mrs Charles Francis Adams
(1808–89)

RIGHT: Charles Francis Adams
(1807–86)

Westminster government and administration, greatly increased
his understanding, his judgement and his philosophy when he
returned to the United States and eventually took up the first
office of the land. Britain and America were his training grounds
to the benefits of America and Britain.

John's son, John Quincy Adams (1767–1848), later to become the sixth President of the United States, was also to serve
with distinction as American Minister to Great Britain. He was

Henry Adams (1838–1918) in his den at Beverly Farms, photographed by Mrs Adams.

described by Alfred Steinberg as 'a short, stout, bald, brilliant and puritanical twig off a short, stout, bald, brilliant and puritanical tree. Little wonder that he took the same view of the office of President as his father.' He started political life by being appointed by George Washington as Minister to the Netherlands in 1794 and then was sent to Prussia from 1797 to 1801. After a period back in the United States teaching at Harvard, he was President Madison's envoy to Russia from 1809 to 1815, and then to England in 1815, arriving *en poste* immediately after the war between the two countries. He was less social and more austere than his father, living in the then country town of Ealing rather than in Grosvenor Square, but making quite sure his sons stayed to be educated at English schools, thereby ensuring, to quote Gore Vidal again 'that the mark of English schooling on Charles Francis's character was life-long, and perhaps saved the nation from a third Adams Presidency'. John Quincy was a man of some culture, even a poet, respected for that, too, on both sides of the Atlantic.

> Alas! how swift the moments fly!
>   How flash the years along!
> Scarce here, yet gone already by,
>   The burden of a song.
> See childhood, youth, and manhood pass,
>   And age with furrowed brow;
> Time was – Time shall be – drain the glass –
>   But where in Time is now?

One son, the anglicized Charles Francis Adams (1807–86), also became Minister in London from 1861–8 over the equally difficult period when Cobden and Bright were so active and when most Britons favoured the Confederate side in the American Civil War. He conducted his mission with great diplomatic skill and

Brooks Adams (1848–1927)

coolness from a house in Upper Portland Place, and won himself much respect both in Britain and in the United States. His son, in turn, the famous historian and novelist, Henry Adams (1838–1918), who once described politics as 'the systematic organization of hatreds', served as his father's secretary in London, one of his tasks being to manipulate the British press, with the ubiquitous help of Cobden and Bright, so that they supported the Northern cause.

Henry's brother Brooks (1848–1927) was also a historian, who in 1900 wrote that China would be the great problem country of the future and that Russia and the United States would be the great power-bloc rivals for world supremacy. In terms of the old world and the new, his prophecy of 1902 had great vision. 'We are penetrating into Europe and Great Britain especially in gradually assuming the position of a dependency . . . The United States will outweigh any single empire, if not all empires combined. The whole world will pay her tribute. Commerce will flow to her from both east and west, and the order which has existed from the dawn of time will be reversed.'

Thus three, indeed four generations of the same family served in London during periods of crisis, helping to rebuilt a relationship that had changed out of all recognition after 1776. They were not mere diplomats sent to lie abroad for their country; they provided a continuous and very special kernel of influence that was to mark Anglo-American relations for many generations.

*   *   *

Show me the country in which there are no strikes and I'll show you that country in which there is no liberty.

SAMUEL GOMPERS

With all their faults, trade-unions have done more for humanity than any other organisation of men that ever existed. They have done more for decency, for honesty, for education, for the betterment of the race, for the developing of character in man, than any other association of men.

CLARENCE DARROW

In striving for the rights of man, one of the most important British contributions to the making of modern America was in the formation and development of trade and labour unions. It was, after all, British immigrants who constituted the central core of the skilled working class. Indeed many of the industrial immigrants had already been members of trade unions or similar bodies in Britain before they left; some unions had a regular policy of helping unemployed members to emigrate by providing them with free passage and creating American branches to help such workers when they arrived. And, if British workers formed the membership, so they naturally provided most of the leadership with their methods of organizing and their political motivations.

The process began with groups of working-class immigrants from Britain founding Co-operative Movements, Friendly Societies and then Labour Unions to defend themselves in a hostile and competitive world. This was particularly true as the threat increased when larger numbers of immigrants began arriving in the United States from other parts of Europe and from the wider world. One of the first co-operative movements was the Fall River Workingman's Association, formed in 1867 by mill hands who had emigrated in large numbers from Lancashire. (Massachusetts authorities had to set up six episcopal churches for that group alone, during the last quarter of the nineteenth century.) The ideas of the English Rochdale pioneers were also exported to the United States, with many examples of consumer

I WILL WIN

co-operatives: one vote per shareholder and dividends paid out on purchases.

Among the many outstanding British-born nineteenth-century labour leaders in America was Richard F. Trevellick (1830–95), who came from St Mary's in the Scilly Isles, the son of a peasant farmer. In his early twenties he travelled widely as a seaman and ship's carpenter, acquiring a reputation as a union agitator as far away as New Zealand and Australia. In Melbourne in 1855, he was prominent in the fight for an eight-hour day. In 1857 he landed in New Orleans and within a very short period of time he had become President of the Ship Carpenters' and Caulkers' Union, leading a successful campaign for a nine-hour day.

Moving to Detroit during the Civil War, he became the first

OPPOSITE ABOVE: 'I will win' – the slogan of the Industrial Workers of the World (IWW), organised in 1905.

OPPOSITE BELOW: American workers at a sawmill in Clatsop County, Oregon in the 1880s.

LEFT: The first Labor Day Parade in New York, 1882.

President of the Detroit Trades' Assembly in 1864, in which year he was delegate to the Louisville Convention which set up the short-lived International Industrial Assembly of North America.

In 1865 he became President of the National Union of Ship-workers and Caulkers. Two years later he was representing the Michigan Grand Eight Hours League and the Detroit Trades' Assembly at the congress of the National Labour Union, the NLU. By 1869 this highly militant and energetic man had become the NLU's President, a position he was to hold on two other occasions, in 1871 and 1872. Later he was to work for the reformist Knights of Labour over half the leaders of which, from the craft unions, the mill-workers and especially the miners, even as late as the turn of the century, were British-born, a statistic which well reflected the ethnic origins of the majority of its members.

In 1868 Trevellick played a leading role in one of the first successful labour lobbies, helping to get through Congress a statute instituting an eight-hour day for all federal workmen. As leader of the NLU he opposed the importation of Chinese contract labour, but not, as happened in California, the complete exclusion of all Chinese. By contrast, he advocated the abolition of the colour bar which prevented negro workers from joining most labour unions, maintaining that the negro had always 'stood his ground nobly when a member of a trades' union'. This was around the time when that other British-born Labour, leader, Samuel Gompers, a bastion of reaction in America, was saying 'Caucasians are not going to let their standard of living be destroyed by Negroes, Japs or any others'.

Following the collapse of the NLU and the decline of American trade unionism after the economic collapse in the early 1870s, Trevellick fell under the influence of the Greenback movement, which advocated relieving industrial and agrarian depression by means of inflationary price-boosting schemes. In 1876 he helped establish the Greenback Party and two years later he presided over the convention at Toledo which amalgamated the Greenbacks with the National Labour Reform Party, to form the National Greenback Party. Their broad platform included many labour demands and, while keeping a primarily agrarian character, they attracted much popular support in its early years, though never becoming a significant force at the polls.

Trevellick made an outstanding contribution to the American labour movement during some of its most difficult years. As a ceaseless promoter and organizer of unionism, with his striking black beard, fiery eyes and stirring rhetoric he became well known to workers all over the United States. In 1868–9 alone he delivered nearly three hundred addresses to labour meetings and, in the process, organized forty-seven local unions during a major tour of the west. In 1870 he helped establish a further two hundred local unions in over sixteen states and, as the *Dictionary of American Biography* says, his 'sense of the need for combined industrial and political activity, his ability for organization, and his rhetorical powers made him one of the first great labor agitators in America'.

What so many of the diplomats and British-American political figures mentioned in this chapter shared was a realization that it was not just a common language that made the dialogue easier for them and for their successors. It is that the whole basis of the society with which they were dealing was so similar to their own: their principles, their rights, their beliefs, their freedoms and their goals. It applies even to a shared sense of humour. Can one imagine any other two countries whose heads of government would communicate as Franklin Delano Roosevelt did in acknowledging a sixtieth-birthday greetings telegram from Churchill in the middle of the war in 1942, with the message: 'It's fun to be in the same decade as you'? Yet, while Paine, Cobden and Bright wanted to create in Britain what they believed existed in a utopian America, the Trevellicks and the Adamses moulded them-

The emblem of the United Mine-Workers of America, whose first president was the Scottish emigrant John Rae, who later became a State Senator for Illinois, a prosperous entrepreneur, oil executive and philanthropist.

selves to accomodate the differences of their new environment, and blended in when they had to blend. As Churchill said in a speech in the House of Commons in 1947, 'The Americans took little when they emigrated from Europe except what they stood up in and what they had in their souls. They came through, they staked the wilderness, they became what old John Bright called, ''A refuge for the oppressed from every land and clime.'' They have become today the greatest state and power in the world, speaking our own language, cherishing our common law, and pursuing, like our great Dominions, in broad principle, the same ideals.'

Politicians and governments, both directly and through diplomatic channels, learn from the mistakes and achievements of their fellows on the other side of the Atlantic, not just in terms of current problems and policies but also in points of principle and in matters of style. It is only necessary to look at the increasing adoption by British political parties of American electioneering methods and, in particular, the impact of Presidential-style politics in the United Kingdom to see one major contemporary example of it. In the beginning the influence was of British political thinking, British governmental institutions, British politicians. Thereafter, the very existence of republican America has determined the ways in which the Rich Tide, and in particular its support for the basic rights of men and women, has flowed.

CHAPTER FIVE

An Intellectual Democracy

Both countries would be highly benefited by borrowing from each other; England by adopting the American system of instructing all the people, and the United States by cultivating that higher species of learning, which has rendered the English scholars, for a series of ages, so particularly pre-eminent. JOHN BRISTED, 1815

From the earliest days of the British in North America, the shared educational heritage has been among the strongest of all the links between the two countries. This has led to their cultural and other intellectual values becoming so intertwined as to make them inseparable. While the foundation of a school was one of the first prerequisites of even the most rudimentary early settlements in North America, for the first two centuries, since there were few American colleges or universities in existence, many students had to go to Britain for their higher education. Even as late as the War of 1812, and thereafter at post-graduate level, this continued to be the case. Additionally, a majority of teachers, lecturers and professors at all levels and in all disciplines came from or had studied in Britain. That the contemporary American school and university owe much to English and Scottish models is, therefore, far from surprising. And today's British students benefit greatly from this, since to them the American system is more accessible than to students from almost any other country in the world, even though such common antecedents certainly do not mean that identical institutions and practices pertain in both countries today. The balance of educational exchange that now takes place in both directions means that the United States is paying back its inherited educational debt many times over.

There were many different strands in the creation of an American educational system, from the influence of the early New England puritans on the development of popular education,

OPPOSITE: John Blair, founder of the college of William and Mary. Oil painting by Charles Bridges, c. 1725.

to the highly significant effect of the democratic Scottish educational system. It was, above all, a concentration on the availability of education for all that dominated the process. It started early. Within only thirty years of the founding of the first Massachusetts Settlement in 1620 all towns in that state were required to hire a schoolmaster, while larger towns were equally strictly bound to found grammar schools to prepare children for university. Just over a century later, any new settlements had, by law, to set aside land for public schools.

In the colonial period, while many students still went to British universities, Harvard had come into being in 1636 (though not so named until a few years later) and William and Mary College in 1693. By the time of Independence there were no less than fourteen seats of higher learning, the number more than doubling by the turn of the century. While most of these owed much to Britain, it is important to recognize that from the outset they differed from the traditional English model in that they were (and with few exceptions are) regional rather than national, each thereby varying to a considerable degree in what it offered. Thus Latin went with agricultural sciences, law with home economics or (later) business administration with journalism, according to the particular needs of the community it served. And this was even more true of the grammar and high schools that were set up throughout the new land, each State of the Union being responsible for and regulating its own schooling standards and curricula.

Taking one strand of what is an enormous spectrum from the early colonial period, the Scots and the Scots-Irish had a unique part to play. The democratic attitude towards education that is now particularly American owed much to the influence of the Scottish and, in particular, the Scottish presbyterian ideal of the free school, where no one was denied basic education because he lacked status or money. In the colonies Scottish teachers were frequently regarded as the best – and there were many of them because of that very educational system. Indeed, in the 1770s, the Virginians, for example, imported all their senior tutors and schoolmasters from Scotland, mainly presbyterians who thought of themselves as cultural missionaries and who taught the basic elements of learning against a heavy background of religious instruction. But it was at university level that the Scots and the Scots-Irish made their greatest impact.

The founder and first President of William and Mary College, the second-established seat of higher education in America, was the Aberdeen-born and Edinburgh University-educated episcopalian James Blair (1655–1743), who arrived in Virginia in 1685 as an emissary of the Bishop of London, in whose diocese it

THE ROOM FORMERLY OCCUPIED BY JOHN RANDOLPH, OF ROANOKE, AT WILLIAM AND MARY'S COLLEGE, VIRGINIA.

'The room formerly occupied by John Randolph, of Roanoke, at William and Mary's College, Virginia', c. 1856.

was, to reform the church there. This he did admirably – securing better salaries for the clergy, filling vacant parishes with able believers and ensuring a strict observance of orthodox liturgical practice. As part of his enterprise he founded William and Mary College to train Anglican clergymen, obtaining a charter from the King and Queen in 1693, and a handsome grant comprising £2,000, 20,000 acres of land and the revenue of one penny per pound of Virginia's and Maryland's tobacco exports. This was despite considerable opposition. According to Esmond Wright 'It is said that when he brought an order to the Lord of the Exchequer for the £2,000 which the King and Queen had granted to the college, the latter demurred strongly. "But, my Lord," said Blair, "the college is designed to educate young men for the ministry, and we in Virginia have souls to be saved as well as you in England." "Damn your souls," was the reply, "make tobacco." '

Blair was a very difficult and irascible man, honoured but feared by students and staff alike. He had an unrivalled influence on the intellectual development of Virginia and would have gone on perfecting the institution he had founded. But he was not a man who believed in quiet compromise, and in 1697 he fell out with the Governor and was recalled to Britain.

*   *   *

In broad terms it can be said that the Scots-Irish made these
contributions to Colonial America: they settled the frontiers,
they founded the kirk and they built the school.

ESMOND WRIGHT

The lively impact of the Scots and Scots-Irish on American university education can be further illustrated by looking at the establishment and emergence of Princeton University, which, again to quote Wright, was 'decisively Presbyterian and Scottish in character, virtually a foster child of Scotland'. The roots of the university are to be found in the famous 'Log College' of the Scots-Irishman, William Tennent (1673–1745/6). 'Hell-Fire' Tennent, as he became known, was born in Ireland, the cousin of influential Quaker Secretary of Pennsylvania, James Logan. Educated at Edinburgh University, he was ordained a deacon in the Church of England in 1704 and became a priest in 1706. But, unable to find a parish and unhappy about the direction his church was taking, he emigrated to Pennsylvania some time between 1716 and 1718 along with his wife and four sons. In 1718 he joined the Presbyterian Synod of Philadelphia and eight years later he became pastor of the Presbyterian Church at Neshaminy, a settlement twenty miles north of Philadelphia. In 1736 he built a school 'no more than twenty feet square', on a tract of land he had been given by his distinguished cousin, with the intention of educating prospective Presbyterian ministers.

The best contemporary description of the Log College was provided by George Whitefield, who visited Tennent in 1739. 'The place wherein the young men study now is, in contempt, called the log college. It is a log house, about twenty feet long, and nearly as many broad, and, to me, it seemed to resemble the schools of the old prophets. That their habitations were mean, and that they sought not great things for themselves, is plain from that passage of Scripture, wherein we are told, that at the feast of the sons of the prophets, one of them put on the pot, whilst the others went to fetch some herbs out of the field. From this despised place seven or eight worthy ministers of Jesus have lately been sent forth; more are almost ready to be sent; and a foundation is now laying for the instruction of many others.'

The Presbyterian Synod insisted on an educated ministry, but because there were no adequate colleges except in New England or abroad it was difficult to increase the supply. Tennent's Log College was set up as an independent attempt to meet this problem. His establishment did not have a charter nor did it

The Log College at Neshaminy, the modest beginnings of Princeton University.

confer degrees, so it could not be classified as a college; rather, it was a sort of academy, at which theology, the classics and the arts were taught. It is hardly surprising, therefore, that from its earliest days the Log College was attacked by those ministers who opposed the evangelical wing of the Presbyterian church, with which Tennent and his sons were allied. Other critics were genuinely concerned that the level of instruction at the College was not of a sufficiently high standard.

In 1738, after investigating the status and work of the College, the Philadelphia Synod issued an edict which stipulated that, in future, all candidates without diplomas from British or other Old World universities, or from Harvard or Yale, could only be approved for the ministry with their approval. It was a direct challenge to Tennent's enterprises, but gradually the edict was opposed or ignored, and as the Presbytery of New Brunswick was largely composed of Log College men the argument became a symbol of the schism that was later to divide the Presbyterian church.

When Tennent died in 1746 his Log College ceased to exist; but that same year some of its supporters, including Tennent's sons, William and Gilbert, united with others at the New Light Synod of New York to set up what they called the College of New Jersey. The new establishment opened in Elizabethtown in 1747 in the home of one Jonathan Dickinson, then moved to the Newark parsonage of Aaron Burr in 1748, before finding its permanent home at Nassau Hall, Princeton, in 1756. Two years

ABOVE: John Witherspoon, (1723–99). Oil painting by Charles Willson Peale.

BELOW: Nassau Hall and the President's House at Princeton, the Dawkins engraving of 1786.

later the Synod of Philadelphia relented as regards this off-spring of the Log College and authorized it to teach and receive funds for the education of young Presbyterians entering the ministry. From its inception the aim of the College was to provide a non-denominational higher education, in which training for the ministry, however prominent, would only be part of the syllabus. Its charter guaranteed 'free and equal liberty and advantage of education to persons of all sects'. Besides Princeton, Tennent's energy and drive, coupled with his evangelical zeal, ensured that the Log College concept became something of a model for many early institutes of higher learning in the United States and provided an impetus to what was to follow.

The College of New Jersey or Princeton had an uncertain start and did not achieve much stability until the long and distinguished presidency of the Reverend John Witherspoon (1723–94), who served in that post from 1768 to 1794. Born at Gifford near Edinburgh, he was educated at Haddington Grammar School and Edinburgh University. Following his ordination he served in various west-of-Scotland parishes and in 1759 became Moderator of the Synod of Glasgow and Ayr. A strict Calvinist

A North West Prospect of Nassau-Hall, with a Front View of the Presidents House, in New Jersey.

from an equally strict family background (at one time he believed himself to be a direct descendant of John Knox), he allied himself with the conservative Popular Party and published tracts attacking lax Presbyterian Moderates, thereby attracting a sizeable following in orthodox Scottish Presbyterian circles.

In 1766, the trustees of the College of New Jersey invited Witherspoon to be their new President. At first he refused largely because of his wife's 'insuperable aversion' to leaving her homeland. Apparently the mere mention of going to America sent her into fits of hysterics. However, thanks to the charm and diplomatic proddings of the young Benjamin Rush, then a Princeton graduate studying medicine at Edinburgh, she changed her mind.

Coming fully prepared for his task, Witherspoon took up his post in August 1768, and held it until his death over twenty-five years later. During his long term of office he revitalized the college, increased the number of students, brought in new endowments, and broadened the basis of the curriculum, introducing many new subjects to the syllabus. Coming as he did straight to his task from the Old World his was very much a new broom. He was a forceful and decisive leader who brought with him the styles of teaching common to Scotland – lectures rather than disputations, backed by frequent examinations and tests of the student's abilities. He was instrumental, from the outset, in building up a fine library and ensuring that the facilities and equipment available to the faculties were the best available. Witherspoon ruthlessly imposed his philosophical ideas on the College, replacing the idealism favoured by many of the tutors and students with a Scottish common-sense realism. His greatest contribution, however, was to direct the College in a way that would serve both Church and State. As a sign of his success, among his graduates, thirteen became College presidents, six became delegates to the Continental Congress, twenty-four representatives, twenty senators, ten cabinet officers, thirteen state governors, three justices of the Supreme Court, one Vice-President (Aaron Burr) and one President (James Madison).

Witherspoon himself was to sign the Declaration of Independence, the only clergyman to do so, and as a member of the Continental Congress he helped to draw up the Articles of Confederation and served on several Congressional committees of the new republic. Before and during the Revolution he wrote extensively on the conflict between the American colonies and the mother country. Princeton under Witherspoon thus became a sort of production line for men of public affairs, men who went on to run the American nation. Later Woodrow Wilson, who himself was of Scots-Irish descent and Witherspoon's most eminent successor as President of the University (1902–10), saw Princeton under Witherspoon as 'a seminary of statesmen'. It was only natural, therefore, that from its earliest days Princeton, its non-denominational standing still maintained, established close links with Edinburgh University, links which are still maintained today.

Two other of America's most famous seats of higher learning had their foundations in England, their founders Englishmen. The oldest of these institutions was founded in 1636 with a grant of a mere £400 made by the General Court of Cambridge, Massachusetts. It is named after the son of a humble London butcher, John Harvard (1607–38). After studying at Emmanuel College, Cambridge, the young Harvard married and emigrated to New England in 1637 where he became a teaching elder at Charlestown Church, and a member of the town committee which helped to compile the Body of Liberties. The year before his arrival, a college had already been founded in the colony which opened its doors in a small house in Cambridge. But because Harvard left half his estate (a modest few hundred pounds) plus his library of some four hundred volumes to the college after his death a short time later, and because his bequest exceeded all others to the college at that time, it was named after him.

Some sixty-five years later, a group of Congregational ministers set up a 'collegiate school' at Saybrook, Connecticut. It was later to be named after Elihu Yale (1649–1721), whose parents had emigrated to New Haven and then Boston in 1637. Elihu's father objected to the theocratic government of Massachusetts

A memorial to John Harvard: a stained glass window in Emmanuel College chapel, Cambridge, England.

RIGHT: Harvard – 'A View of the Colleges taken Near the Craigie Bridge, 1821.' Painting by Alvan Fisher.

that prevailed at the time and so returned with his family to England in 1652. Elihu therefore was educated in London. He later acquired a reputation as a philanthropist through his gifts to schools, churches and missionary societies. Approached by one Jeremiah Dummer, then Connecticut's agent in London, for support for the struggling collegiate school at Saybrook, he sent a small gift of forty volumes to it in 1714.

Four years later, the trustees of the College's new building at New Haven asked for more support, intimating that 'the name of Yale College might easily adorn his munificence with a fame more enduring than the pyramids'. Yale duly sent over three bales of goods, some books and a portrait of George I by Kneller, a gift in itself worth some £800. (Though the goods were actually sold for £562, they were the largest contribution made by a private individual to the College in over a century.) In September 1718, the building and school consequently received their new name of Yale.

At university level, while even for a long time after independence America relied heavily on Britain for higher educational support, there was much evidence of the Rich Tide turning long before the obvious and undoubted influence provided by American talent, skills and money that has flowed eastward in the

Governor Elihu Yale (1649–1721). Oil painting by Enoch Zeeman, 1717.

LEFT: A front view of Yale College and the College Chapel, in New Haven, 1786.

twentieth century came to full flood. Francis Gilmer (1790–1826), for example, who came to Britain to recruit university staff, influenced the formation of University College, London. Gilmer was born in Virginia in 1790. Having lost both his parents in early childhood, he became a protégé of Thomas Jefferson, who had been a close friend of his father.

As a youth Gilmer showed great academic potential, and after graduating from William and Mary in 1810 he went to Richmond to read law. While he achieved considerable success at the Bar, he took a close interest in the non-sectarian University of Virginia which was being established at Charlottesville by Jefferson and others. In 1824 Jefferson, who saw Gilmer 'as one of the best, and to me, the dearest of men', offered him the professorship of law at the new institution. Gilmer was reluctant to abandon his practice, declined the offer, but did agree to go to Britain to recruit professors and acquire books and apparatus for the new university. Leaving in the spring of 1824 he brought with him Jefferson's *Rockfish Gap Report*, which outlined the plans for the new university.

Arriving in London in June, he visited Cambridge, Oxford and Edinburgh before returning to London in late August. While in the capital he met, among others, the Benthamite reformers Lord Brougham and George Birkbeck, and the poet Thomas Campbell. Three years later when these men helped found University College, London, England's first non-sectarian university, they were undoubtedly influenced by Gilmer's views and Jefferson's *Report*. Equally, there is no doubt that until Gilmer's arrival most educational reformers who were opposed to the religious tests which made Oxford and Cambridge preserves of the established church accepted the situation and sent their children to European or Scottish universities instead.

Of the group, Thomas Campbell was particularly sympathetic and helpful, not surprisingly, given that he had strong family connections with Virginia – his father had been involved in the Virginia trade, one brother lived there, and another relation had married the son of Patrick Henry. As the historian of University College, London, has written, Campbell saw Gilmer as 'a fellow in the faith, and what was more, a witness to the practicability of what men said was a dream. That which could be done in Charlottesville could surely be done in London.' Gilmer's real mission was also a success and four British professors were recruited, but the trip ruined Gilmer's already poor health. After abandoning his practice and at last accepting the professorship of law at Charlottesville he died on 26 February 1826, before having had a chance to deliver his first lecture.

Francis Walker Gilmer (1790–1826)

BELOW: An artist's impression (*c.* 1820) of University College, London.

There is a strong and significant flow and counter-flow once again here. If Gilmer's importance lay in bringing American ideas to the formation of University College, London, and to the University of London itself, the latter was, in turn, to become more of a model for the new non-denominational American universities than Oxbridge ever was, even following the abolition of the religious qualifications for entry to them after 1871. The first non-religious schools in Britain, along with the 1870 Act (which was the greatest of all moves towards secularization), were, therefore, re-imports into the United Kingdom of those ideas of religious toleration and secularization that went out with the original settlers.

Mass Education

Joseph Lancaster (1778–1836)

One of the problems of the pursuit of a literate democracy which the Industrial Revolution in Britain, and later in the United States, brought in its wake was that of the education of a new teeming urban population, given the limited supply of teachers and money. One way of coping with it was by the introduction of a monitorial system whereby older children were instructed to teach younger ones the rudiments of reading, writing and arithmetic. A key figure in introducing this 'emergency' measure, which helped to alleviate the problem though not to solve it, was Joseph Lancaster (1778–1838). He was born in Southwark, London, the son of a shopkeeper who had served in the American war. As a child he developed strong religious beliefs, at the age of fourteen running away from home hoping to sail to Jamaica 'to teach the poor blacks the word of God'. However, lacking the money to pay his passage, when he got to Bristol he enlisted as a naval volunteer, and made one voyage before friends intervened to release him from further service. Back in London he joined the Society of Friends, and while still a teenager he started bringing poor children into his home to teach them to read. From this, in 1801, he established a school for poor children in the Borough Road, and to overcome the problem of staffing and financing the school he developed his monitorial system.

The school was divided into small classes (which were minutely graded into those learning one-, two- or three-syllable words) each under the care of a monitor. A group of these classes was superintended by a head monitor and there were numerous other sub-categories, including monitors for discipline. (Lancas-

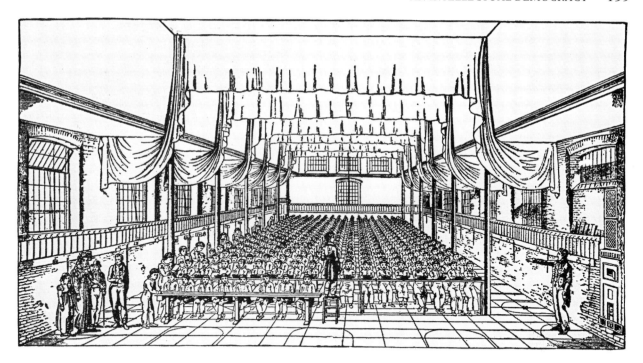

ter's school was known for its strict, almost military approach where, at a word of command from their teacher or monitor, the pupils were marched, brought to silence, made to stand up or made to sit down.) Additionally, every pupil and monitor had to be occupied constructively at all times. Heavy use was made of competition, and Lancaster devised an elaborate system of punishments, some of them very bizarre indeed, like shutting miscreants into wicker-work cages which were then suspended from the classroom ceiling. More peacefully, to encourage hard work, he used badges, offices and orders of merit, which inevitably tended to favour the more ambitious children at the expense of the less determined.

The Lancasterian Model School in Borough Road, Southwark, London. There were 365 pupils in a room 40 × 90 feet in size, who sat at 20 desks, each 25 feet long. The boys of each row were divided into two 'drafts' of eight or ten, each in the charge of a monitor.

While the essential idea of the monitorial system was first expounded by Andrew Bell in a pamphlet published in 1797, Lancaster was the first to implement the system fully. By its nature, the system was limited and mechanical, with much learning by rote. But it did have certain advantages; in particular, it was inexpensive and went some way toward meeting the problem of the mass education of Britain's industrial poor.

Any spare time Lancaster had was spent lecturing and fund-raising for the establishment of new schools. In 1803 he published his first pamphlet entitled *Improvements in Education*, in which he describes his experiences at Borough Road. News of Lancaster's work soon spread, and he won the support and attention of the

Dukes of Bedford and Somerset and others. In 1805 George III met him at Weymouth, promised him his patronage and support and told him that it was his wish 'that every poor child in my dominions should be taught to read the Bible'. Until 1810 Lancaster travelled widely to lecture, fund-raise and found new schools. However, despite this energy and the King's help, his enterprise was never particularly secure and he was always in need of money. In 1808 his financial situation was so bad that two fellow Quakers, Joseph Fox and William Allen, came to his assistance, paid his debts and took over the responsibility of running the model school, which was thereafter called the Royal Lancasterian.

Lancaster's schools were non-denominational and therefore attractive to the Dissenting churches. The Anglican church was drawn to retaliate in a constructive manner by setting up schools using Bell's name and system rather than Lancaster's, all firmly under the aegis of the established church. In 1811 they formed themselves into the National Society for Promoting the Education of the Poor, and in the following year, to Lancaster's chagrin, the Royal Lancasterian Society, which rapidly lost most of its royal and aristocratic support to its Anglican rival, became the British and Foreign School Society.

Lancaster, embittered by losing control of his enterprise and frustrated by the financial restrictions the trustees imposed on him, left the Society to set up a private school near Tooting. When this also failed and made him bankrupt, he became desperate. In 1816 he printed a bitter and petulant attack on his former friends and associates, its title summing up his troubled state of mind – *Oppression and Persecution, being a Narrative of a Variety of Singular Facts that have Occurred in the Rise, Progress, and Promulgation of the Royal Lancasterian System of Education*. His problems were further exacerbated by ill health, poverty, a period in gaol for debt, and the mental instability of his wife. So in 1818 he decided to emigrate to the United States in the hope that his luck would change.

The Lancaster system had already preceded him there. Introduced to New York in 1806, it had spread to Philadelphia and Boston. Thus, when Lancaster arrived in America, he was warmly received, with the influential educationalist and Governor of New York, De Witt Clinton, calling him the creator of a new age in education, 'the benefactor of the human race', whose system 'was a blessing from heaven to redeem the poor of this world from the power and domination of ignorance'.

At the beginning, Lancaster was employed as the Head of a recently established model teacher-training school in

OPPOSITE: *John Adams in London* Oil painting by John Singleton Copley, 1783 *(see page 112)*.

Philadelphia. But after lecturing in New York and Philadelphia he went on to Baltimore where he founded the Lancasterian Institute there. This, too, was beset by problems, both financial and as a result of his own ill-health, and the enterprise was eventually abandoned. When he had made a partial recovery, Lancaster moved on, surprisingly, to Caracas in Venezuela, because its President, Bolívar, when he had visited the Borough Road in 1810, promised him very large amounts of money to set up schools in his own country. But the President failed to honour his pledge, and Lancaster made his way back to the United States. After various wanderings in New England and Canada, he again failed to establish himself and ended his days, poor and despondent, in New York, where on 24 October 1838 he was killed, run over by a carriage in the street.

Though he had spent his last few years in poverty and obscurity, Lancaster's move to America for a time rejuvenated his career and, in the 1820s, helped spread the monitorial system to most of America's principal cities. As well as in New York and Philadelphia, the system was used in Albany and elsewhere in New York State and at other schools as far away as Cincinnati and Detroit. Lancaster's pupils were to continue the campaign which eventually led to the establishment of a nationwide public education system. In the long run its defects – poor and mechanical methods of teaching – led to it being abandoned. But it had served its purpose.

In September 1838, only weeks before his death, Lancaster had written to a friend in England: 'With properly trained monitors I should not scruple to undertake to teach ten thousand pupils all to read fluently in three weeks to three months, idiots and truants only excepted.' His exultant optimism was sadly misplaced, and he was left a broken man ignored by former friends and with his monitorial system a spent force in America and a declining one in his native country. Nevertheless, despite its shortcomings, his system, in the short term, helped to overcome the problem of educating the poor of Britain's and America's towns and cities. Moreover, the cheapness of the system convinced many that the cost of universal popular education would not be prohibitive.

The flow of men and ideas on matters of public mass education was seldom rivalled in other fields. For example, Lancaster's efforts apart, it has been argued that Americans were better equipped and disposed than the British to respond to the problems of popular education presented by the Industrial Revolution. This is suggested by what came to be known in Britain as the American System – a scheme based on popularly elected

OPPOSITE: Classroom in America around the time of Horace Mann's reforms. *The Teacher* by Charles Frederick Bosworth, 1852.

ABOVE: Horace Mann (1796–1859)

BELOW: Mary Peabody, Mrs Horace Mann, Mann's second wife and a sister-in-law of Nathaniel Hawthorne, who took a close and active interest in her husband's educational schemes.

schoolboards administering non-sectarian schools for everyone. It was a system that owed much to the efforts of the Massachusetts-born Horace Mann (1796–1859), who came from Franklin, Massachusetts. After an unhappy childhood characterized by poverty and repression, he won a place at Brown University, thanks to the tuition of a talented itinerant teacher. There he excelled, achieving a top-class degree and, following a spell teaching at his university, he entered law school and in 1823 was admitted to the Bar.

While embarking on what was to become a successful legal career, Mann became involved in public affairs. Winning a place on the Massachusetts State Legislative, he served in the House from 1827 to 1833 and in the Senate from 1833 to 1837. As President of the State Senate (1835–7) he encouraged and eventually signed a revolutionary education bill which became law in April 1837, which set up a state board of education whose secretary would make annual reports to the State Legislature. Mann then promptly abandoned both his lucrative legal practice and political career to become the board's first secretary. While this decision surprised many of his contemporaries, he explained that, since his childhood, he had been 'consumed with a desire to do something that would be of positive benefit to mankind'.

Mann's basic mission was the revival of the once proud Massachusetts tradition of public education which had been languishing since the revolutionary period, after a decline in both public interest and financial support for the states' free schools. As the population and wealth of the inhabitants increased, new private schools had been built at their expense and, starved not only of money but of the best teachers and pupils, the standards and reputation of the free schools had inevitably dropped. Mann believed that the only way to stop the rot was to develop a universal, compulsory, non-sectarian system of elementary education under the strong central control of the state government. And so, as one commentator wrote, 'clothed with almost no authority except to collect and disseminate information, he brought to his new duties such a degree of courage, vision, and wisdom that during the brief period of twelve years in which he held office, the Massachusetts school system was almost completely transformed'.

To achieve this, Mann's first move was to try to stimulate and educate public opinion as to the value and needs of free education. Thus he organized annual educational conventions in every country in the state for teachers, school officials and parents, which were addressed by him and by leading lawyers, clergymen and academics. In 1838 he started and edited a maga-

(handwritten annotations on photograph: Horace Mann Teachers' Institute Lecturers; Herman Krüsi; Arnold Guyot; Dana P. Colburn; Samuel S. Greene, Grammar, Worcester Academy, Brown; Louis Agassiz; Barnas Sears; Wm Russell, founder of Am. Jour. of Ed.; Jno B. Swenson.)

zine, the *Common School Journal* – in order to make the public more aware of the value, problems and needs of the public school. Rather like the educational writings of Mann's English contemporaries – James Kay Shuttleworth, the Secretary of the Committee of the Privy Council on Education, and Matthew Arnold, the poet, critic and England's most famous schools inspector – they show the passion of the crusader and reformer who, for once, was also successful. (Mann was also a vigorous temperance and anti-slavery campaigner.)

When he became Secretary, one sixth of the children in Massachusetts were being educated in private schools with another third deprived of any educational opportunities whatsoever. In many districts the school year only lasted two or three months and most elementary teachers received very low wages. In 1839 Mann forced an Act through the State Legislature which

Teachers' Institutes holding short courses were set up by Mann in 1845. These gathered some famous teachers in America, for example the Swiss naturalist Louis Agassiz, seated second on the left, who came to Boston in 1846.

1859

June 30. Sunday. Yesterday went to Lexington in company with Mr. Pierce to make preliminary arrangements for the opening of his school there, which is expected to take place on Wednesday next, when I must be there again as one of the Visitors.

Tomorrow evening I have engaged to lecture at Andover before an association of Young Men belonging to the Teacher's Seminary. This is indeed going into the Lion's den. May I come out like Daniel.

July 2. Tuesday. Tomorrow, we go to Lexington to launch the first Normal School on this side the Atlantic. I cannot indulge, at this late hour of the night, & in my present state of fatigue, an expression of the train of thoughts, which the contemplation of this event awakens in my mind. Much must come of it, either of good or of ill. I am sanguine in my faith, that it will be the former. But the good will not come alone. That is the reward of effort, of toil, of wisdom. These, as far as possible, let me furnish. Neither time, nor care, nor such thought as I am able originate shall be wanting to make this an era in the welfare & prosperity of our schools: — & if it is so, — it will then be an era in the welfare of mankind.

July 3. Have been at Lexington. The day opened with one of the copious of rains during this rainy year. Only three persons presented themselves for examination for the Normal School. In point of numbers, this is not a promising commencement. How much of it is to be set down to the weather, how much to the fact that the opening of the school has been delayed so long, I cannot tell. What remains but more exertion, more & more! until it must succeed.

established a minimum school year of six months, while, during his reign as Secretary, some two million dollars was spent on building schools and purchasing new equipment, the state budget for public education was more than doubled, and the salaries of masters greatly increased. With many new schools established, the opportunities for free public secondary education increased dramatically, particularly since teacher training was also put on a firm basis. In a report to the Massachusetts State Board of Education in 1848, he spelled out his views with some precision:

> Education, beyond all other devices of human origin, is a great equalizer of the conditions of men – the balance wheel of the social machinery . . . Without undervaluing any other human agency, it may be safely affirmed that the common school, improved and energized as it can easily be, may become the most effective and benignant of all the forces of civilization.

In 1849, following his election to the United States House of Representatives, Mann resigned from the secretaryship. After failing to win the election for the Governorship of Massachusetts in 1852, he served as President of the newly established Antioch College in Ohio. In 1859 he died soon after an illness had forced him to retire from his post.

Mann's contribution to the Rich Tide emerged through the way in which his 'Massachusetts System', as it came to be known, became the main model for reformers seeking to implement a system of public education in Britain. That it received so much attention owed much to the friendship forged between him and the Scottish philosopher and phrenologist, George Combe. Just at the time when Mann was about to take up the secretaryship he read Combe's *Constitution of Man*, which had an immense impact on him. In it, Combe maintained that the mind was made up of more than thirty faculties such as 'combativeness' and 'self-esteem' which could be determined by measuring the part of the head which housed it. As soon as a person's faculties were known it was possible, through education, to bring out the more beneficial aspects and repress the more detrimental ones.

According to Mann's biographer, Jonathan Messerli, Combe's book was 'both revelation and reassurance to Mann, reaffirming his older beliefs and raising his sights to even greater possibilities for human perfectability'. He sent his sister a copy of the *Constitution of Man*, together with a plaster-of-Paris head with all the phrenological propensities carefully mapped out 'I know of no book written for hundreds of years which does so much to "vindicate the ways of God to man",' he assured her. 'Its

OPPOSITE: Horace Mann's Journal for 2nd July 1839, the day of the launch of the first Normal School: 'Much must come of it, either of good or ill. I am sanguine in my faith that it will be the former. That is the reward of effort, of toil, of wisdom.'

THE

SCHOOL LIBRARY,

PUBLISHED UNDER THE SANCTION

of the

Board of Education

OF THE STATE OF

MASSACHUSETTS.

BOSTON.

MARSH, CAPEN, LYON, & WEBB.

Copy Right Secured.

Title page of *The School Library*, one of the books issued by the Massachusetts Board of Education.

philosophy is the only practical basis for education.' So complete a convert did he become that he claimed the doctrines advanced in the *Constitution of Man* would 'work the same change in metaphysical science that Lord Bacon wrought in natural'.

In October 1838 Mann attended a series of lectures given by Combe in Boston, and was so impressed that he wrote to the Scotsman and they later became life-long friends. Combe, impressed in turn by the educational work of his disciple, agreed to publicize the Massachusetts System in Britain, and later wrote in the *Edinburgh Review* and elsewhere to bring Mann's work to the public at large. He also urged his radical friends such as Richard Cobden, who was, after his 1835 trip, already a firm admirer of American education, to agitate for a similar system in Britain. In 1848, the article written by Combe in July 1841 for the *Edinburgh Review* was used as a draft for a scheme of universal education produced for the Manchester Committee, which first grew into the Lancashire Public School Association and then into the National Public School Association.

In May 1843, soon after marrying his second wife, Mann travelled to Europe partly on honeymoon but also in order to observe the different education systems. Visiting England, Ireland, Scotland, Germany, France, Holland and Switzerland, he was, like many British educational reformers, highly impressed with the Prussian system of education with its advanced teaching practices and curricula and emphasis on strong central control. He thought the standard of elementary education provided by the voluntary societies to be extremely poor. However, in Britain he visited many schools and colleges copiously recording all his findings in a journal, and met up with his friend Combe and other reformers who had heard about his work in Massachusetts, and during his time in London was shown around by none other than Charles Dickens, someone who was also much taken by his theories and practice. The Manns were lavishly entertained, but in his background and attitudes he was not always prepared for London Society. At a charity ball Mann and his wife attended, he was disturbed by the low-cut dresses of the women. 'About twenty ladies were beautifully and tastefully dressed', he conceded, but 'the money of the others apparently did not hold out; for their dresses rose just above the waist'. He was equally unimpressed by much of the squalor, the workhouses and prisons of Victorian England, a view shared by his guide, Dickens.

Seven years later, on 17 April 1850, Mann's 'Massachusetts Plan' was introduced in a House of Commons bill, which was effectively blocked by the resistance of the churches to what was seen as a thoroughly secular system of state education. The

The Scottish phrenologist George Combe (1788–1858), who had a profound influence on Mann's ideas. After hearing him speak for the first time in Boston in 1838 Mann told Combe that 'there will be a new earth, at least, if not a new heaven, when your philosophical and moral doctrines prevail.'

conflict, one of the most prolonged reform issues in Victorian history, was not resolved until the famous Education Act of 1870. The pressure group which was instrumental in getting the Act passed – the National Education League – agitated for a system of free non-sectarian schools on the American model. In its campaign the League more often referred to the schools of Boston than to those of any other city, since that city had the essential features of the reform advocated by the League – representative government, free admission and compulsory attendance. In the end, the 1870 Act owed much to the reforming zeal of Mann and the Massachusetts System. An arguable but appropriate inscription is carved on the bust of Mann in the Hall of Fame: 'The Common School is the greatest discovery ever made by man.'

The links, born of contacts built and developed by the British founders of American institutions of higher learning, by the resulting bonds between actual institutions, such as Edinburgh and Princeton, and by those driven by a common resolve to bring about mass literacy, have produced a deep and lasting effect. In this century, there has been a remarkable American influence on all aspects of university education, especially in the technical sphere, with emphasis on practical and vocational subjects as opposed to purely academic disciplines. Equally, the contemporary development of advanced research degrees and co-education owes a very great deal to the American experience.

Finally, in a broader way, Andrew Carnegie's bequests to British libraries and universities, the Rockefeller and Carnegie Fellowships and Trusts, the Rhodes Scholarships (established early in the century by Cecil Rhodes to provide American and Commonwealth students 'who would be potential leaders of great character' with two years of study at Oxford), the Commonwealth Fund Fellowships, and the Fulbright Awards run by the United States–United Kingdom Education Commission to provide British students with the opportunity to study in the United States have all contributed to the continued expansion of educational exchange between the two countries. The history of educational ideas, reforms and practice has been common to both countries. Given the nature and expectations of both societies and the degree of exchange between them, it is inconceivable that this process will not continue long into the future.

CHAPTER SIX

A Genius Shared

The American is only the continuation of the English genius into new conditions, more or less propitious.

RALPH WALDO EMERSON

In 1901, Nobel Prizes for Physics, for Physiology and Medicine and for Chemistry, along with those for Peace and Literature, were first awarded from a trust fund established under the terms of the will of the Swedish scientist, Alfred Nobel, the inventor of dynamite. Since that time three countries have dominated the lists of winners in the scientific categories. Until 1985, in Physics, America had won 47, Great Britain 20 and Germany 15; in Physiology and Medicine America had won 57, Great Britain 19 and Germany 10; while in Chemistry America had won 27, Great Britain 22 and Germany 24. Other countries, most notably France, came well behind. In such an arena where the barriers of language are much less, yet where the degree of co-operation and the cross-frontier flow of knowledge is very high, these figures say much about the pattern of movement of the men and women behind twentieth-century scientific knowledge and invention. Setting aside the German scientific connection with the United States as we must (which came into its own from the middle of the nineteenth century), what of the historical background to this phenomenon, and how and when did the rich scientific tide flow?

During the early colonial period, the settlers were forced to rely on the skills, tools and technologies of the mother country in order to meet the challenge presented by the New World. Gradually, however, they became less dependent, and by the outbreak of the American War of Independence had achieved a high degree of self-sufficiency though they were still far behind Britain in every way. There was a spirit among many of the colonists which made them determined to provide for themselves. They had to come to America to acquire the freedom to live as they wished and to enjoy the fruits of their labours to the full without being subject to the restrictions of class, land or ownership that operated in the Old World. They were confident that they possessed the expertise to create almost everything that they needed, a charac-

teristic which came to be known as 'Yankee ingenuity'. This was, to a large extent, a product of the colonists' response to the problems of utilizing America's vast natural resources. Faced with the task of clearing and then farming great areas of land, but lacking the necessary manpower, they were forced to develop new labour-saving devices, improving the traditional tools and techniques imported from the Old World. For instance, the colonists developed sharper and better-balanced axes to clear the dense forests of the frontier and a new harvesting tool, the 'cradle', replaced the clumsy hand-scythe still favoured throughout Europe. Using this implement American farmers were able to bring about a huge increase in the amount of acreage given over to grain. The colonists also developed new ways of growing crops, processing wool and flax, and tanning leather. Thus American inventiveness, especially in the early colonial period, and in the western frontier country in later periods, was very much an expedient, a question of survival, as well as being the key to prosperity.

At national level, too, an independent economic structure had been virtually achieved by the time of the Revolution. Sawmills and glassworks had long been established, while shipbuilding and ironworking had become so profitable that the British Government, worried about the developing competition from American iron masters, passed an Act in 1750 to restrict the output and construction of ironworks in the colonies. From such small beginnings American farmers, millers, artisans, printers and manufacturers, always particularly alive to the newest scientific advances, began the process that was to revolutionize the lifestyles and manufacturing systems not only of the New World but also of the Old. ·

Yet even at the time of Independence America was still largely under-developed compared with Britain, and the colonists still, therefore, needed much of the technical knowledge of the Old World. Later Americans borrowed what they could and brought whom they could, often deviously, from Britain. In particular, they went to considerable lengths to get their hands on the inventions that had revolutionized the textile industry in Britain – Arkwright's water frame and Cartwright's power loom (thus suggesting comparisons with modern Japan in taking, perfecting and inexpensively manufacturing from the ideas and inventions of others). Alive to the danger to its own position, the British Government forbade the exportation of such inventions and banned the emigration of the men who could make and operate them.

Inevitably many escaped the net: in about 1785, for example,

OPPOSITE: The American James Watson and the Englishman Francis Crick standing by their model of the NDA molecule at the Cavendish Laboratory, Cambridge, England, in 1953. This outstanding example of Anglo-American scientific co-operation won the Nobel Prize for Watson and Crick in 1962.

the Scottish-born inventor and manufacturer, Hugh Orr (1715–98), who had come to America as a young man, induced three highly skilled Scottish mechanics, the brothers Robert and Alexander Barr and Thomas Somers, to come to America to construct textile machinery. (To some, this is a typical example of an early brain drain from Britain to America, a phenomenon usually associated with the present century. If so, it was a brain drain of a somewhat different category from the more recent westwards exodus: a better contemporary parallel would be the export of British talent, architects and engineers to Third World and developing countries.)

Not long after Independence Americans first began making an international impact with their own inventions. In 1793, for

Eli Whitney (1765–1825). Oil painting by Samuel F. B. Morse.

Eli Whitney's cotton gin.

example, Eli Whitney invented the cotton gin, a labour-saving device which revolutionized the cotton industry with enormous implications for the world trade in that commodity. Again, in 1798, Whitney introduced a system of interchangeable parts for muskets at his New Haven firearms factory, a new technique which made mass production possible and which was widely adopted, not just in America but in Britain and elsewhere, becoming known as the 'American system'.

Thus, while for approximately two hundred years British and European technology had been exported – legally and illegally – to America, by the middle of the nineteenth century the tide was beginning to turn. Evidence of American ingenuity was particularly provided at the Great Exhibition of 1851. While there were only a few American exhibits (some 3 per cent of the total) they won a high proportion of the awards, and the British public, proud of their own progress and inventive genius, still could not fail to be impressed by the brilliance of many of the American exhibits. *The Times*, commenting on a new reaping machine, said that it was 'worth the whole cost of the Exposition', while other American inventions such as the sewing machines and Colt's revolver also won high praise.

From the middle of the nineteenth century on, the flow of American technology into Britain gathered momentum, and began to take the lead in a number of important areas – particularly in electricity, communications, transport, steel manufacturing and the new petroleum technology. Thus by the time of the

The United States stand at the Great Exhibition of 1851.

great international expositions at the end of the century America was no longer the young, somewhat uncivilized upstart, but the nation which now set the standards for inventiveness.

The twentieth century has witnessed the emergence of America as a great world power, a rise that owes much to the advances it has made in applied science and technology. The inventive genius of the American people has meant that they have been closely involved in all the major technological developments since 1900 – in manned flight, automated transport, motion pictures, radio, television, radar, the production of synthetic materials, atomic energy, computer technology and space flight. British inventors have often only continued to make important contributions through one of her most successful exports to America – her technological expertise – rather than through the finished product!

*   *   *

The true men of action in our time, those who transform the world, are not the politicians and statesmen, but the scientists.

W. H. AUDEN

With science, the colonies for long depended upon the practices of the mother country, but a man like John Winthrop, Jr (1606–76) was the equal of any of his European contemporaries. The first scientist of note in the American colonies, he was born in Suffolk, England, the son of Sir John Winthrop, later the Governor of Massachusetts. Becoming involved in the Society for the Promotion of Knowledge, the forerunner of the Royal Society, and a group which included Robert Boyle and Sir Christopher Wren, he, with his fellows, sought to promote 'Natural Knowledge and Experimental Philosophy', and advocated the doctrine that scientific enquiry must serve practical ends. The Royal Society was the focus of English scientific endeavour, yet welcomed the development of science in the colonies and often elected distinguished American scientists as fellows.

John Winthrop Jnr (1606–73). Anonymous contemporary oil painting.

In 1631 Winthrop emigrated to the Bay Colony to join his father, but kept in touch with his fellow scientists in England, and when the Royal Society was formally established in 1660 he was elected as an 'original' member. He was a natural choice, a notable collector of mineral and plant specimens to be found in the New World, and author of numerous papers based on his observations. He was particularly known for his ideas on the best methods for growing maize, methods of making sugar from cornstalks and his writings on the flora and fauna of the New World. On one of his trips back to England, Winthrop carried with him a mineral collection which he exhibited, as well as finding time to deliver papers to the Royal Society on such arcane subjects as 'The Manner of Making Tar and Potash'. Above all, Winthrop is seen as the founder of industrial chemistry in the United States, particularly for his attempts at producing salt, saltpetre, indigo and other products, including iron and graphite. (He was also the chief medical authority in New England, and operated what was probably the first large telescope in America.)

During the eighteenth century American interest in science grew. In 1744 the American Philosophical Society, modelled partly on the Royal Society, was established in Philadelphia, while the American Academy of Arts and Sciences, founded in 1780 in Boston, further stimulated scientific activity. One of the founders of the American Philosophical Society was Benjamin Franklin (1706–90), America's Newton and the father of American science and invention. Franklin was born on 17 January

1706 in Boston, the son of Josiah Franklin, a soap- and candle-maker, who had come to New England from Northamptonshire, England, in about 1682. When still only twelve he was taken on as an apprentice to his brother James, who was a printer, and by the age of sixteen he was already writing an anonymous weekly column for a journal which he and his brother produced. But after a row between the brothers – James was jealous of his writing success – Benjamin left Boston before completing his apprenticeship, and eventually found his way to Philadelphia 'with only a Dutch dollar and a copper shilling to his name'.

But he soon found work at his trade, and was so successful that he was urged to set up a printing business of his own by the eccentric governor of Pennsylvania, Sir William Keith. In 1724, on Keith's advice, he went to England to obtain type and establish contacts with London stationers and booksellers. Though he had promised to furnish Franklin with money and letters of introduction, the governor never fulfilled his pledge, but, undismayed, Franklin was soon printing in London. With this experience he returned to New England in 1726, where, within four years, he had established himself as the sole proprietor of a printing business and a journal, the *Pennsylvania Gazette*. Extending his operations, he became public printer for Pennsylvania, New Jersey and Delaware, and had a number of other successful money-making ventures, which allowed him, when still only thirty-four, to amass enough money to decide to retire from active business.

He first found real fame as the author of *Poor Richard's Almanack*, a light but instructive book of maxims and proverbs – such as the familiar 'Early to bed and early to rise, Makes a man healthy, wealthy and wise'; 'It is hard for an empty sack to stand upright'; 'Three may keep a secret, if two of them are dead'; and 'For want of a nail the shoe was lost, for want of the shoe . . .'. The book established Franklin as one of the most popular writers in the Americas, and is considered to have had a seminal influence on the development of homespun American humour. Determined to employ his knowledge of science to improve the social conditions of the time, in 1727 he organized the Junto, a debating club that discussed the practical uses of science and invention. Four years later, he helped establish the Library Company of Philadelphia, the first circulating library in the American colonies, and over the subsequent years he also managed to sponsor a city police force, a volunteer fire company, a city hospital and an Academy for the Education of Youth, which was the precursor of the University of Pennsylvania.

Franklin's interest in science probably dates back to his first visit to England in 1724 where he had met several members of the

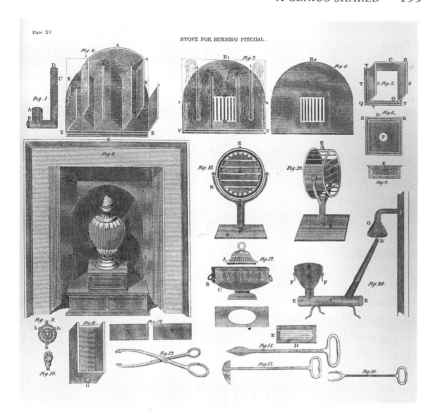

Benjamin Franklin's design for a 'Stove for Burning Pitcoal'.

Royal Society, and once back in America he became interested in every kind of natural phenomenon. By 1737 he was writing articles in the *Pennsylvania Gazette* on earthquakes and meteorology, and the concepts of high and low pressure in the atmosphere also originated with him.

In the early 1740s he turned his attention to the study of heat, noting 'that air, heated, becomes rarified and rises'. Realizing the implications of his discovery for domestic heating, he built a stove with a rear airbox which trapped the rising, heated air, stopped it from disappearing up the chimney and instead let it circulate (through the use of side-shutters) around the room. The stove, invented in 1774, but never patented, became known as the Pennsylvania fireplace or Franklin Stove, and was the forerunner of several modern systems of central heating. But Franklin's reputation as a leading scientist rests most on his pioneering work on electricity, in which he first became interested in the early 1740s. At that time electricity was a fascinating new subject which nobody fully understood. Franklin probably became familiar with the latest discoveries in this field through the *Transactions of the Royal Society*, the main source of new scientific knowledge for colonists interested in science.

After witnessing a demonstration of electricity in Boston, Franklin wrote to his English correspondents to ask for apparatus. Equipped with an 'electric tube' sent to him from England, Franklin started investigating electrical phenomena, and soon became an acknowledged expert on the subject with his observations recorded in a series of letters to his English correspondents and read before the Royal Society or printed in the *Gentleman's Magazine*. In 1751 these writings were collected together and published in London as *Experiments and Observations on Electricity, Made in Philadelphia in America by Mr Benjamin Franklin*. The book was acclaimed on both sides of the Atlantic, went through five editions in English, and was translated into French, German and Italian. Joseph Priestley later wrote that it was easily the most widely read book on the subject, and for many years afterwards textbooks on electricity constantly referred to it.

The initial publication of the book was entirely brought about by Franklin's English admirers, emphasizing the close relations between scientists on both sides of the Atlantic even then. In 1753, Franklin was awarded the prestigious Copley Medal by the Royal Society and in 1756 he was elected a Fellow of the Royal Society. These distinctions were as a result of his greatest scientific achievement, which was to formulate a theory of the nature of electricity, namely that electricity and lightning were identical. Others had suggested this, but Franklin proposed a method of testing the hypothesis by placing an iron rod on a high tower or steeple. He also devised his famous kite experiment (what has been called 'the first great American scientific legend') which was described by Joseph Priestley as follows:

> To demonstrate, in the completest manner possible, the sameness of the electric fluid with the matter of lightning, Dr Franklin, astonishing as it must have appeared, contrived actually to bring it from the heavens by means of an electrical kite, which he raised when a storm of thunder was perceived to be coming on. Preparing, therefore, a large silk handkerchief and two cross-sticks of a proper length on which to extend it, he took the opportunity of the first approaching thunderstorm to take a walk in the fields, in which there was a shed for his purpose . . . the kite raised, a considerable time elapsed before there was any appearance of it being electrified. One very promising cloud had passed over it without any effect; when, at length, just as he was beginning to despair of his contrivance, he observed some loose threads of the hempen string to stand erect, and to avoid one another, just as they had been suspended on a common conductor. Struck with this promising appearance

Franklin's famous experiment, June 1752, demonstrating the identity of lightning and electricity, from which he invented the lightening rod.

he immediately presented his knuckle to the key, and the discovery was complete. He perceived a very evident electric spark. Others succeeded, even before the string was wet, so as to put the matter past all dispute, and when the rain had wet the string he collected fire very copiously. This happened in June 1752.

Before this success, Franklin had made several other important discoveries in the science of electricity, including that of electrostatic induction and the importance of insulation in electrical experiments. Additionally, many of the terms we employ today when discussing electricity – such as positive and negative, plus and minus charge, armature, electrical battery, condenser, conductor, charge and discharge – were coined by him.

In Franklin's mind the division between science and invention did not exist, this attitude typifying the American approach to science. Indeed, to him a scientific discovery had no value whatsoever unless it could be of use to man. Thus, out of his study of heat, he developed the Franklin Stove, and from his research in electricity in 1753 he invented the lightning conductor – a device which was soon adopted in the American colonies and in Britain.

After about 1755 Franklin turned his attentions to politics and diplomacy. It was a decision that, in later life, was to be his one major regret – since he wished that he could devote himself totally 'to those subjects [science] that are more agreeable to me than political operations. Then I will be happier than all the grandees of the earth.'

Franklin's political and diplomatic activities took him back to

London for long spells from 1757 on, particularly to argue for the redress of Pennsylvania's many grievances, particularly the degree to which the Penn family should continue to rule that State. There, based at his house in Craven Street, he was received, first and foremost, as one of the world's greatest scientists, and his fame as a diplomat and politician followed, to a certain extent, as a consequence of his scientific reputation. He argued for the repeal of the Stamp Act before the British Parliament in February 1766, impressing, in his subdued dress and somewhat old-fashioned white wig, even those hostile to him, with his native wit. The exchange went thus:

> 'If the act is not repealed, what do you believe the consequences will be?'
> FRANKLIN: 'The total loss of the respect and affection the people of America bear this country.'

> Then a friend asked: 'What used to be the pride of Americans?'
> FRANKLIN: 'To indulge in the fashions and the manufactures of Great Britain.'
> 'What is now their pride?'
> FRANKLIN: 'To wear old clothes over again until they can make new ones.'

These words had their effect and, with the help of his Parliamentary friend the Marquis of Rockingham, the Stamp Act was repealed, delaying by ten years the revolution that was to come.

Franklin became such a familiar figure in London after the repeal of the Stamp Act, that Staffordshire potters were able to sell iconographic statuettes of him, as 'the personification of the American gentleman', and he made more of a name for himself with his wit in mocking the British for their ignorance of things American. Thus, he wrote to a British newspaper in 1765. 'The grand leap of the whale up the Fall of Niagara is esteemed, by all who have seen it, as one of the finest spectacles in nature.'

He kept up with the latest scientific developments, even in Britain, and became close friends with Joseph Priestley, who, he encouraged to write the 'history of electricity'. But his main concern was the growing deterioration of relations with the mother country, about which he wrote both in prose and in verse:

> Great empires crumble first at their extremities. I would try anything and bear anything that can be borne with safety to our just liberties, rather than engage in a war with such near relations, unless compelled to it by dire necessity in our own defence.

A contemporary English figurine of Franklin.

We have an old Mother that peevish is grown,
She snubs us like Children that scarce walk alone;
She forgets we're grown up and have Sense of our own;
Which nobody can deny, deny,
Which nobody can deny.

There is no doubt that on his return to America in March 1775 he felt that he had failed in a great mission, so much so that at his final meeting with Priestley on his last day in London, according to a friend, 'he was frequently unable to proceed for the tears literally ran down his face'. But his understanding of British political thinking, from his years spent there, and an equal knowledge of how to play the French along to American advantage, made a masterful contribution to the events of 1776 and thereafter. In later life he did not entirely stop his research and continued to make contributions in many fields, including

The American negotiators at the Treaty of Paris, 1783, which formally ended the War of Independence: John Adams, John Jay, Benjamin Franklin, Temple Franklin (Benjamin's grandson and secretary to the delegation) and Henry Laurens. An unfinished group portrait by Benjamin West, 1784–5.

medicine, engineering, agriculture, nutrition – even, at the age of 83, inventing bifocal glasses. Becoming increasingly annoyed that he had to use two pairs of glasses – one for reading and one for long distance – he adopted the simple expedient of inserting a half lens of each kind into the one frame.

He also found time to write, in 1782, a pamphlet for potential British emigrants with 'Information to Those Who Would Remove to America'.

It cannot be worth any Man's while, who has a means of Living at home, to expatriate himself, in hopes of obtaining a profitable civil office in America; and, as to military Offices, they are at an end with the War, the Armies being disbanded. Much less is it adviseable for a Person to go thither, who has no other quality to recommend him but his Birth. In Europe it has indeed its Value; but it is a Commodity that cannot be carried to a worse Market than that of America, where people do not inquire concerning a Stranger, What is he? but, What can he do?

This acerbic style carried through with Franklin till very late in his life. At nearly eighty he was, with his tongue firmly in his cheek, commenting in a letter to his daughter on the very Symbol of America: 'I wish the bald eagle had not been chosen as the representative of our country; he is a bird of bad moral character; like those among men who live by sharping and robbing, he is generally poor, and often very lousy. The turkey is a much more respectable bird, and withal a true original native of America.'

Later Thomas Jefferson said of Franklin: 'I succeeded him: no one could replace him, for no man was so accomplished, charming and amusing.' It was said that he acquired his polish and his dress sense in London but, if that was so, his humour and style were very American. He was, above all, not just an intellectual, but a practical man who always used his skills for the common good, a man who was ahead of his time in almost every aspect of his remarkable career. And, it must be remembered, one of his last political actions (some would argue that it was his greatest invention) was no minor one – he also produced the framework for the Constitution of the United States. When he had signed the Declaration of Independence he turned to John Hancock and said: 'We must indeed all hang together, or, most assuredly, we shall all hang separately.' There was one particular eulogy after his death which summed him up well:

Antiquity would have raised altars to this mighty genius, who, to the advantage of mankind, compassing in his mind the heavens and earth, was able to restrain alike thunderbolts and tyrants.

* * *

For some years after Independence, America remained reliant on Britain in that the new republic lacked well-funded colleges, museums and libraries, scientific journals and even textbooks; and to get their work published American scientists still had to go to Britain. While successive American governments were keen to promote the pursuit of science if it had an end use (Washington and Jefferson were keen practical scientists) it took some time before they could provide the facilities and patronage found in Britain. Things changed the more quickly because American science was also benefiting directly from the political events that were then taking place in Britain just as it was to do, in much more dramatic fashion, in the 1930s, when many European scientists, particularly Jews, fled from Fascist Europe to find their refuge in the United States.

One such political refugee was Joseph Priestley (1733–1804), the Yorkshire-born radical Unitarian minister, scientist and friend of Franklin, who came to the United States in 1794, three years after he had to flee with his family when his Birmingham home was burned and destroyed by a mob who were incensed at his open support for the French Revolution. By this America gained not just one of Britain's leading radicals but also one of Europe's greatest scientists. He is often portrayed in history books as the most eminent of America's early scientists after Franklin, though he in fact never relinquished his British citizenship nor did he achieve any of his great scientific breakthroughs during his time in the United States. Nevertheless, his emergence as a scientist contributed much to the Rich Tide and owes much to the results of his open advocacy of the rights of the American colonists.

Joseph Priestley (1733–1804)
Pastel by Ellen Sharples.

Priestley first became interested in science while teaching at a Dissenting Academy in Nantwich where he began to entertain his pupils and friends with scientific experiments. It is said that he was accidentally attracted to the subject because he lived beside a brewery and he noticed that lighted tapers would become extinguished in the gas coming from the fermenting vats. But it was not until December 1765 that he became involved in serious, systematic research, when on a trip to London he met Franklin, who encouraged him to write his popular history of electricity. While working on the book, Priestley carried out a number of original experiments which led to his nomination to the Royal Society. Proposed by Franklin and others, he became a Fellow in June 1766. The book, *The History and Present State of Electricity* (1767), was a major work on the subject for many years and went through five editions during Priestley's lifetime. Priestley remained close friends with Franklin, and kept in touch until the latter's death in 1790.

After 1770, Priestley turned to chemistry, in particular becoming absorbed with the theory of combustion, during the study of which he discovered oxygen (or, as he called it, 'dephlogisticated air'. Its present name was first used by his great rival Lavoisier). A year later he isolated nitrous oxide and hydrochloric acid and went on to identify other chemicals including ammonia, sulphur dioxide and hydrogen sulphide. Later in America he also identified carbon monoxide and wrote extensively on this among many subjects. One of his friends recalled him thus: 'a more amiable man never lived; he was all gentleness, kindness and humility. He was once dining with me when someone asked him, rather rudely, how many books he had published. He replied, ''Many more, Sir, than I should care to read.'' '

Another great scientist, Cuvier, said of Priestley: 'He was the father of modern chemistry . . . who would never acknowledge his daughter.' By that was meant that, while the modern science of chemistry on both sides of the Atlantic owes much to Priestley's pioneering work, his one weakness was that, contrary to the usual American practice, he could not see the full implications of his discoveries.

In 1794 Priestley was followed to the United States by his friend and fellow radical and chemist, Thomas Cooper (1759–1839), who had no such lack of understanding of the practical end uses of his inventions. Born in London and educated at Oxford, Cooper, who eventually became a barrister, settled near Priestley in Pennsylvania where he farmed, practised law and also worked as a consulting physician. Eventually, as well as holding office as a state judge, he became Professor of Applied Chemistry and Mineralogy at the University of Pennsylvania and later, from 1819 to 1834, held the exciting varied posts of Professor of Chemistry, teacher of political economy and President of South Carolina College which is now the University of South Carolina. His major achievements in the scientific field included developing the use of chlorine in bleaching and he was also the first person to prepare potassium in the United States. But it is perhaps as a promoter of scientific information that he is best remembered as he also helped publish a number of American editions of English textbooks on chemistry and wrote several theoretical works of his own on the subject. Cooper was another who adopted the American approach, emphasizing the importance of chemistry to industry and to everyday life. In his *Introductory Lectures on Chemistry* he declared that the science of chemistry 'enters every workshop, every factory, every home . . . and we must look to chemistry for future improvements in agriculture, in manufactures, and in all that tends to render human existence more desirable'.

As the nineteenth century progressed, America acquired its own scientific societies, journals and textbooks, and, most importantly, the wealth and interest to patronize its own scientists. Interest in science – both at a scholarly and a popular level – grew rapidly. It was greatly stimulated by the establishment of the Smithsonian Institution in 1846 whose function was to explore every field in the realm of art, science and invention. It was founded thanks to the large bequest of the British chemist and mineralogist James Smithson.

American scientists were among the first to be influenced by the new scientific thought – especially the theories of organic evolution that were being developed in Britain and Europe in the second half of the nineteenth century. The writings of Darwin, Huxley and Herbert Spencer were highly influential in America; the American role in this new scientific awakening was exemplified by the fact that it was to the American scientist Asa Gray that Darwin, in September 1857, wrote his famous letter in which he first set out his theories of the evolution of the species by natural selection. Throughout this period American scientists continued to come to Britain and Europe to study and to meet

Thomas Cooper, (1759–1839) in old age in South Carolina. Silhouette done from life by William H. Brown.

James Smithson (1765–1829) when a student at Oxford. Smithson was a scientist and the illegitimate son of the first Duke of Northumberland. He never saw America, yet bequeathed in his will his entire fortune, which amounted to about £100,000, or then roughly $550,000, to that country 'to found at Washington, under the name of the Smithsonian institution, an establishment for the increase and diffusion of knowledge among men.' The bequest, according to the terms of his will, passed to the United States in 1835, but it took a further eleven years before the Smithsonian was incorporated by Congress.

OPPOSITE: 'The Artist in his Museum', a self-portrait by Charles Willson Peale, the prolific painter, writer, inventor and principal founder of the Pennsylvania Academy of Fine Arts and the Philadelphia Museum (depicted here). The Scottish ornithologist Alexander Wilson (see below) used the Museum's excellent collection of American birds painted by Peale in reconstruction of their natural habitats.

with the leading figures in their field. In turn, British scientists such as the physicist John Tyndall, with Huxley and Herbert Spencer, came to America where they were received often with more enthusiasm than in their home country.

As with pure science, so, too, with the natural sciences where even the American Revolution did not lead to any major breaks in personal relations between pioneers in those fields. These relations had always been particularly close in natural history, with British natural scientists co-operating closely with their American counterparts and their botanists, for instance, long continuing to

Catesby's humming-bird on a trumpet-flower. Of the humming-bird Catesby writes: 'There is but one kind of this bird in Carolina. The body is about the size of a Humble Bee.' Of the trumpet-flower: 'These plants climb upon trees . . . the humming bird delights to feed on these flowers, and by thrusting themselves too far into the flower, are sometime caught.' From Catesby's *Natural History of Carolina*, 1731.

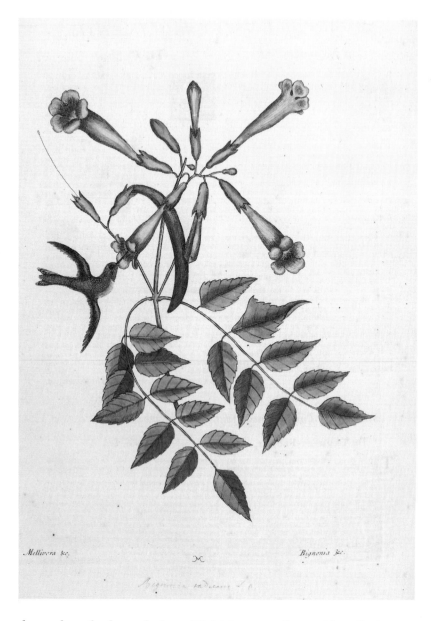

Mellivora &c.   *Bignonia &c.*

depend on the knowledge of British naturalists to identify American plants. For the British, America was a rich and inviting treasury of new flora and fauna and several crossed the Atlantic to explore the American continent while others depended on the despatch to Britain of collections from American amateur naturalists and enthusiasts. The politician, religious leader, physician and scientist, Cotton Mather (1663–1728), for example, sent collections of skeletons, plants, snakes and information on the moose to London while also describing the Indian use of herbal remedies. Again, John Winthrop Jr's great-grandson, another

John Winthrop, sent hundreds of carefully classified specimens of fossils, shells and minerals found in America. So much so that the fortieth volume of the Royal Society's *Transactions* was entirely dedicated to him and his famous ancestor. The preface to the volume includes the following words, which illustrate both the esteem with which the Winthrops were held in the mother country and the importance of America to British scientists.

> You have initiated the example of your worthy ancestor, and have increased the riches of the repository [of the Society] with above 600 curious specimens . . . accompanied with a list containing an accurate account of each particular, thereby showing your great skill in natural philosophy and at the same time intimating to England the vast riches which lie hidden in the lap of her principal daughter.

The botanist and ornithologist Mark Catesby (*c*.1679–1749), who came originally from Essex, went to Virginia in 1712 to join his sister and, while there, explored much of the new colony. He paid visits to Bermuda and Jamaica and these plus a further trip to South Carolina, Georgia, Florida and the Bahamas some three years later, mainly to collect plants, led to the eventual publication of his classic book *Natural History*. This he illustrated himself, and his ornithological work was later used by Linnaeus as the main source of classification of American birds. Catesby returned to England in 1726, where he spent the rest of his life writing and illustrating his *Natural History of Carolina, Florida and the Bahama Islands*, which was published in 1731–42. Catesby was a great exponent of the exchange of trees and shrubs between Britain and America, as was the American John Bartram (1699–1777), who was considered the world's greatest naturalist by his peers, and who travelled the colonies collecting specimens which were sent to the Royal Society, Kew, and to the private gardens of the English aristocracy. Much of his pioneering botanical work was also published in the *Transactions* of the Royal Society.

After Independence the progress of the natural sciences continued to depend heavily on the combined efforts of British and American scientists and, as one historian (John C. Greene) has written, 'the garnering of the first harvest in American natural history' was performed by outsiders, 'who, unhampered by the daily demands of a practical calling, were free to indulge their passion for exploring the varied productions of nature in a new world'. Many of these people were 'scientific adventurers' like the ornithologist, Scotsman Alexander Wilson, who was born in 1766 near Paisley, Renfrewshire, the son of a poor Scottish distiller. At the age of thirteen he was apprenticed to a weaver.

John Bartram, (1699–1777). Oil painting attributed to John Wollaston, 1758.

Drawn from Nature by A. Wilson.   1. Snow Owl.   2. Male Sparrow-Hawk.   Engraved by A. Lawson.

32

LEFT: Alexander Wilson, (1766–1813). Oil painting by Rembrandt Peale.

OPPOSITE: The Snow Owl, from Alexander Wilson's *American Ornithology*. He wrote: 'Nature, ever provident, has so effectually secured this bird from the attacks of cold that not even one point is left exposed. The bill is almost completely hid among a mass of feathers that cover the face; the legs are clothed with such an exuberance of long thick hair-like plumage, as to appear nearly as large as those of a middle-sized dog, nothing being visible but the claws.'

After ten years as a weaver and peddler, both occupations which he hated, Wilson, while striving to become a successful poet, became involved in the liberal movement then sweeping Britain after the French Revolution. He wrote a poem in defence of the radical weavers of Paisley, accusing one of the town's prominent businessmen of cheating his employees. After losing the ensuing court case and spending three months in the town gaol for libel, Wilson decided to emigrate to America, a bitter and resentful man. Unattractive and poor, he wrote that poverty, that 'haggard harlot', was his only mistress.

He arrived in Delaware in July 1794, journeying on to Philadelphia on foot. On his journey he was astounded by the beauty of the countryside, and by the species of birds he had not encountered before. He eventually found work as a schoolmaster, teaching in small village schools in New Jersey and eastern Pennsylvania and alleviating this daily drudgery by studying the plants, animals and birds of the local countryside.

In 1802, after moving to a small settlement on the Schuylkill River near Philadelphia, Wilson got to know the American botanist, William Bartram. Encouraged by Bartram, Wilson decided to

White-headed Eagle.

The white-headed, or bald eagle, from Wilson's *American Ornithology*. Wilson wrote: 'This distinguished bird, as he is the most beautiful of his tribe in this part of the world, and the adopted emblem of his country, is entitled to particular notice.' Niagara Falls are in the background.

OPPOSITE: *Blue Jay*. Plate I of Alexander Wilson's *American Ornithology*, 1808–14. 'This elegant bird, which, as far as I can learn, is peculiar to North America, is distinguished as a kind of beau among the feathered tenants of our woods, by the brilliancy of his dress; and, like most other coxcombs, makes himself still more conspicuous by his loquacity, and the oddness of his tones and gestures.'

write a book on the birds of the United States. In doing so, he was embarking on an enormous task, and he certainly did not appear to have either the money, the scientific knowledge, or the artistic training required. But with Bartram's advice and encouragement he learned the hard way how to classify and name. In April 1806, a Philadelphia publisher offered Wilson the post of assistant editor of a new American edition of *Rees's Encyclopaedia* and with this financial help the first volume of his own project was published in 1808. (The eighth volume would be in the press when he died in 1813.)

After the first volume had been published, as he had to find subscribers for future books, Wilson travelled the north-eastern states and by March 1809 had obtained enough subscriptions – over two hundred (including Tom Paine) at a hundred and twenty dollars a set – to be able to continue with the project. His

1. *Corvus cristatus,* Blue Jay. 2. *Fringilla Tristis,* Yellow-Bird or Goldfinch.

3. *Oriolus Baltimorus,* Baltimore Bird.

Drawn from Nature by A. Wilson.   Engraved by A. Lawson.

1

travels gave him the opportunity to discover several new birds and to establish a network of correspondents who promised to keep him informed if they saw any new varieties of bird in their vicinities. In Georgia he befriended John Abbot, an English-born Savannah planter who, before coming to America, had achieved something of a reputation as a painter of butterflies and rare insects. In America, Abbot, who made an invaluable contribution to Wilson's work, did hundreds of bird paintings for English collectors, sending stuffed birds, mounted insects and numerous drawings and paintings of American insects back to his native country.

Following the publication, in January 1810, of the second volume of *American Ornithology*, Wilson embarked on a new expedition to the south-west to collect more material, where, in Louisville, he met up with the young John James Audubon, who noted with some astonishment that this man, with projecting cheekbones, hooked nose, and hollow but keen and lively eyes, appeared with a tame parakeet on his shoulder. On the trip he amassed a large amount of material on the birds of south-western America, but it was a labour of love, and until the remaining volumes were published neither he nor his publisher made any profits from them.

As an example of his dedication, after returning from a particularly exhausting later trip to New England, Wilson discovered that the colourists had stopped work on the plates for the sixth volume of his works and that if the project was to continue he would have to complete them himself. He thus spent the daytime gathering material for the later volumes on water birds, and the evenings colouring plates. By April 1813, the sixth and seventh volumes had been published and, optimistic that his work was near completion and happy that he had achieved recognition by being elected to the American Philosophical Society, he set off for Cape May to obtain the necessary information for the last two volumes. It was to be his last expedition. On his return to Philadelphia he worked feverishly but, totally exhausted, he died on 23 August 1813, and the last volumes were completed by his friend, the Philadelphia scholar-businessman, George Ord.

Wilson's *American Ornithology* was a truly heroic achievement. It was no systematic natural history, but he made remarkably few mistakes in classification. While he was not the great artist Audubon was, he was, according to some, a better field naturalist and, as his biographer points out, Wilson described in picturesque details 264 of the 363 species of bird found in the United States in his time, adding over forty new species and christening them with

OPPOSITE: *Benjamin Franklin*
Oil painting by Charles Willson Peale, 1789 *(see page 152).*

the popular names by which they are still known. *American Ornithology* only covered the eastern United States, north of Florida, but during the next hundred years other ornithologists were only able to add twenty-three indigenous land birds to his list. (His poetry, long forgotten, was respectable by American standards of the time, and his *Poems, Chiefly in the Scottish Dialect*, published in 1816, were also widely appreciated in his homeland.)

American Ornithology was unsurpassed until John James Audubon's masterpiece, the *Birds of America*, was published between 1827 and 1838. Rather than thinking of the two as rivals, as history has sometimes done, it is important to recognize that Wilson was an important influence on Audubon, that Audubon might not have done what he did without Wilson, for, as Audubon's biographer, John Chancellor, has written, 'when Audubon turned over the pages of Wilson's first two volumes, he must have realized that here was a man who had made a profession out of a hobby. Audubon was still more of a sportsman than a naturalist and his drawings were haphazard and unsystematic. The sight of Wilson's first two volumes pointed out to him the direction which his work could take.' Wilson's birds were neither as splendid nor as lively as Audubon's, but it was the former who led the way in terms of a scientific approach to the subject.

Audubon himself was an American of French descent, born in Haiti, but his success would have been impossible if he had remained in the United States. In 1826, he had to come to Britain

Wilson's phalarope, from John James Audubon's *Birds of America*.

in order to get his *Birds of America* published since there was no American capable of producing life-size colour engravings from his drawings. In 1827, the London engraver, Robert Havell, was consequently engaged to start work on Audubon's illustrations but it was to take eleven years for all the 435 mammoth plates to be printed and published. During this time Audubon travelled frequently between Britain and America obtaining subscriptions and adding extra drawings. Much of his time in Britain was spent in Edinburgh where he worked on his five-volume *Ornithological Biography*. The history of the production of Audubon's master-piece further emphasizes the importance of Britain to America during the early years of the Republic. It was only in Britain that he could find an engraver, a publisher, the financial backing and a market to sustain the production of his work.

*   *   *

Medicine, the only profession that labours incessantly to destroy the reason for its existence.
JAMES BRYCE (1914)

The links between British and American medicine have always been strong and there is not a field, be it surgery, anatomy, gynaecology, immunology or pharmacology, in which doctors, professors, students (and, indeed, patients) did not travel back and forth across the Atlantic with their skills, knowledge and diseases. In the nineteenth century these close links found par-ticular expression in the efforts to open up the medical profession to women. Two names stand out in the pages of the history of medicine: Elizabeth and Emily Blackwell. Elizabeth was born in February 1821 at Counterslip near Bristol, England, the third daughter of a wealthy Nonconformist sugar refiner, who was himself an active supporter of liberal causes such as social reform, women's rights, temperance and, in particular, the abolition of slavery. Samuel Blackwell's progressive views and strong social conscience made a deep impression on Elizabeth and her brothers and sisters. (Her brother, Samuel, married Antoinette Brown, America's first woman minister; another, Henry, married an American feminist, Lucy Stone, while her sisters, Ellen and Marion, also became active feminists.)

In 1832, after their sugar refinery was destroyed by fire, the Blackwells emigrated to America where they set up a sugar refinery in New York City. Elizabeth's father soon became in-volved in the anti-slavery movement, befriending William Lloyd Garrison and several other persecuted abolitionists. From New York the Blackwells moved on first to New Jersey, and then to Cincinnati, but Elizabeth's father's pro-abolition views alienated

Elizabeth Blackwell (1821–1910)

many of his business associates and he suffered badly during the depression of 1837. Shortly after their move to Ohio in May 1838 his health deteriorated and three months later he died leaving Elizabeth and the other older Blackwell children to help her mother support the rest of the family.

Elizabeth began by helping her mother run a small school but then she moved on to a teaching post in Kentucky. Soon becoming bored with this, and, as she said, 'disinterested in the prospects of marriage', she determined to become a doctor, motivated as much by wanting to open up the prospects for women in medicine as by any fundamental urge to cure the sick.

Between 1845 and 1847, while teaching in the Carolinas, she spent her spare time studying medicine, first with the physician – clergyman John Dickson and then with his brother Samuel Dickson, a distinguished Charleston physician. In May 1847 she moved to Philadelphia where two prominent Quaker physicians, Joseph Warrington and William Elder, tried to get her admitted to one of the city's medical schools. But none was yet prepared to accept a woman, however talented she was, nor were the medical schools of New York, Harvard or Yale any more flexible. Unbowed, she moved to study anatomy at a private medical school while continuing to apply to rural medical schools, and to her joy and surprise she was eventually accepted by Geneva College in New York State. Later she learned that the college's administrative board had put her application to the students, who accepted it with much amusement, believing it to be a prank concocted by a rival school.

Elizabeth began her studies there in November 1847. Initially she was not admitted to classroom demonstrations, but gradually she won the respect of the staff and her fellow students and in the summer of 1848 she was accepted by the Philadelphia Hospital. There she gained her first practical experience of working with patients, and in January 1849 she received her medical degree, with her thesis published shortly thereafter.

In April 1849 she decided to go to Europe to advance her medical education, and was welcomed by hospitals both in Birmingham and London. Moving to Paris, she gained further practical experience as a student midwife at La Maternité, a large state institution, but she was forced to give up her training when she contracted an eye disease, which eventually led to the loss of the sight of one eye. This was a great blow: she could now no longer aim to become a surgeon. Back in England in October 1850 she was admitted to the wards of St Bartholomew's Hospital and while in London became friends with, among others, Michael Faraday and Florence Nightingale.

Elizabeth returned to America in 1851 hoping to commence her career as a doctor, but no institution would accept her, she was barred from practice in hospitals, ignored by her fellow doctors and insulted in anonymous letters. After failing even to find anyone who would rent decent consulting rooms to a female physician, she bought a small house in a poor district of New York and, in 1853, opened a small dispensary there. In the first year, with help and encouragement from Florence Nightingale, she treated over two hundred women patients and after four years of fund-raising and help from her Quaker friends she expanded the dispensary into a hospital – the New York Infirmary for Women and Children – modelled after the Children's Hospital in London where Elizabeth's sister, Emily, had worked under Dr William Jenner. There, too, she provided clinical experience for other aspiring women doctors.

Emily Blackwell (1826–1910)

Emily, the fourth Blackwell daughter, had, meanwhile, followed her sister into medicine. After being turned down by many medical schools, including Elizabeth's Geneva College, showing a determination similar to her sister's, she was eventually accepted by Rush Medical College in Chicago where her attendance caused such opposition that she was not admitted for her second year. After gaining practical experience at Elizabeth's New York dispensary, however, she was able to complete her course at the Western Reserve University in Cleveland and in March 1854 she came to Britain where she was accepted as a student by the distinguished Edinburgh physician, Sir James Young Simpson. During her stay she turned down an offer to assist Florence Nightingale in the Crimea, and in 1856, after visits to London, Paris and Germany, she returned to help her sister with her New York project.

Elizabeth's venture increasingly won the moral and financial support of several influential New York figures – leading city physicians even served as consultants. With the hospital now on a firm footing, in August 1858, leaving the management of it to Emily, Elizabeth returned to Britain determined to help advance the professional opportunities for women there. Early in the following year she became the first woman to have her name entered on the Medical Register of the United Kingdom – an important landmark in British medical history. In achieving this she inspired several other women, including her friend Elizabeth Garrett, to follow in her footsteps.

She was back again in the United States in the following year, this time determined to establish a medical school, a nursing school and a chair of hygiene for women. While the Civil War interrupted these plans, it did open up other opportunities to

RIGHT: An anatomy class at the Women's Medical College of Pennsylvania. This photograph of 1900 shows the class, entirely of women, dissecting several cadavers on the tables.

BELOW: A student of anatomy at the Women's Medical College of Pennsylvania, c. 1885.

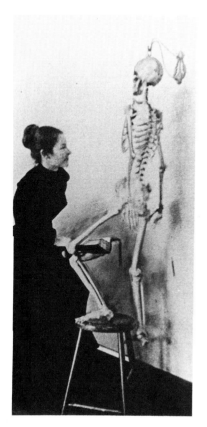

increase the involvement of women in medicine, and she ran intensive short-term training courses for female nurses who wished to work in military hospitals. As well as founding the Women's Central Association for Relief, a forerunner of the American Sanitary Commission, in 1868, Elizabeth founded the Women's Medical College of Belleview, the New York Infirmary. Now, for the first time, women in America could obtain a good medical education and practical training. Her task complete, as was becoming her habit, she left the infirmary and college in the capable hands of Emily, and returned once more to Britain, and for the next thirty years it was Emily who held the post of Dean and Professor in Obstetrics and Diseases for Women (later gynaecology) in New York. In 1874 the infirmary moved to larger premises and soon it was dealing with over seven and a half thousand patients a year.

Elizabeth and Emily had always believed that women should be taught alongside men, so when in 1898 the new Cornell University Medical College in New York accepted women on equal terms Emily arranged for the transfer of all her students there. During its thirty-one-year existence, the Women's Medical College had graduated 364 women physicians. The New York Infirmary for Women and Children stands as a lasting tribute to the contribution of the Blackwell sisters to American medicine.

In London, Elizabeth soon built up a large and successful practice and in 1871 she helped establish the National Health Society dedicated to promoting the importance of hygiene. Four years later she accepted the Chair of Gynaecology at the New Hospital and London School of Medicine for Women, but, unfortunately, she had to retire in 1876 because of ill health and moved to Hastings on the Sussex coast where she spent much of her later years writing on medical and moral issues. In the summer of 1910, at the age of eighty-nine, she died. She was buried at Kilmun in Argyllshire where she had spent many of her summers. Three months later, in September, Emily died in Maine at the age of seventy-three.

Neither Elizabeth nor Emily made a major contribution to medical research, though their emphasis on the importance of preventive medicine, sanitation and public health was progressive and advanced for their time. Elizabeth's particular achievement was, however, to open up the medical profession to women on both sides of the Atlantic. Breaking down the barriers of prejudice and custom she inspired many other women to follow in her footsteps – in America such women as her friend, the brilliant gynaecologist, Dr Elizabeth Cushier, and Mary Jacobi; in Britain, Elizabeth Garrett and Sophia Jex-Blake.

While Emily is not as well known as her sister she, too, made a great contribution to women's medicine in America, and indeed, without her help, Elizabeth would not have been free to make her long and frequent trips to Britain to promote the cause there. Together their careers were the epitome of genuine Anglo-American achievement.

ABOVE: Mary Putnam Jacobi, (1842–1906), the pioneering woman physician, who was born in London of American parents and practised at Elizabeth Blackwell's New York infirmary for women and children.

LEFT: 'The Feminine "Faculty"', a *Punch* cartoon on lady doctors: *'New Housemaid (to her Master) Oh Sir! I'm glad you've come in. There's a party a waiting in the Surgery to see you. I think (shuddering) it's a Man in Woman's Clothes, Sir!'*

Many famous male doctors also made their contribution in every field of medicine. Remember only the English physician William Worrall Mayo (1819–1911) who came from Manchester in the year 1845 to study at the University of Missouri. His contribution, which has become a household name, was to establish, with the indispensable help of his sons William and Charles, the Mayo Clinic near Rochester in Minnesota, a group surgical practice which has become world-famous. He was additionally in his own lifetime a pioneer in abdominal surgery.

In the wider fields of discovery and invention there is no aspect or area of activity that has not been affected by the Rich Tide. Equally, innovation has gone hand in hand with the desire to market patentable inventions on both sides of the Atlantic, since inventors were often also businessmen who wished to produce, or indeed mass-produce, what they discovered or designed. In the eighteenth and nineteenth centuries, the particular need was to build an efficient communications infrastructure – good roads, railways, canal systems, hygienic water and efficient power supplies – and this was a further impetus to new ideas and inventions crossing the ocean with or without their inventors. Inventions, as with talent, were bought, irrespective of where they originated, particularly so in this field that was so critical to a continent as large as the United States.

Inevitably, in the development of various forms of mechanical transportation, the United States increasingly played a pre-eminent role. The dashing and ambitious Robert Fulton (1765–1815), developer of the steam-propelled boat and inventor of the submarine was born in Pennsylvania, and first came to London in 1786 actually to study painting under his fellow-countryman, Benjamin West (see p. 253 below). While supporting himself by this means he also studied all the latest engineering developments and became friends with both Lord Stanhope and the Duke of Bridgewater, both sponsors of any new 'useful arts'. He became particularly involved with the Duke, both in the West Country and later in Birmingham, in that great canal builder's projects, and, developing an interest in canal engineering, he invented an apparatus that was later to be built in both Britain and the United States for raising and lowering canal boats, as well as a dredging machine or power shovel for cutting canal channels, a device long used for this purpose on both sides of the Atlantic.

Fulton also wrote extensively on the subject of canal navigation, illustrating his works himself, and setting out the costs and what he saw as the huge political and social benefits of a country building a major network of inland waterways. He put forward many precise proposals to the British Government including a

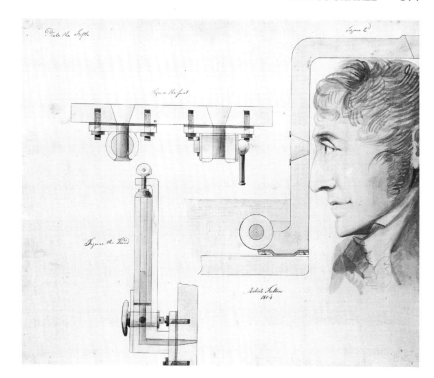

Robert Fulton, in a plate from a prospectus on his submarine, the *Nautilus*, which shows him looking through a periscope. (1804)

major one in 1796 to the Board of Agriculture, which advocated the construction of cast-iron aqueducts. One of these was eventually erected, eighteen spans of fifty-two feet, with the central span a hundred and twenty-six feet high, over the River Dee near Chester. Not content with this, in 1794 he began corresponding with James Watt among others about buying a steam engine to be used to propel a boat. His other interests continued to be very varied as his medal-winning patents for sawing marble, spinning flax and making rope demonstrated.

While he is often remembered for his sojourn in France where he constructed his submarine *Nautilus*, he failed to get any financial backing there, and returned to Britain when the British Government expressed interest in his invention. He attempted to demonstrate how useful it could be in a trial expedition against the French fleet in Boulogne harbour in 1804, but this ended in failure when the torpedoes failed to operate. Despite a successful demonstration a year later when he blew up a ship near Deal, the British authorities were too cautious to adopt his invention.

Disappointed, he returned to the States in 1806, but he brought with him a steam engine he had bought from James Watt and his partners. It was thus a British Boulton & Watt engine that powered *Clermont*, known to his critics as 'Fulton's Folly', the double-sided paddle-wheel steamer that, in August 1807, made

Fulton's steamboat *Clermont* on the Hudson. Watercolour, 1861.

its memorable voyage up the Hudson. On that occasion Fulton wrote of his snub-nosed vessel: 'My steamboat voyage to Albany and back has turned out rather more favourable than I had calculated. The distance from New York to Albany is 150 miles; I ran it up in thirty-two hours, and down in thirty hours; the latter is just five miles an hour. I had a light breeze against me the whole way going and coming, so that no use was made of my sails, and the voyage has been performed wholly by the power of the steam engine. I overtook many sloops and schooners beating to windward, and passed them as if they had been at anchor.'

It was thus a combination of British and American engineering skills, directed by the inspired and indefatigable energy of Fulton, an American who had gained much of his training and experience in Britain, that ushered in the new era of power navigation.

The history of the humble sewing machine further illustrates the Rich Tide in action. The first one patented was devised by the Englishman Thomas Saint in 1790, though it was never put to practical use, and it was in 1829 that a Frenchman, Barthélemy

Thimmonier, devised one of the first workable machines. But, while Isaac Merrit Singer is the better-known name, it was the Massachusetts-born Elias Howe who pioneered their development in the United States. Howe was born in Worcester County, Massachusetts, the son of a none too wealthy owner of a small grist-mill and sawmill. Ill health prevented him from undertaking heavy farm work but from an early age he was fascinated by anything mechanical, and in 1835 he ran away to the famous Lowell factories in Massachusetts where he became an apprentice at a cotton machinery plant.

From there he moved on to Boston to apprentice himself to the eccentric but ingenious Ari Davis, a maker of watches and scientific apparatus. At this workshop where Howe became a skilled machinist and developed an appetite for invention, it is said that one day he overheard Davis urge a would-be inventor to

Elias Howe (1819–69).

Isaac Singer and his first sewing machine.

OPPOSITE: Elias Howe with his sewing machine – a poster issued by his son in the late 1860s.

make a sewing machine. Inspired, Howe set about inventing such a machine that would sew with the same movements as the human hand. He started out by attempting to copy the movements of his wife's hands as she sewed, but as this inevitably did not provide an answer he devised a machine with an eye-pointed needle united with a shuttle, an idea he had been familiar with while working at Lowell.

Giving up his job with Davis in order to concentrate on his invention, Howe managed to get a friend, George Fisher, to become a partner in his scheme. Fisher advanced him $500 towards buying materials and tools, and by 1845 Howe had devised a successful machine which sewed accurately and well. To promote his invention, in July 1845, he challenged the Quincy Hall Clothing Manufacturing Company to a sewing race, and duly defeated five of the firm's fastest seamstresses, reaching speeds of 250 stitches a minute. While his machine impressed the onlooking manufacturers, none of them placed an order. At $300 it was too expensive. Disappointed, Howe decided to try his luck in England. In October 1846 he sent his brother over to London; he managed to sell the machine and the British patent rights for £250 (plus £3 for every machine sold) to William Thomas, a manufacturer of corsets, shoes and umbrellas. Thomas saw the possibilities of adopting it for leather and induced Howe to come to England for this purpose. After working for eight months at $15 a week Howe fell out with his employer and was sacked while Thomas went on to make a million pounds from the machine. Destitute, Howe pawned his model and patent papers so that his wife and children could be sent back to America, and a few months later he himself returned, paying his way by cooking for the crew.

Back in the United States, Howe learned that all his family's belongings had been lost in a shipwreck and his wife lay dying. But at least in business all was not lost. While Howe had been in Britain, certain American manufacturers, including Singer, finding out about the success of his machine, were already making and selling similar models. On his return, Howe, who had received an American patent in 1846, sued them for infringement of rights, an action which resulted in one of the most protracted fights in the history of American patent law, lasting five years and dubbed the Sewing Machine War by the press. In the end he was victorious, his patent was upheld, and he himself was given a royalty for every machine that infringed it. By the 1860s this was bringing in $4,000 a week in royalties and Howe was able to die a rich man, in Brooklyn, New York in 1867. (From his royalties he financed an infantry regiment in the Civil War, in which he himself served as a private.)

Transatlantic genius, both domestic and industrial, has cross-pollinated in every field of activity, with the output largely international, from the car (Ford), the aeroplane (the Wright Brothers) on to the pneumatic tyre (Dunlop) and the work of Elisha Graves Otis of lift/elevator fame. There have been electric light bulbs (Edison and Swan) to brighten the world just as the achievements of Samuel Colt and Richard Gordon Gatling cast their shadows.

There are differences of course. Britain has long been accused of failing to take the best commercial and entrepreneurial advantage from the inventions that first saw the light of day there. Too often they have, as with John Logie Baird's television, had to travel the Atlantic to be made commercially viable. Perhaps this is no twentieth-century phenomenon, for in 1862 Anthony Trollope was writing of the American: 'In his mind he is quicker, more universally intelligent, more ambitious of general knowledge, less indulgent of stupidity and ignorance in others, harder, sharper, brighter with the surface brightness of steel, than is an Englishman; but he is more brittle, less enduring, less malleable, and I think less capable of impressions. The mind of the Englishman has more imagination, but that of the American more incision. The American is an observer, but he observes things material rather than things social or picturesque . . . In his aspirations the American is more constant than an Englishman – or I should rather say he is more constant in aspiring. Every citizen of the United States intends to do something.'

The Anglo-American genius, born out of British genius and implanted into 'new conditions', is not only shared; at its best, it is also complementary.

CHAPTER SEVEN

The Gospel of Wealth

The Almighty Dollar, that great object of universal devotion.
WASHINGTON IRVING

Enterprise means, at root, making money out of new ideas, inventions and processes. The history of the Anglo-American relationship reveals a close and productive pattern of influence in this field. The commercial and financial giants, the people who operated and benefited from transatlantic trade and investment, the many British-born entrepreneurs who had to emigrate in order to find success, are as much part of the Rich Tide as any other. The British Industrial Revolution led the way for an American industrial take-off, with the pre-eminent example of the development of the American cotton industry, bound to an essential British market, having a profound effect on bilateral relations over very many years. At a later stage it was not trade with America so much as American business methods that had a devastating impact in Britain. Advertising, retailing, pressure salesmanship, accounting methods by firms such as Westinghouse and National Cash had as revolutionary an effect on British business as did American scientific management, commercial and industrial mass production, standardization procedures, time and motion studies and the use of ever more efficient methods of business administration and communications.

There is circularity about the process. At the present day, the importance of American multinationals like IBM to the British economy is second to none, particularly in the new industries such as American mining technology in the development of North Sea oil. In historical terms, this is a relationship that can, with relevance, be compared to the enormous financial investment and the technological contribution made by Britain to the development of mining and processing in eighteenth- and nineteenth-century America. British money largely financed the new America, its great drive to industrialize and its push westwards. It helped create the conditions that produced American money which in turn started arriving in Britain after the First World War, borne by a vast and increasing flood of businessmen and financiers. Here we almost stop looking at the mere origins and birthplaces of the people who were part of the Rich Tide of enterprise, for increasingly they were becoming totally transatlantic in their ideas, their areas of activity and their effects.

*   *   *

However unimportant America may be considered at present, and however Britain may affect to despise her trade, there will assuredly come a day when this country will have some weight in the scale of empires.

GEORGE WASHINGTON

The achievements of Samuel Slater (1768–1835) provide a useful focus on the relationship at the time of the Industrial Revolution. Slater, sometimes called the 'Father of American Manufacturers', was born in Belper, Derbyshire, the son of an independent farmer. As a child he showed an aptitude for mathematics, so in 1783, on the completion of his schooling, his father apprenticed him to a friend and neighbour, Jedediah Strutt, who was a partner of Richard Arkwright, the famous designer of cotton manufacturing machinery. Strutt took the young Samuel under his wing, and from the start Slater displayed a remarkable talent for things mechanical. Strutt himself was particularly pessimistic about the whole future of cotton manufacturing in England, despite the fact that the development of the industry was the key force behind the Industrial Revolution. Influenced by these views and attracted by the advertisements and reports of bounties and rewards offered by American state governments for experienced textile mechanics and machinery, Slater decided to emigrate.

As it was illegal to export textile machinery from Britain, Slater first familiarized himself with the inventions that were revolutionizing the English textile industry – including Arkwright's water frame, Crompton's spinning mule and Hargreaves's spinning jenny. Slater completed his apprenticeship and gained further experience by the supervision of Strutt's mill, which provided him with additional knowledge of production processes and the design and layout of mills. In the autumn of 1789, without even telling his family, he finally left for America, disguised as a farm labourer, since the emigration of skilled textile operatives was also prohibited, taking with him in his head the blueprints for cotton machinery. Arriving in November, he first found work at the New York Manufacturing Company, and then

Van Slyck & Co. Boston.

Samuel Slater

Samuel Slater (1768–1835)

in January 1790 he met up with Moses Brown of Providence, Rhode Island, the owner of an established cotton mill, who engaged him to reproduce Arkwright's cotton machinery. Slater told Brown that he 'could give the greatest satisfaction in making machinery that would manufacture a good yarn, either for stockings or twist, as any that is made in England'. Despite the lack of skilled mechanics and tools, within a year Slater built his first mill at Pawtucket, Rhode Island, with a spinning frame of seventy-two spindles, which, shortly afterwards, he modified to be driven by water power.

The old Slater Mill at Pawtucket

A treadmill of the type
which powered Samuel Slater's first
cotton mill at Pawtucket. Engraving
c. 1835.

In October 1791, Slater married Hannah Wilkinson, an enterprising lady who had herself developed the idea of making sewing thread from fine cotton yarn instead of from linen. She had so impressed her brothers with the quality of the thread that she produced that together they set up a factory to make it. By 1789 Slater had established a partnership with his brothers-in-law, known as Samuel Slater and Company, which, building all its own machinery, opened several new cotton and spinning mills in Rhode Island, New Hampshire and Massachusetts.

According to Alexander Hamilton, America's first Secretary of the Treasury, in his famous 1791 document 'Report on Manufacturers', Slater was recognized as the 'first to introduce into the United States the celebrated cotton mill'. But Slater, by also bringing the factory system to the United States, must be seen as one of the founding fathers of America's industrial revolution. It was not that he himself was an inventor so much as the fact that he used the ideas of others in a most successful entrepreneurial way. As the *Encyclopaedia of American Biography* says, it is a prime example of the 'export of highly trained capital from a nation in which supplies of this capital were plentiful to one in which supplies were scarce and dear'. His is but one prime example among many; the influx of his fellows, skilled citizens from Britain, millworkers, miners, ironworkers, potters, was in very many ways the key to the early stages of the American industrial revolution.

On the British side of the Atlantic the cotton trade went through Liverpool, whose rich merchants were closely involved with their fellows in New York, Philadelphia and elsewhere. Trade in other goods followed naturally – pottery, British manufactured hardware and other commodities, with the axis that particularly linked Liverpool to New York growing in strength, especially after the 1812 War. It was an axis that was a central factor in bringing about the pre-eminence of New York on the eastern seaboard.

Through such trading links, one British merchant, Jeremiah Thompson (1784–1835), was to become one of America's largest shipowners and merchants. He was born in Rawdon in the West Riding of Yorkshire, the son of William Thompson, a Quaker woollen manufacturer. In 1798, soon after the opening of the Leeds and Liverpool Canal across the Pennines, his uncle, Francis Thompson, went to New York as an agent for the family business, where, in 1801, Jeremiah joined him. They soon became involved in an informal business partnership with Isaac Wright, a New York merchant and fellow Quaker (whose daughter married Francis) and also with Benjamin Marshall (1782–1858), a

New York Harbour in 1827. Oil painting by Thomas Birch.

Huddersfield-born cotton merchant who came to America in 1803. In 1807, the Thompsons, with Wright, acquired *Pacific*, a fast transatlantic sailing ship, used for importing dry goods, including woollen manufacturers, from the family mill in Yorkshire. After 1815 the Thompsons increasingly used their English connections to establish themselves as one of the leading houses in the Atlantic trade with Jeremiah its main driving force.

In January 1818 the partners set up the Black Ball Line, with three additional packet ships which were to make regular monthly sailings from New York and Liverpool. They used only the most modern sailing vessels which were faster, more reliable, gave more room for cargo, and were more economical to build and run than previous transatlantic vessels. Jeremiah also introduced regular sailings, with fixed, announced times of departure, and these measures proved so successful, further strengthening the pre-eminence of Liverpool and New York, that other similar lines were established, sailing from Boston and Philadelphia to other British and European ports. Thus, speed and the regular delivery of cargo and mail by sail and later by steam brought about

a fundamental change in transatlantic trade. But its full success was not assured until 1822, when, in the face of new competition, the fleet was doubled to provide regular fortnightly sailings.

Over the next few years Jeremiah rapidly expanded his operations, helping establish other packet lines from Liverpool to Philadelphia and from Belfast and Greenock to New York, and by 1827 he had become one of the largest shipowners in the United States. To exploit his growing success he had made a second important innovation: most of the cargo flowed westwards and, wanting to find suitable cargo to fill his eastbound ships, he started to deal in raw cotton. His colleague, Benjamin Marshall, who had sound experience of the Lancashire cotton industry, spent the winter months in Georgia purchasing cotton which was shipped to New York and transferred into Thompson vessels bound for Liverpool. There, the cotton was sold to pay for British dry goods, some of which were exported to the South. It was a

New York Harbour c. 1860, by which time its traffic had increased dramatically.

Advertisement for the Black Ball Line, published in the *Liverpool Mercury*, December 1817.

For NEW YORK,

To sail on the 1st of January,

The COURIER,

WILLIAM BOWNE, Master;

Burthen 380 tons.

To sail on the 1st of February,

The PACIFIC,

JOHN WILLIAMS, Master;

Burthen 370 tons.

In order to furnish more certain Conveyance for Goods and Passengers, between Liverpool and New York, the owners of the American Ships, COURIER, PACIFIC, JAMES MUNROE, and AMITY, have undertaken to establish between the two Ports, a regular succession of Vessels, which will *positively sail, full or not full*, from Liverpool on the 1st, and from New York on the 5th of every month, throughout the year.

These Ships were all built in New York, of the best materials, and are coppered and copper-fastened; they are all remarkably fast sailers; their accommodations for passengers are uncommonly extensive and commodious, and their commanders are men of great experience and activity. These recommendations, and the dependance which may be placed upon the periods of their departure, afford to these conveyances advantages of so much importance to the Manufacturing Houses, and to the Shippers of Goods generally as it is hoped will secure to them general support.

The Courier now lies at the east side of the King's Dock.—For further particulars, apply to Capt. Bowne, on board, or to

CROPPER, BENSON, & CO. and RATHBONE, HODGSON, & CO.

(*One property.*)

great success and by 1827. Thompson was recognized as the largest cotton dealer in the world, and the main entrepreneur behind the development of this so-called 'Cotton Triangle'.

His position was impressive – and short-lived. Wild price fluctuations made the cotton market far from steady, and in the

UNION LINE.
FOR PHILADELPHIA,
AND
BALTIMORE,
At 11 o'clock, A. M.
25 Miles Land Carriage.

Steam-Boat BELLONA—*Capt. Vanderbilt,*
Steam-Boat PHILADELPHIA—*Capt. Jenkins.*
The only Steam-Boat Line,
Via New-Brunswick, Princeton & Trenton,
FARE THROUGH $3.

The Passengers will leave the city, foot of Courtlandt street, every day, (Sundays excepted) at 11 O'CLOCK, A. M. in the POWLES HOOK Steam boats, for Jersey City, where they will meet the Bellona, and proceed direct to New-Brunswick, where they will take Post Coaches to Trenton, and lodge, and arrive at Philadelphia in the Steam-boat, by 10 o'clock, in time to take the Baltimore Union Line Steam-Boat which leaves Philadelphia at 12 o'clock (noon) daily.

For Seats, apply at the YORK-HOUSE, No. 5, COURT-LANDT-STREET, SECOND OFFICE FROM THE CORNER OF BROADWAY, and at the Steam Boat Hotel, (up stairs) foot of Marketfield street.

WM. B. JAQUES, Agent,
For LETSON, BAYLES & SHUFF,
PROPRIETORS,

NEW-YORK, JULY 25, 1821.
⁎ All Baggage at its owner's risk.

Thompson's 'Union Line for Philadelphia and Baltimore.' Advertisement published in New York, July 1825.

same year the Liverpool House, to which Jeremiah had consigned his cotton, refused to accept his bills with the result that the whole Thompson empire rapidly collapsed, Jeremiah became insolvent and all his shipping interests were sold. Fortunately, however, the lack of bankruptcy law in New York State at that time allowed him to free himself from his debts and re-establish himself in business. Unable to match his previous achievements, he joined Francis Thompson in establishing an immigrant business, which his cousin Samuel later expanded into a regular line of immigrant packets – the Union Line. Previously British and Irish emigrants had usually travelled in cargo ships – now their transportation had become big business, though travelling conditions for long remained poor.

Jeremiah died, unmarried, in New York City on 10 November 1835. But, though his business crumbled, his creative career epitomized the development of Anglo-American trade: more than anyone else he made the cotton trade work, and in the process of bridging the Atlantic he helped make New York what it is today, the gateway to America.

These are no small achievements, but his multi-faceted place in the Rich Tide is also reserved because he was one of the first great entrepreneurs in the greatest of all markets. He always saw his opportunities not just in terms of the land of his birth or of his adoption, but in a more far-sighted global context. In this he was the progenitor of the great multi-nationals that were to come, adroitly meshing his various interests together both in Britain and the United States, using the needs and skills and output of both countries to their greatest possible mutual advantage.

Three years before his death, Frances Trollope had written:

> I heard an Englishman, who had been long resident in America, declare that in following, in meeting, or in over-taking, in the street, on the road, or in the field, at the theater, the coffeehouse, or at home, he had never over-heard Americans conversing without the word DOLLAR being pronounced between them. Such unity of purpose, such sympathy of feeling, can, I believe, be found nowhere else, except, perhaps, in an ants' nest.

Jeremiah Thompson was not one who would have understood that this was meant as criticism. For it was his creed.

*   *   *

It is the best country for a Rothschild I ever knew.
MATTHEW ARNOLD

There is a strange contrast, in historical terms, between America's heavy financial dependence on the United Kingdom, particularly around the middle of the last century, and the way the balance has swung in the twentieth century. Some historians have indeed argued that the contribution made by British capital to the development of the United States was greater in real terms than Britain's debt to America now. Certainly for many years Americans were heavily dependent upon British money, unable as they were to compete with the very low interest rates and attractive credit terms offered by British houses. In the development and opening up of the frontier, for example, British capital and investment was of unique importance, being used by state governments to finance capital projects and to build that infrastructure so essential to commercial development – roads, canals, railroads, harbours and bridges. It was especially important in the development of the American railroad; indeed, without British funds the great American railway boom would not have been possible.

Although North Atlantic trade and capital investment in America depended on the powerful London money market, trade and commerce were not exclusively run by British houses. Many were already truly Anglo-American. The 'Three W's', the houses of Wildes, Wilson and Wiggin, for example, were American companies founded in London, while the powerful Brown Brothers was originally founded by Alexander Brown (1764–1834), a linen merchant from Country Antrim, who emigrated to Baltimore at the end of the eighteenth century. The firm expanded from linen to general merchandise before moving into merchant banking. One of Alexander's four sons, William, operated the Liverpool branch of the company, while the others, James, John and George, operated the American branches. In 1837, Brown Brothers were able to use their London connections to survive the panic which led to the downfall of the 'Three W's'. That same year, too, as we will see, the American, George Peabody, settled in London to establish himself as one of the most important merchant bankers in the City.

Alexander Baring, 1st Lord Ashburton (1774–1848)

That said, from the second quarter of the nineteenth century, the financing of American trade and the marketing of American securities were long dominated by the British House of Baring. In particular, for the supply of both long- and short-term credit which was one of the main reasons for the very rapid economic development of the United States, Barings were the leading link between British capital and American entrepreneurs. The company first became involved in American investment in the 1790s when the young Alexander Baring, later Baron Ashburton (1774–1848), like several other wealthy English families, invested heavily in American land. Although Barings established some important and close connections with America then – the company was for long the sole fiscal agent in Britain of the United States Government – until 1828 they were mainly preoccupied with European trade and finance. That same year, which was marked by the retirement of Alexander Baring and the arrival at their offices in Bishopsgate Street of an American banker, Joshua Bates (1788–1864), their American activities began to expand.

Joshua Bates, (1788–1864), the stern Bostonian who joined Barings in 1828. He and Thomas Baring formed the greatest partnership in the history of the bank. From 1803 until 1871 Barings were the London financial agents for the United States government. One of their duties was to make various diplomatic payments for the Government, included among which was a loan to James Monroe supported by the promissory note on page 195. Monroe was at the time the America's Ambassador in London and subsequently became her fifth President.

Bates came from near Boston, Massachusetts, the only son of a retired Army colonel. At the age of 15 he had joined the Boston counting house of William R. Gray, and shortly afterwards was employed as a clerk by Gray's father, William Gray, one of New England's leading shipping merchants. In his early twenties Bates established a partnership with a Captain Beckford of Charleston, but their firm, Beckford & Bates, was, like hundreds of other businesses, a victim of the financial collapse during the War of 1812. Re-employed by William Gray, who had by then become one of the largest shipowners in America, he was sent in 1816 or 1817 to Europe as Gray's general agent. Bates's subsequent astute handling of Gray's business interests was soon recognized in the City, and his reputation and career blossomed. At the same time he acquired a useful knowledge of European markets.

In Paris he met by chance Peter Caesar Labouchère, a relation of the Barings by marriage, and a senior partner in the important house of Hope & Company of Amsterdam. Impressed by the young American, Labouchère recommended him to the Barings, who were seeking a partner for John, the third son of Sir Thomas Baring. When in early 1826 Samuel Williams, a wealthy American banker and merchant dealing with American business accounts in London, went bankrupt, Bates saw his opportunity and borrowed £20,000 from Labouchère and formed a partnership with John Baring. Specializing in American securities they soon captured a sizeable amount of the American financial market in London, and by 1828 their partnership had become so successful that it was absorbed by Baring Brothers & Company.

When Bates joined Barings the company was in a state of decline. In its American sphere it faced tough competition from a growing number of other merchant banks who could offer – as Baring & Bates had done – specialized services to American businesses and banks. Alexander Baring was on the point of retiring and there were few men of genuine ability within the firm. As Bates himself later said, the House of Baring when he joined had the 'highest fame for respectability and wealth' yet 'for business, however, it did not stand very high' (a familiar diagnosis in the City of London to this day!). Bates was taken on as part of a major reorganization designed to reinject vigour into the company and to win a larger proportion of the American market. He was to remain with the company for the rest of his life, quickly becoming a senior partner and over the years acquiring a considerable fortune. (In 1858 he said that he had started from his native town with only five dollars and now had four million.) As Baring's main strength, he helped it to become the leading Anglo-American merchant bank, seeing it through the panic

of 1837, and defending it against the formidable challenge of N. M. Rothschild & Son who had moved into the American securities market in the mid-1830s.

Of Bates's relationship with Thomas Baring one of the company's American agents wrote, 'They were warmly attached to each other; each had the greatest respect for the other's qualities, which were strikingly different, Mr Baring being a man of brilliant and active mind and keen perceptions; while Mr Bates was the

Barings were a major supplier of capital for the construction of the United States' railway network through the issue of securities of railway companies or of the stock of individual states who then lent on to these railway companies. In some instances, as in the case of the South and North Alabama Railroad Company, Barings acted as paying agents.

thoroughly trained merchant, with a steadiness of mind that made him the balance wheel of the concern.' To Bates, banking and commerce were everything. Although he came across as rather a dry individual, he achieved considerable social success in England, becoming close friends with Louis-Napoleon (Napoleon III) and even going bail for him when the latter was arrested in connection with a projected duel. Bates bought a fine London house in Portland Place and a country estate. While he might not have been the most stimulating character to meet, he was probably the most influential foreigner in the British Isles. Eventually he became a British citizen, preferring the social and political institutions of his adopted country, but that did not stop him working to improve relations between America and Britain.

Bates Hall in Boston Public Library.

Bates is perhaps best remembered in his native country for his important role in the establishment of the Boston Public Library, America's first public library. In 1852, the City of Boston was negotiating a loan with Baring Brothers, and in their correspondence the Americans mentioned a projected plan for such a library. Bates immediately offered $50,000 for the purchase of books if the city would provide and maintain the building, and he followed this up a few years later with a further donation of 27,000 books. After his death on 24 September 1864, the trustees acknowledged him as the Founder of the Boston Public Library, calling the large library hall the Bates Hall. In a letter to the Mayor of Boston, Bates indicated why he had given his help. As a child, 'having no money to spend and no place to go, and not being able to pay for a fire or light in my own room, I could not pay for books, and the best way I could pass my evenings was to sit in a book store and read, as I was kindly permitted to do'.

When Bates left the City, his place as the leading American banker in London was taken by another man with humble origins, George Peabody (1795–1865), from South Danvers (now Peabody), Massachusetts. At the age of eleven Peabody was apprenticed as a grocer, and while still in his teens he became manager of a wholesale dry goods warehouse in Georgetown, DC, soon thereafter being made a partner. From such poor beginnings, by the age of 32, his business had expanded rapidly and he not only owned a number of small stores in Washington and Baltimore, but had also become involved in banking.

He made his first visit to England in 1826, and on a second visit started a small import/export company – George Peabody & Co., winning a small share of a market that at that time was dominated by Brown Brothers. In 1835 he again came to England, hoping to sell bonds to finance the new Chesapeake and Ohio Canal. He arrived at a time when the City had lost confidence in American securities, so he had to work hard to restore faith in his country's probity, personally assuring British investors that Maryland – then on the verge of bankruptcy and with much British money invested there – would honour their bonds. To boost confidence further he backed American securities with his own funds and later made a great deal of money when the market improved. Against the odds he eventually negotiated a loan of $8 million for Maryland. Two years later, now with an excellent and reliable reputation, he settled permanently in Britain, and his company, based in the City, soon emerged as an important challenge to the British houses of Baring and Rothschild in the market for American securities. During the severe financial panic of that year, he, more than any, helped restore confidence in American credit.

George Peabody (1795–1865).

By 1850, Peabody had become one of the most important and respected figures in the City and, looking forward to his retirement, began looking for a successor who would ensure the stability of his company and leave him free to concentrate on his growing philanthropic activities. In May 1853, after much deliberation, he invited the forty-year-old Boston merchant, Junius Spencer Morgan, to join his firm as a full partner. Morgan was just the sort he was looking for, a man already well regarded by both American and British businessmen, trustworthy, with good judgement and, most importantly, the breeding and manners to mix with the gentlemen of the British business community. Morgan willingly took up Peabody's highly attractive offer (which included a $25,000-a-year allowance for entertainment).

Peabody and Morgan faced their greatest crisis during the financial panic of 1857 but, on the point of collapse, Peabody at

Peabody Square Model dwellings, Blackfriars Road, London, 1872.

The portrait of Queen Victoria which she gave to Peabody, a watercolour on enamel by F. A. Tills, 1867, set in gold and velvet.

the last moment managed to negotiate a loan of £1 million from the Bank of England. That he was able to secure such a deal, which was virtually unprecedented, owed much to the friendship he had struck up over the years with Thomas Hankey, Jr, the Governor of the Bank of England. From this low point, Peabody & Co. went from strength to strength, so that when Peabody retired and handed over the business to Morgan (who changed the name of the house to J. S. Morgan & Co.) they were second only to Rothschilds.

Peabody, a reserved man who would take a packed lunch with him to his office and preferred whist and fishing to grand company (though he could and did arrange and finance sumptuous Anglo-American dinners and parties), was, after Bates, one of the first Americans to take the City by storm. He lived only for his work and his devotion to the betterment of Anglo-American relations, and, specifically, the image of America in Britain. Thus, in 1851, when Congress failed to vote monies for an American stand at the Crystal Palace Exhibition, a shocked Peabody financed most of the costs himself. Apart from funding the 1852 expedition to search for Sir John Franklin, the British Arctic explorer, and setting up institutes of learning at Harvard, Yale and elsewhere in the United States, his greatest benefactions were in Britain with the gift to the City of London of $2½ million, a breathtaking sum at that time, for building workingmen's houses, tenements that can still be seen today in many parts of London as his lasting memorial.

It was, in essence, Britain's first large-scale housing development for the less well off, and for this great enterprise, which encouraged subsequently greater efforts by the British government in this direction, he was made a Freeman of the City of London, while a statue of him, unveiled by the Prince of Wales, was erected by the Royal Exchange. He refused to accept both a baronetcy and the Grand Cross of the Order of the Bath, because this would have meant him having to give up his American citizenship, asking merely for a miniature portrait of Queen Victoria, which she had commissioned and sent to him. But when he died in London in 1869 his funeral service was held in Westminster Abbey, the first for an American, before his body was taken to the United States for burial in his native Massachusetts.

'The funeral of Mr Peabody in Westminster Abbey.'

Andrew Carnegie

'How much did you say I had given away?' he asked his secretary.

'324,657,399 dollars,' said the secretary, his taste for figures being precise.

'Good heavens!' answered Carnegie. 'Where did I get all that money?'

BURTON J. HENDRICK, Life of Andrew Carnegie

After banking, there is no doubt that, in terms of nineteenth- and early-twentieth-century Anglo-American or, more precisely, Scots-American entrepreneurship, there is one real giant, the supreme example of the barefoot Scots immigrant who was to reach the very pinnacle of late-nineteenth- and early-twentieth-century American industrial society. The life of Andrew Carnegie (1835–1919) spans the years during which the greatest contribution was made by British immigrants to the development of the United States. Born in November 1835 in Dunfermline, Scotland, he was the son of a poor damask linen weaver who, with other members of the family, was much involved in radical politics. His father was an Anti-Corn Law Leaguer and local Chartist leader and his grandfather, Thomas Morrison, was one of Scotland's most outspoken radical agitators, and a friend of William Cobbett. One of Carnegie's earliest memories was that of being awakened in the night with the news that his uncle, Bailie Morrison, had been taken and gaoled for sedition. The radicalism of his family and of the Scottish artisans made a deep impression on young Carnegie. He later said, 'As a child I could have slain king, duke, or lord, and considered their death a service to the state.' Carnegie attended a local parish school as well as a Lancasterian school, but it was through his uncle George Lander that he was introduced to Scottish and Celtic history, and, more importantly, to the wonders of the United States.

Carnegie's family were poor, and the emergence of the factory system meant that the days of the individual handloom weaver were numbered. Carnegie's father found it increasingly difficult to find work, and the family was kept going by Andrew's determined and resourceful mother who stitched shoes and sold sweets and groceries to make ends meet. Seeing no future in Scotland or in the Chartist movement, she persuaded her husband to sell up their possessions and emigrate to the United States, where her two sisters and a brother already lived. They left Scotland in May 1848 and, arriving in New York, they made their

Andrew Carnegie (1835–1919) at the age of 33.

way to Allegheny City, Pennsylvania, which is now part of Philadelphia.

Carnegie, then thirteen, first found work as a bobbin-boy in a cotton factory, earning a mere $1.20 a week. He moved on to a bobbin manufacturing establishment, where his duties included the firing of a furnace in a hot, evil cellar. To use his own words, 'feeling like a bird in a cage', he applied for and gained a post as messenger boy in Pittsburgh's telegraph office in 1850. That same year a Colonel James Anderson, who had founded free libraries in Western Pennsylvania, announced that he was going to open up his private library to 'the working boys of Pittsburgh', but as telegraph messengers did not actually work with their hands it was proposed to exclude them. The precocious Carnegie wrote a letter to the *Pittsburgh Dispatch* arguing that telegraph messengers were indeed working boys, and so impressed was the Colonel that he forthwith included them. It was from this first-hand experience of the benefits of free libraries that Carnegie was driven to found the huge number of libraries that he endowed in his later life.

When he was only eighteen, Carnegie moved to being employed by Thomas A. Scott, the superintendent of the Pennsylvania Railroad and an influential Pittsburgh businessman, as his telegraph operator and personal secretary. Scott had a reputation as one of America's most daring railroad executives. He taught Carnegie the skills of speculation and business manipulation. In 1855, for example, Scott asked him whether he could find $500 to invest in railroad stock: this Carnegie did, at the dangerous expense of mortgaging the small cottage which his family had by then acquired. In 1859 Scott promoted him to the post of superintendent of the western division of the Pennsylvania Railroad, and the following year Carnegie made his first major financial killing by acquiring an interest in the Woodruff Company, who held the original patents for Pullman sleeping cars.

During the Civil War, Scott, now the Assistant Secretary of War, employed Carnegie as the superintendent of military transportation and the director of communications. Because of the war, iron was fetching record prices and new rails were a scarce commodity. Among the first to recognize the potential, Carnegie organized and financed a rail manufacturing company, and at the same time set up the Pittsburgh Locomotive Works. A series of catastrophic fires, which destroyed a number of existing wooden railway bridges, also led to him forming the Keystone Iron Bridge Company in 1865. He also diversified by successfully selling railroad securities in Britain and Europe (usually dealing through J. S. Morgan & Co.), and helping expand the Western Union

The Edgar Thomson steelworks, the heart of the Carnegie empire, named in honour of the President of the Pennsylvania Railroad Company, in 1875.

Telegraph Company. Wealth flowed in to Carnegie from all these concerns and, by both scrupulous and unscrupulous means, he and his colleagues moved on to further profitable investment in the oil wells of Pennsylvania and Ohio. While he later popularized the maxim, 'Put all your eggs in one basket and then watch that basket', at this stage in his career he was doing the exact opposite. Above all, he had quickly earned himself a reputation as a shrewd, courageous and dashing businessman even though the more conservative members of the Pennsylvania business community considered him a reckless gambler.

While on one of his trips to Europe, Carnegie met up with Sir Henry Bessemer whose 'Bessemer process' was revolutionizing the British steel industry. Seeing the enormous possibilities of this for America and deciding at last to put all his eggs in one basket, in 1872–3 he diverted all his resources into steel, forming a new consortium and raising capital for the Edgar Thomson Steel Works, which were erected on a huge site near Pittsburgh. It was a wise move, and by 1881 Carnegie had become the foremost iron and steel master in America, the capital assets of his companies standing at an estimated $5 million. A mere seven years later, his wealth had increased some sixty times over so that in 1899, when his various interests were vested in the Carnegie Steel Company, the profits alone were $40 million.

Carnegie's business life from the 1870s to 1900 matched the industrial history of the United States over the same period. When he started out in steel, the industry was totally dominated by Britain, but by 1889 America was already leaving her lagging

far behind. Carnegie made Pittsburgh America's steel capital, with the largest Bessemer plant, the largest crucible plant and the largest steel freightcar works in the world. Quite simply he was able to produce more and better-quality steel at a lower price than anybody, by sacrificing everything to reducing the costs of production, and adopting the latest technological processes, instantly discarding costly equipment if something better appeared. Thus by the end of the century the Carnegie Steel Company controlled every essential part of steel manufacturing – transportation, raw materials, distribution and finance. He owned ore mines, coal fields, lake steamboats, the whole of Conneaut Harbor in Ohio, and the very railway linking that harbour with Pittsburgh.

OPPOSITE: Making Bessemer steel: the converter at work.

LEFT: A *Punch* cartoon, titled 'The MacMillion'. 'Mr Carnegie, the Scottish-American millionaire, has provided £2,000,000 for the establishment of free education at four of the Scottish universities – Edinburgh, Glasgow, St Andrew's, Aberdeen.'

Another key to Carnegie's success was due to his old-fashioned partnership organization. He owned 58 per cent of his company, his partners were all active managers, and so, unlike the other emerging modern-style corporations, he was not inhibited by hundreds of absentee stockholders. He was thus virtually free to plough all the profits back into the company and, as he himself said, he thus owed his success to the people he employed and to his efficient organization – 'Take from me all the ore mines, railroads, manufacturing plants, but leave me my organization, and in a few years I promise to duplicate the company.' Ultimately, as his biographer Joseph Wall said, his success was due 'to Carnegie himself – to his drive, his imagination, his boldness and innovative daring, and above all to his insatiable appetite for more – more iron, more rails, more customers, more power.' He was a great empire-builder, the Napoleon of industry who ruthlessly and rapidly defeated his opponents whether they were a rival company or a labour union.

In December 1868 Carnegie wrote a memorandum to himself which is worth quoting at length –

> By this time two years, I can so arrange all my business as to secure at least $50,000 per annum. Beyond this never earn, make no effort to increased fortune, but spend the surplus each year for benevolent purposes. Cast aside business forever except for others. Settle in Oxford and get a thorough education, making the acquaintances of literary men – this will take three years' active work – pay especial attention to speaking in public. Settle then in London and purchase a controlling interest in some newspaper or live review and give the general management of it attention, taking part in public matters, especially those connected with education and improvement of the poorer classes. Man must have an idol – the amassing of wealth is one of the worst species of idolatry – no idol more debasing than the worship of money.

Of course, Carnegie did not give up business two years after writing the memorandum. But as he continued to build up his steel empire his sense of guilt certainly did not disappear. Feeling the pull of his family's radical roots, he began to try to help reform Britain's political and social institutions. In the 1880s he bought a string of newspapers which advocated the abolition of monarchy. In 1886 he published *Triumphant Democracy*, which aimed to demonstrate the superiority of republican over monarchical institutions, and in particular the American system over the British. The book offended many people in Britain but it sold over 40,000 copies in the United States. At one stage he even thought about

Dec 'lt?
St Nicholas Hotel N.Y.

Thirty three and an income of 50,000$
per annum,
By this time two years I can so arrange all,
my business as to secure at least 50,000$ per
annum — Beyond this never earn — make no
effort to increase fortune, but spend the
surplus each year for benevolent purposes,
Cast aside business forever except for
others, —
Settle in Oxford & get a thorough education
making the acquaintance of literary men
this will take three years active work —
Pay especial attention to speaking in public,
Settle then in London & purchase a
controlling interest in some newspaper or
live review & give the general management
of it attention, taking a part in public
matters especially those connected with
education & improvement of the poorer
classes —
Man must have an idol — The amassing
of wealth is one of the worst species of
idolatry — No idol more debasing than the
worship of money — Whatever I engage in I must
push inordinately therefor should I be careful
to choose that life which will be the most elevating
in its character — To continue much longer
overwhelmed by business cares and with most
of my thoughts wholly upon the way to make
more money in the shortest time, must degrade
me beyond hope of permanent recovery,
I will resign business at Thirty five, but during
the ensuing two years I wish to spend the afternoons
in receiving instruction, and in reading systematically

Carnegie's 1868 memorandum,
written from the St Nicholas Hotel,
New York, where he and his mother
made their home for several years.

returning to Britain, reclaiming his British citizenship and stand-ing for Parliament as an anti-monarchist. Above all he found it increasingly difficult to reconcile the accumulation of wealth and power with his democratic (though never socialist) feelings and tendencies. This self-questioning, as he called it, was not resolved until the appearance of his article the Gospel of Wealth in 1889. Encouraged by his friend, Gladstone, among others, this was published in the *Pall Mall Gazette*. In the article, Carnegie argued that the accumulation of wealth was necessary for human prog-ress but it was the moral obligation of the wealthy to dispense their money for the good of society.

> This, then, is held to be the duty of the man of wealth: to set an example of modest, unostentatious living, shunning dis-play or extravagance; to provide moderately for the legiti-mate wants of those dependent upon him; and, after doing so, to consider all surplus revenues which come to him simply as trust funds – the man of wealth thus becoming the mere trustee and agent for his poorer brethren, bringing to their service his superior wisdom, experience, and ability to administer, doing for them better than they would or could do for themselves.

In the decade following the appearance of this article Car-negie's wealth continued to multiply. But eventually, in January 1901, after one or two abortive attempts, he finally sold the Carnegie Company for a massive $89 million to the newly formed United States Steel Corporation, and retired from business.

In his 'Gospel of Wealth' Carnegie had emphasized the im-portance of education as a way of curing some of the ills of society. In particular, he stressed the need for every community to have a free public library. Before writing his essay he had already built libraries for Dunfermline, Scotland, and Braddock, Pennsylvania. Within five years of proclaiming his gospel he had established eight more libraries in Scotland and two more in America (he would only provide the library building, insisting that the town should tax itself for books and maintenance). After 1901 Carnegie and his various corporations and trusts were to provide for 2,811 free public libraries (1,946 in America, 660 in Britain and Ireland, and 205 in the British colonies) at a cost of nearly $45 million. Virtually non-existent before him, the free library, as a result of his philanthropy, became as much a part of both urban and rural Britain and America as the school or the church.

Carnegie made numerous other benefactions, to individual colleges, to the Carnegie Institute of Pittsburgh and the Carnegie Institution of Washington, to the Endowment for International

The first library founded by Carnegie, in his home town of Dumfermline, 1911.

Peace (he was a staunch pacifist from beginning to end), to the Scottish Universities Trust, the United Kingdom Trust, the Dunfermline Trust, and to his Hero Funds. This last benefaction set up 'to compensate those injured in helping their fellow men' pleased Carnegie the most because, as he said, 'it came up my ain back'.

Despite being hurt by much bitter criticism resulting from his munificent charity – 'Pity the poor millionaire, for the way of the philanthropist is hard,' he said – and the dictatorial or anti-democratic way in which some people believed it was distributed, Carnegie continued to covet the various honorary academic degrees and other accolades that were showered on him. He became friends with many distinguished people throughout his life including Theodore Roosevelt, Mark Twain, Gladstone,

Carnegie at Skibo.

Matthew Arnold, Herbert Spencer and, above all, John Morley. He relished the company of the intelligentsia while he found his fellow millionaires and businessmen dull and intellectually limited, claiming that they had 'never read any book except a ledger'.

A particular characteristic of his later life was his strong attachment to Scotland. Behind his hard exterior he was a romantic at heart and this led him to purchase the Skibo Estate in Sutherland where he built a much ridiculed Scots baronial mansion and increasingly delighted in maintaining the kilt and bagpipes traditions of a Scottish Highland laird. Carnegie had written in his 'Gospel of Wealth' the famous and widely quoted lines that

The south wing of Skibo Castle.

'Surplus wealth is a sacred trust which its possessor is bound to administer in his lifetime for the good of the community'. He went on to say, 'The man who dies leaving behind him millions of available wealth, which was his to administer during life, will pass away "unwept, unhonoured, and unsung", no matter to what uses he leaves the dross which he cannot take with him. Of such as these the public verdict will then be: "The man who dies thus rich dies disgraced."' When he passed away in 1919 the world discovered that he had died in a state of grace. Of the $350 million in United States Steel first mortgage bonds he had owned, not one was left.

*   *   *

That tall Liberty with its spiky crown that stands in New York Harbor and casts an electric flare upon the world, is, in fact, the liberty of property, and there she stands at the Zenith.

H. G. WELLS

Along with banking and industry, retailing is an essential component of any modern industrial society, for ultimately the prosperity of a country depends upon, among other things, its ability to distribute the fruits of mass production. Britain was the first country to enter the industrial age, but, famous as the nation of shopkeepers, she was peculiarly slow to develop the retailing techniques which would have enabled her to exploit this position to the full.

In contrast, America's economic strength today owes much to

the successful development of the retailing techniques which it pioneered in the nineteenth and present centuries. Americans have, as one commentator has written, 'led the world in advertising, the use of electric lights, plate glass, packaging, air-conditioning, self-service, refrigeration, credit, parking lots and other devices for painlessly bringing together buyers and sellers'. The British have been especially receptive to American innovations, partly perhaps as a consequence of their own deficiencies in this area, but largely because of the close economic and social relationship between the two countries.

One of the most important retailing innovations in the nineteenth century was the department store, which sold a variety of merchandise. Here, too, the Rich Tide played its considerable part on both sides of the Atlantic. While Bon Marché, founded in Paris in 1852, was probably the world's first, their defining characteristics emerged out of British enterprise in the United States in the second half of the nineteenth century. It is not easy to identify the first American department store. Some say it was Macy's, others Wanamaker's, but most historians of the subject agree that A. T. Stewart's, founded by a Scots-Irish immigrant, has the strongest claim to the title.

Alexander Turney Stewart
(1803–76)

Alexander Turney Stewart (1803–76) was born in Lisburn, County Antrim, of Scottish Protestant parents. He was sent to an academy in Belfast with a view to entering the ministry, but after the death of his grandfather who had brought him up he decided to go to the United States. But, following a spell teaching in a private school in New York, he returned to Ulster to claim an inheritance of about £5,000. With this money Stewart returned to America in 1823 and opened a small shop on lower Broadway selling imported Irish lace. Soon after, he moved to larger premises and by 1850 he was operating the largest retail store in New York. Thirteen years later, in an eight-storey building covering a whole block between Ninth and Tenth Streets, Broadway and Fourth Avenue, he opened the largest retail store in the world, and America's first department store.

The scale of his operation was remarkable for the time, with about 2,000 employees and built at a cost of nearly $2,750,000. The store concentrated on selling quality dry-goods, much of them imported from Britain and Europe. Stewart was also involved in related enterprises, establishing or acquiring a controlling interest in several textile mills in the northern states, soon becoming America's leading retail merchant and one of its richest men. During the Civil War when he won substantial army and navy contracts, his annual income averaged nearly $2 million. His success owed much to hard work but he was also a shrewd and

highly capable businessman, and he was always quick to assess the market or spot a change in fashion.

Stewart's Store before its final enlargement.

Stewart was a strict disciplinarian; his employees were harshly treated, receiving fines for lateness and mistakes, and were badly paid. However, he proved himself in other ways to be a generous man, sending shiploads of food to Ireland during the Great Famine, and aiding the injured of the American Civil War and the Franco-Prussian War. In 1869 he was appointed Secretary of the Treasury by President Grant, but was unable to take up the position because of a provision prohibiting a man engaged in business from holding the post. He died in 1876. Two years later, on 7 November 1878, his body was stolen from the family vault and held for a reward. When this was paid in 1880 the body was returned and reburied at the Episcopal Cathedral which he gave

Marshall Field (1835–1906)

to Garden City, a model town he built for people of modest means on Long Island.

In the second half of the nineteenth century, following Stewart's example, department stores were established in all the major American cities, with one of the largest and most successful to emerge in this period being Marshall Field of Chicago, once called 'the Cathedral of all the Stores'. Its rapid growth owed much to the genius of its founder Marshall Field (1835–1906), a man quick to spot and nurture talent among his employees. One of them was Harry Gordon Selfridge, who in his turn was to become one of Britain's great merchant princes.

Selfridge (1858–1947) was born on 11 January 1858 in Ripon, Wisconsin, the only son of Robert O. Selfridge, who owned a small dry-goods business. At the age of fourteen he became a junior bank clerk, though his ambition was to join the navy. He applied to the Naval Academy at Annapolis, but was turned away because he was under the required height. According to one commentator, this was a traumatic experience for him and thereafter Selfridge harboured an irrational hostility to men taller than himself, who were automatically debarred from senior executive positions. He then joined the Chicago mail order business of Field, Leiter & Co. (from 1881 Marshall Field & Co., Retailers), as an apprentice clerk earning $10 a week. From an early stage he displayed such a genius for merchandising that he was noticed by Marshall Field himself, who in 1886 made him the manager of his enormous department store in State Street. Four years later, when Selfridge was thinking about establishing his own business, Field made him a junior partner.

Selfridge's greatest asset was his imagination and innovative mind. He introduced the novel idea of holding special sales to bring the crowds in, and established a bargain basement or budget floor, as it came to be known, which grew to become the largest single salesroom in the world. He employed brilliant shop window dressers and got Field to increase the amount spent on advertising, writing much of the copy himself. He even persuaded Field to open a tearoom on the third floor of his stores, arguing that it would prevent their customers from cutting their shopping and going home or elsewhere for refreshment. The novelty soon caught on, and within months they were serving 1,500 people a day. (In 1966 Field's boasted the largest restaurant operation in the world.) In 1903, while still in his early forties, he sold his share in Marshall Field intending to retire with his fortune of about $300,000. But retirement did not suit 'Mile a Minute' Harry (so-called because of his speed of working) and after various business deals in Chicago and elsewhere he began travelling,

H. Gordon Selfridge (1858–1947) in his prime.

entertaining and adding to his collection of orchids, a lifelong obsession. (Selfridge would wear a fresh orchid in his button-hole every day.)

In 1906 Selfridge went to London for a holiday and to survey the commercial scene there. He saw one or two good general stores and luxury shops but realized that the capital lacked a department store run on American lines. He immediately felt that, using his American training and experience, he could find a huge market. After much careful research he found a site on the north side of Oxford Street, which at that time was not a major shopping district. Told by his London friends that his scheme had no hope of succeeding as the capital already had too many shops,

VALUE

THE Great Store is built, and stands strong in stone and steel four square to all the world.

The Business is yet to build, and we mean to found and foster it by establishing Public Confidence in all we say and all we do.

We have everything to win, and —*we shall win.*

Already in the gathering of vast stocks of merchandise from every quarter of the world have been practised sound business principles that make for confidence.

For months our Buyers have been busy at every fountain head of best supply. Every ebb and flow of market value has been used to the best advantage, with the result that here assembled are the largest, most keenly bought and best assorted stocks of dependable merchandise ever seen in London under one retail roof.

In distribution to the Public, the next great step, we shall begin to prove our principles by offering in our hundred separate Departments goods absolutely dependable in freshness, style and quality at London's Lowest Prices.

This is Merchandising as we believe in it; the straightforward way of dealing with the Public that establishes implicit confidence, and the rule of Value-giving that leads to permanent success.

SELFRIDGE & CO.
OXFORD STREET, LONDON, W.

he tried to explain that a department store was a very different concept. The leading Chicago architect Daniel Burnham was commissioned to design a spectacular structure and, in March 1909, Selfridge & Co commenced business with 130 departments and £900,000 capital. It aimed to cater for all tastes, from restaurants to American-style barber shops, a library, an information bureau and a roof garden.

A great deal of attention was paid to display, his windows were dressed elaborately and left to be seen at night when the usual British practice was to cover them with blinds. Advertising was a vital ingredient of his marketing operation, and he invested heavily in the press. For twenty-six years he wrote a daily column in *The Times* under the pseudonym 'Callisthenes'. His articles did not contain any overt advertising and simply began: 'This space is occupied every day by an article reflecting the policies, principles, and opinions of his House of Business upon various points of public interest.' In order to gain as much publicity as possible, especially when launching a new promotion, Selfridge provided special facilities, telephones, typewriters and briefing rooms for the press. He also entertained and befriended many of Fleet Street's most influential editors, including his fellow expatriate Ralph D. Blumenfeld.

Without being overtly paternalistic, Selfridge took a particular interest in the welfare of his staff and, as well as giving them incentives to progress within the firm, he provided a sports ground at Wembley and set up societies and clubs. Staff tours to

Gordon Selfridge celebrates his store's 28th birthday by inspecting specimens of a £30,000 collection of Crown Jewel replicas at the store.

Selfridge and the Midnight Folly
Girls help to pull down the old
Selfridge building.

the Continent and to the United States were organized to broaden
the minds of his employees, all this at a time when the working
conditions of shopworkers in Britain were exceedingly poor.
Selfridge was a success from the start. Londoners, formerly conservative in their shopping habits, were quickly won over by this
new type of store. After the First World War, Selfridge acquired a
number of London suburban and provincial stores, and established a chain of 3*d* and 6*d* John Thrifty stores on the model of the
Woolworth 5 and 10 cent stores.

In America, Selfridge had been totally absorbed by business or
what he called the *Romance of Commerce*, the title of a book he
published in 1918. In Britain he continued to be captivated by
commerce but after a while he seemed to become more interested
in spending money rather than in making it. One of his major
problems, as he entered old age, was women. He was especially
drawn to the stars of the theatre and showbusiness, and fell for
the beautiful French cabaret star, Gaby Deslys, then with an
American nightclub entertainer, Jenny Dolly, who achieved
great popularity in London in the 1920s in a revue with her sister
Rosy. Selfridge poured out his money on them for jewels, houses
and furs, and within ten years his girlfriends had managed to
spend over £2 million of his fortune.

Though not suffering from the chronic delusions of grandeur
that beset that other American expatriate, William Waldor Astor,

Selfridge did not spare anything on entertainment. He took over Lansdowne House from Astor and acquired Highcliffe Castle in Hampshire, also purchasing a site on the south coast near Bournemouth where he hoped to build a large castle. He was a constant giver of lavish parties, especially with the élite of the Tory party, to whom he was particularly attracted.

In 1927 Selfridge sold the control of his company, and by 1937, the year he took up British citizenship, he was heavily in debt. While the store continued to thrive, the other partners, including his son, could just afford to tolerate Selfridge's indebtedness, but when the country was plunged into war in 1939 he proved to be too much of a burden. In early 1940 he was given an ultimatum by his board: he had to repay at once the £118,000 owed to the company or resign from active management and accept the honorary title of President and a salary of a mere £2,000 a year. With no real choice, Selfridge retired. After moving to a flat in Park Lane he moved away from his beloved West End to a room in the Putney home of his daughter. As Richard Kenin has written, 'Selfridge could no longer afford boxes at the theatre stocked with iced bottles of champagne. Instead he spent hours in the darkened recesses of cinemas, frequently in the cheapest seats, a lonely, isolated, and generally unrecognized figure stripped of the polished top hat, frock coat and striped trousers which had been his hallmark.' (*Return to Albion*)

On 8 May 1947 he died. Though the major British papers carried obituaries he was almost a forgotten man. Nevertheless, to paraphrase his own words, Selfridge had left his native country and unfurled the American flag of commerce over shopkeeping London. He helped to initiate a revolution in British retailing. It was said in the introduction to this book that the Rich Tide was concerned with people as vehicles for ideas. Selfridge certainly carried the ideas he acquired in the United States to Britain and instigated them in Oxford Street. Selfridges started business as an alien American innovation; now it is a British institution.

One man in the Selfridge mould was the British grocer and retailer, Sir Thomas (Tommy) Lipton (1850–1931). Born of a poor Glasgow family he went to New York at the age of fourteen, returning some four years later with experience of advanced American book-keeping and retailing methods. He opened his first shop in Glasgow in 1871 and by the turn of the century he owned some four hundred shops up and down the country, using many American-style promotional and marketing devices. He expanded into the United States where his assets included two meat processing factories in Chicago. In later life his many yachting challenges for the America's Cup won him a wide

'Sir Thomas Lipton entertains Chicago nurses and doctors at his new Southgate Residence', June 1917.

international reputation, and particularly endeared him to the American public.

*   *   *

We shall not make Britain's mistake. Too wise to try to govern the world, we shall merely own it. Nothing can stop us.

LUDWELL DENNY

In pre-Civil War America there was a certain degree of interest in developing commercial outlets in Britain, but when one examines this trend more closely the real aim of such endeavours was to attract funds for the development and opening up of the United States. Surprisingly, the claim to be the first proper British branch factory of any American company, using American methods and machinery, probably goes to Samuel Colt (1814–62), who established a London gun factory in 1852. Though it was not a success and soon sold out to the London Pistol Company, who continued to manufacture Colts, it was an indication of a trend to come.

More notably, Isaac Merrit Singer's achievements (1811–75) may have been known to every British householder over the last century and more. In the 1860s Singer opened up several sales outlets in Britain benefiting from the very favourable exchange rate prevailing at the time. The establishment of a small Singer factory in Clydebank, Scotland, in 1867/8, which was controlled, not by a British holding company but by the parent company in America, was a new development that makes Singer one of the first American multi-national corporations. Over the next decade the output of that factory increased enormously, with twenty-six major British offices by 1879, apart from the London headquarters.

By the 1880s, many other American companies were either directly exporting to, had established agencies in, or were actually manufacturing in Britain – companies such as the National Cash Register Company, the Otis (Elevator) Company, Babcock &

COLT'S
NEW "SERVICE"
·455 Cal., as supplied to Her
Majesty's War Department.
NEW "POCKET"
REVOLVERS
AND
LIGHTNING MAGAZINE RIFLES.
Price Lists Free.
COLT'S PATENT FIREARMS M'F'O CO.,
26, Glasshouse Street, Piccadilly Circus, London, W.

Singer Sewing Machine factories: (top left) Cabinet works, Govan, Glasgow; (top centre) Glasgow; (top right) South Bend, Indiana; (bottom) Elizabethport, New Jersey.

Silas M. Burroughs (1846–95)

Henry Solomon Wellcome
(1853–1936)

Wilcox, and many others. Alexander Graham Bell had his own representative in Britain, an American colonel, William Reynolds, who tried to attract finance to form a company to develop Bell's telephone system there. In direct competition with him was another American colonel, George Gourard, who was Thomas Edison's British agent, and who formed the Edison Telephone Company in London in 1879.

The two American-led companies, both busy installing telephone systems and exchanges in London, were at first bitter rivals, but soon merged into the United Telephone Company in 1880, though under the British Telegraph Acts of 1870 their operations were to end as a State monopoly. Edison's other operations to market the phonograph, the megaphone and the 'incandescent lamp' with the British Edison Electric Light Company Limited of 1882 were left intact. Shortly thereafter this company merged with its British competitor, the Joseph Wilson Swan Company, in 1883 to collaborate and compete with the established companies who produced and distributed the still cheaper form of lighting gas.

American businesses were expanding in Britain in other fields as well. In 1880, the Americans Silas M. Burroughs and Henry S. Wellcome began introducing American medicines, in pleasant-tasting compressed pill form, to the British market. Until then British-made medicines were known for their huge doses and unpleasant tastes. Burroughs and Wellcome marketed their wares very aggressively: they were the first to sell direct to doctors by the use of free samples. Then in the developing field of photography George Eastman was granted his first British patent for coating photographic plates as early as 1879, and by the mid-eighties he had a permanent representative and sales outlet in London which also imported Kodak cameras from the United States. By 1890 his company started manufacturing cameras and plates at their new factory in Harrow, Middlesex, with finance raised in London, and cheaper British materials, but using American management and imported machinery.

In every possible way, particularly after 1900, the impact of American business initiative on the British economic and commercial scene grew dramatically. It was increasingly called 'The American Invasion' and as *The Times* reported, 'from shaving soap to electric motors, and from shirts to telephones, the American is sweeping the field'. While at the time of the American Civil War it was estimated that there were, at most, about a dozen American firms operating in small ways in the United Kingdom, by the turn of the century they had grown to six or seven times that number, and by the time of economic crash in the early 1930s there were

Burroughs Wellcome and Co. headquarters in London, on the corner of Holborn Viaduct and Snow Hill, *c.* 1900.

over four hundred. Since then, American business concerns and products have become so familiar that British consumers tend to consider them as British: Heinz, Singer, Kelloggs, Black & Decker, and Kodak.

But, undoubtedly, the American company which has, more than any other, made the greatest impact on the British economy is Ford. One of the great American corporations, its actual development in the United Kingdom owes much to an Englishman, Percival Lee Dewhurst Perry. Perry (1878–1956) was born in Bristol and educated at King Edward VI's School, Birmingham. His ambition was to become a lawyer but lack of money forced him to seek an alternative career, and at the age of seventeen he answered an advertisement in the *Birmingham Post* for a job at the

London office of a bicycle and car dealer named Harry J. Lawson. Selling his stamp collection to pay his railway fare to London, he took the post at a pound a week. His employer, Lawson, was attempting to capture the fledgling British automobile industry by purchasing all the patents recently taken out by European manufacturers such as Otto and Daimler.

After gaining a valuable introduction to the motor car business, Perry reluctantly left Lawson and spent a brief and unhappy time working for his uncle's printing firm in Hull. But by 1900 he was again working in the motor industry, and by 1903 he was, with others, involved in an import company, the American Motor Car Agency and Central Motor Car Agency, whose prime concern was to sell and distribute Fords in Britain.

The company failed to prosper, partly because the British considered American cars rather cheap and lacking the style and performance of the Continental models. Using his abundant reserves of energy and imagination Perry did all that he could to boost sales, and in one attempt to draw the public's attention he imported three Model B Fords and put them on the streets of London as taxicabs, one of the first fleets of motor-powered cabs to operate in the capital. The cabs, incidentally, had to be painted white in order that they could be seen by pedestrians. Despite these efforts, sales remained low. So in 1906 Perry decided to go to America to seek financial support from Henry Ford, the man who had said, 'I am going to democratize the automobile. When I'm through everybody will be able to afford one, and about everyone will have one.'

In Detroit, Ford invited Perry and his wife to stay with him and, although the great man was not willing to invest abroad at this stage, the two men established a close friendship. Perry warmed to the American immediately – a man 'to whom you would give your last penny'. Likewise, Ford was impressed by the young Englishman's zeal and enthusiasm. Ford did apparently introduce Perry to Gordon McGregor, the head of Ford in Canada and the owner of the rights to sell Canadian-assembled Fords throughout the British Empire. Generously McGregor ceded his British rights to Perry, saying that the rest of the British Empire was enough for him!

When, in November of the following year, Ford's new mass-produced Model T was exhibited at the Olympia Motor Show in London, its success at last convinced Ford that the time was right to expand his overseas operations and compete with the European manufacturers. Perry was the obvious candidate to become manager of a well-financed branch of the Ford Company in Shaftesbury Avenue, London and he quickly established a

A Ford Model B Taxi in London, 1905.

nationwide network of exclusive Ford dealers. In their first year they received orders for over four hundred Model T's, and soon plans were being made to establish a British assembly plant. Perry found a suitable site on the Trafford Park industrial estate in Manchester and by 1911 the new factory was in operation. With this new venture, sales of Ford cars in Britain rose appreciably, and by·1914 the Model T was the best-selling car in Britain. As a result, Ford decided to replace the British branch with a company, and in March 1911 the Ford Motor Company (England) Ltd was incorporated with Perry as its head.

In the summer of 1912, Henry Ford and his family came to Britain. Perry dutifully showed him the country's historical sites and beauty spots but Ford was more interested in the country's factories and the prospects for his cars in Britain. They inspected the Manchester plant and visited the Midlands, already the heartland of Britain's motor industry. Ford decided that at some stage the English company needed to move to a larger site where there was room for expansion. He also decided to introduce manufacturing to the Manchester factory and in 1913–14, under close American supervision, their new mass-production techniques were introduced to Britain.

The expansion of the English company was held up by the First World War, since Perry was called on to serve as the Deputy Controller of the Mechanical Warfare Department and Director of Traction at the Ministry of Munitions, for which he received a knighthood in 1918. When the war ended, Ford in Britain faced a promising future and in 1918 the Manchester plant was

Percival Perry, early in his career, as a clown in the 1896 Coventry Parade.

expanded and production increased. But the following year Henry Ford clashed with Perry over the future of his company's activities in Britain. Ford wanted to operate the English company as a division of Detroit, which would mean that Perry and the other English executives would become mere managers. Perry, on the other hand, wanted to control and direct expansion in Britain, and with no hope of a compromise he resigned in May 1919. Henry Ford, realizing that it would be very difficult to find someone who matched the Englishman's experience and influence, wrote to Perry expressing regret that their differences had led to the split. Perry went on to lead a group which purchased and successfully developed the Slough Motor Company Repair Depot, and in 1922 he retired to the Channel Island of Herm.

Ford continued to prosper in the United Kingdom and, as the Manchester factory could no longer meet demand, Henry Ford employed one of his managers to find a site suitable for large-scale production. After much research and deliberation, in 1925 a site, mostly Thames marshland, was acquired at Dagenham. After Perry's departure the English company had been run by salaried American managers who tried to duplicate Detroit methods in Manchester. But none of them matched Perry's ability, and in May 1928, while in London, Henry Ford contacted Perry and offered him the chairmanship of his restructured European organization. Perry accepted. Back in America Ford was asked by Sorensen, one of his senior managers, what he had achieved on

Sir Percival Perry inaugurating the Ford site in 1929. To his right (seated) Edsel Ford and Henry Ford II, the small boy in the cap.

Cutting the sod at Dagenham: Edsel Ford, Henry Ford II and Perry.

his European trip. Ford said, 'I've hired Perry again'. To which Sorensen replied, 'That is the best news you could have brought me'.

Under a new strategy, Ford's various European interests were grouped together as the Ford Motor Company Ltd, and this new organization was able to make and assemble Ford products to be sold throughout Europe. Its centrepiece was Dagenham, which was in operation by 1931, and was then the largest factory in the United Kingdom and the largest car plant outside the United States. In order to rid Ford of the image of a foreign corporation, 40 per cent of Ford of England would be held by the British public.

Back in the fold, Perry skilfully masterminded this reorganiz-ation. In many ways his position in 1919 had been vindicated, as he had succeeded in persuading Henry Ford to give Ford subsidiary companies both local management and direction commensurate with economic business conditions in Britain. Thus in 1936 he was able to boast that 'the Ford organization in England has now come to be considered entirely British'. At Dagenham, he ensured that cars such as the Model Y were produced to meet the laws, needs and tastes of the British public. Despite competition from General Motors and European manufacturers, and setbacks caused by the Depression and the rise of nationalist interests in Europe, Ford's European operations progressed. Perry kept the organization's various European directors happy, and at no time during these difficult years did he lose the confidence and respect of the two Fords in America.

During the war, when Dagenham was put on a war footing, Perry continued to run the English company and after VE Day he resumed his co-ordinating role for the company in Europe. In

Aerial view of the Ford works at Dagenham *c.* 1933.

April 1948 Perry retired as chairman of Ford Motor Company Ltd. Ten years before, in January 1938, he had been created Baron Perry of Stock Harvard in recognition of his contributions to the development of the automobile industry and his standing as a businessman. He had been in the vanguard of the modern mechanized age and had, in his way, as much of an effect on twentieth-century Britain as any one man.

Ford Dagenham has been a great success, and despite some well-publicized setbacks the company has brought more income into the British Isles than any other. While the product was largely American, the initiative and drive to bring it to Britain well merits Perry's inclusion in the Rich Tide of transatlantic enterprise. But his story and that of the Ford Motor Company is only one impressive example of American business and manufacturing coming to Britain, and the events described took place against the background of an all-out process during the twentieth century which is called the Americanization of Britain. As we have

Edward, Prince of Wales visiting Dagenham in 1934, being driven in a Ford V8-40 Phaeton with Sir Percival Perry.

BELOW: 'On Tuesday, August 27th, 1946, Dagenham produced its millionth vehicle, a 10hp Prefect. It was driven out of the factory by the Minister of Supply, with Ford of Britain's "Founding Father", Lord Perry, as passenger.'

already seen, British people, ideas, inventions and lifestyles had long been exported and adopted or adapted. Now they were on the receiving end.

In the pursuit of wider markets, a large number of American products and processes began arriving that were to have a fundamental effect on British habits and ways of life. In some British minds this has been a process largely to be deplored. But to the wiser it can be seen as being largely positive. The British live daily with the effects and benefits, for example, of the arrival from across the Atlantic of some primary foodstuffs such as the potato, the tomato and maize (and, of course, tobacco), not to forget the turkey, and of the American processed foods which have had such an impact on British eating habits. And it was in America that the canning industry became a massively economic organization. To take the commonest product, the first canned baked beans (a development from the pork and beans once very popular in American farming communities) were produced in Portland, Maine, in 1875 for supply to the American fishing fleets. Then, in 1895, the Pittsburgh firm of H. J. Heinz started with their famous beans in tomato sauce, the forerunner of very many other varieties of tinned food. Heinz baked beans are indeed now much more popular in Britain than in America.

There were other processes out of America that have, through the development of 'convenience foods' and stimulants like colas and instant coffee, had a very great impact on British shopping habits. Despite Selfridge, this has been in the development of supermarkets rather than specialized butchers, bakers and grocers. Cornflakes, and a whole series of other breakfast cereals, tomato ketchup and peanut butter sit side by side on the shelves with the products of the vast food-freezing industry of today. And credit for the modern expansion of that market must go to Mr Clarence Birdseye who set up the first freezing plant in New York in 1928.

Apart from food, American 'institutions' in contemporary Britain are legion. The popular architecture of such American developments as filling stations, cinemas and laundromats can be despised by their critics but they will long remain with us along with the accessories of advertising, neon lights and hoardings. Otherwise the high streets of the United Kingdom are full of MacDonalds, Kentucky Fried Chicken, Holiday Inns, Avis Car Rentals, Mobil, Texaco, Exxon garages (all satisfied by American Express cards) and the American look in everything from car design to Levis.

American transatlantic influence is everywhere, though this is of course not just a British phenomenon. But, perhaps as a result of all the other things shared, the process has been easier with the British. While much of the Americanization process has been 'trendy' as the result of the all-pervasive images of America provided by film and television, the essential reason for most of these new institutions has been economic. For the members of the Rich Tide carry with them their own gospels of wealth when they come and go. And today both the fact of the wealth and the faith in the gospel happen to reside more in one territory than in the other.

CHAPTER EIGHT

The Emigrant Muse

My choice is the Old World,
My choice, my need, my life.
HENRY JAMES

There is a cynical feeling among some cultural historians that, in different ages, British and American painters, writers and poets have appeared to have but one objective: to become expatriates – either temporarily or more permanently – in the other country. A whole age of Americans, feeling the call to their ancestors, have gone to Britain to find their roots (and a market lacking in the United States), providing *inter alia* a living rebuttal to the British view that all Americans were barbarians. At a later stage the British set off to what they felt was the greater freedom of America but, like the American expatriates, they, too, have found themselves subject to conflicts of loyalties, and often indeed considered traitors to their native land.

It is dangerous to argue about the cultural 'origins' of the United States, but in the historical sense there can be no doubt that British culture was, until perhaps a hundred years ago, the benchmark of American culture. While Shakespeare, Milton and Chaucer never crossed the Atlantic, they are still as much a part of America's cultural inheritance as they are of Britain's. But from roughly the mid-nineteenth century onwards American culture, literature and other art forms have had their own status, with native Americans achieving international stature – like Longfellow, Emerson and Hawthorne.

There have of course been periods of great cultural hostility between the two countries, born of jealousy and fuelled by the writings of a number of well-known polemicists. Arch-villain in the famous 'War of the Reviews' in the second decade of the nineteenth century was the caustic observer Sydney Smith whose diatribes culminated in his famous or perhaps infamous article in the *Edinburgh Review* in 1820:

During the thirty or forty years of their independence they have done absolutely nothing for the sciences, for the arts,

OPPOSITE: *John Singleton Copley.* Oil painting by Gilbert Stuart, *c.* 1784 *(see page 257).*

for literature, or even for the statesmanlike studies of politics or political economy . . . In the four quarters of the globe, who reads an American book? or goes to an American play? or looks at an American picture or statue? What does the world yet owe to American physicians or surgeons? What new substances have their chemists discovered, or what old ones have they analysed? What new constellations have been discovered by the telescopes of Americans? What have they done in the mathematics? Who drinks out of American glasses? or eats from American plates? or wears American coats or gowns? or sleeps in American blankets? Finally, under which of the old tyrannical governments of Europe is every sixth man a slave whom his fellow-creatures may buy and sell and torture?

OPPOSITE: *The Royal Academicians in General Assembly*, 1795.
Oil painting by Henry Singleton. Benjamin West is in the presidential chair. Copley is standing on the right with a staff in his hand.
(see page 253)

Charles Dickens (1812–70)

But there were always as many defenders of things American, including a whole generation of great poets – Wordsworth, Coleridge (who thought of emigrating and founding a utopian community in America, as did Keats), Byron, Shelley and Southey. The early sniping at American literary and cultural attempts died away, it is said, when American writers of great depth and style such as Washington Irving and Fenimore Cooper began appearing on the scene. But still the writings of Scott, Carlyle, Dickens, Burns and the others mentioned above often reached a much wider market in the United States than they did in their homeland.

There was another reason why (as Emerson had complained in *English Traits*) 'every book we read, every biography, play, romance, in whatever form is still English history and manners'. It was in part due to the lack of copyright protection for British authors since, while American publishers were obliged to pay royalties only to American authors, they made their actual profits from publishing British writers. Thus it was commonplace for cheap reprint houses in New York and Philadelphia to pirate important British works and distribute them in pamphlet or newspaper form almost as soon as they had appeared in Britain.

The image of the other country has always been central to the whole Anglo-American relationship. One British writer who wrote and travelled widely in the United States to enormous popular acclaim, more popular indeed than in Britain, yet one who is often thought of as an unqualified anti-American, was Charles Dickens.

Dickens did not see himself in that light:

> Prejudiced, I am not, and never have been, otherwise than in favour of the United States. To represent me as viewing America with ill-nature, coldness or animosity, is merely to do a very foolish thing; which is a very easy one. (*American Notes*)

Dickens first visited America in January 1842. He was still a young man, but he had already written six books, including *The Pickwick Papers* and *Oliver Twist*, which had more readers in America than in Britain. (As the ship carrying the last episodes of *The Old Curiosity Shop* entered New York Harbor thousands lined the quayside yelling: 'Is Little Nell dead?') He was utterly amazed at the enthusiastic reception he got in America.

> How can I give you the faintest notion of my reception here; of the crowds that pour in and out the whole day; of the people that line the streets when I go out; of the cheering

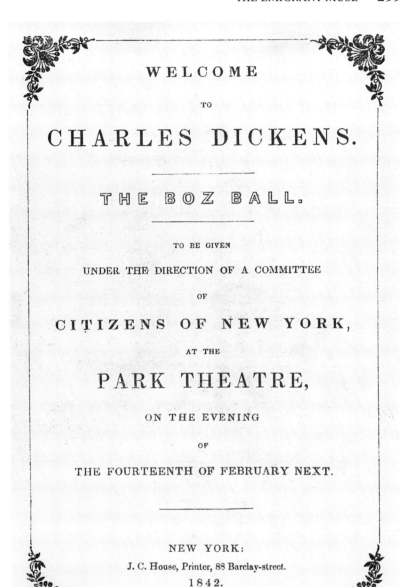

WELCOME

TO

CHARLES DICKENS.

THE BOZ BALL.

TO BE GIVEN

UNDER THE DIRECTION OF A COMMITTEE

OF

CITIZENS OF NEW YORK,

AT THE

PARK THEATRE,

ON THE EVENING

OF

THE FOURTEENTH OF FEBRUARY NEXT.

NEW YORK:
J. C. House, Printer, 88 Barclay-street.
1842.

'Welcome to Charles Dickens: The Boz Ball'. Programme cover for Dickens' arrival in New York City, 1842.

when I went to the theatre; of the copies of verse, letters of congratulation, welcomes of all kinds, balls, dinners, assemblies without end . . . ? I have had deputations from the Far West, who have come more than two thousand miles distance: from the lakes, the rivers, the backwoods, the log-houses, the cities, the factories, villages, and towns. Authorities from all the States have written to me. I have heard from the universities, Congress, Senate, and bodies, public and private, of every sort and kind. 'It is no nonsense, and no common feeling,' wrote Dr Channing to me yesterday. 'It is all heart. There never was and never will be, such a triumph.'

In Boston, on one occasion, a mob of women accosted him and started cutting off pieces of his fur coat to have as souvenirs. Not surprisingly, perhaps, he soon tired of all this attention and longed for privacy. Nevertheless, in many ways he enjoyed being worshipped, wanting the best of both worlds – to be lionized and at the same time left to do as he pleased. While based in Boston, he visited the New England states, New York, Pennsylvania, Virginia, Maryland, Kentucky, Missouri and Canada. On his travels he met a number of leading American writers, several of whom had been influenced by his writings; he was particularly taken by Washington, Irving who had spent many years in England earlier in the century.

Dickens wrote about his visit and published in 1842 *American Notes for General Circulation*. Within two days of its release in America the New York publishers had sold as many as 50,000 copies. In the book, which is largely descriptive, Dickens admires many aspects of American society such as its universities, which, whatever their defects, 'disseminate no prejudices; rear no bigots; dig up the buried ashes of no old superstitions; never interpose between the people and their improvement; exclude no man because of his religious opinions; above all in their whole course of study and instruction, recognize a world, and a broad one too, lying beyond college walls'. But he criticized aspects of its penal system, its yellow press, its dilapidated streets, the prevalence of pigs on Broadway, the corruption of the House of Representatives, the universal habit of spitting, 'their immoral denial', as he held, 'of copyright privileges to English authors' and the entire system of slavery. And at the same time he was writing to a friend in extreme terms that 'I believe there is no country, on the face of the earth, where there is less freedom of opinion on any subject in reference to which there is a broad difference of opinion, than in this'.

The book provoked much anger and criticism in America. Many Americans were deeply offended by it, particularly given the hospitality and kindness they felt they had shown to Dickens during his visit. James Gordon Bennett, for example, after reading the book, called Dickens 'the most trashy . . . the most contemptible . . . the essence of balderdash reduced to the last drop of silliness and inanity', causing Carlyle to say in turn that 'all Yankee-doodle-dom blazed up like one universal soda bottle'.

The American trip provided Dickens with the background material for the American scenes in his next novel, *Martin Chuzzlewit*. In the book Martin, after being stopped from marrying his sweetheart, Mary Graham, by his wealthy grandfather, sails for America with his evil architect cousin, Pecksniff, and his servant Mark Tapley, to seek his fortune. In America Martin is defrauded, loses all his money and almost dies of a fever. But, morally strengthened by the experience, he returns to Britain where his grandfather allows him to marry Mary Graham. In some ways

The Thriving City of Eden as it Appeared on Paper.

'The thriving city of Eden as it appeared on paper.' From *Martin Chuzzlewit*.

The Thriving City of Eden as it Appeared in Fact.

'The thriving city of Eden as it appeared in fact.' From *Martin Chuzzlewit*.

Martin's experience in America caricatures Dickens's visit. For instance, Martin is given an inordinate amount of attention wherever he goes in America. But the parodies of American life in the novel offended many readers in the United States and Dickens himself said that it 'made them stark staring mad across the water'.

'Why, I was a-thinking, sir,' returned Mark, 'that if I was a painter, and was called upon to paint the American Eagle, how should I do it?'

ABOVE: Captain Marryat (1792–1848)

LEFT: Frances Trollope in 1832. A portrait by Auguste Hervieu who accompanied them on their expedition to America.

If it was unfair to accuse Dickens of being anti-American, the same could not be said of two other British writers, Captain Marryat and Frances Trollope. Marryat (1792–1848), the British naval captain and popular novelist, came to the United States and Canada in 1837 to compare the British and American systems of government. His tactless comments and irregular behaviour angered the American press, who retaliated by accusing him of being a spy and assaulting women. In Detroit he was burned in effigy along with his books. His experiences were recorded in his razor-sharp and often very witty *Diary in America, with Remarks on Its Institutions* (1839). In 1827 Frances Trollope emigrated with her husband and three children (including the young Anthony Trollope) to Cincinnati, where, in an effort to recover from a severe financial setback, they set up a fancy goods 'bazaar'. The venture was not a success, and the Trollopes returned three years later to England. In 1832, Frances published her observations of American society in *Domestic Manners of the Americans*. Her unflattering account, according to one source, 'succeeded in angering Americans more than any book written by a foreign observer before or since'. If she was not enamoured of American society, she was certainly fascinated by it, for she wrote four later books with an American theme. Her son, Anthony, was also intrigued by, but less critical of, the United States, its peoples and its customs.

Dickens giving a reading.

'Paint it as like an Eagle as you could, I suppose.'

'No,' said Mark. 'That wouldn't do for me, sir. I should want to draw it like a Bat, for its shortsightedness; like a Bantam, for its bragging; like a Magpie, for its honesty; like a Peacock, for its vanity; like an Ostrich, for its putting its head in the mud, and thinking nobody sees it—'

'And like a Phoenix, for its power of springing from the ashes of its faults and vices, and soaring up anew into the sky!' said Martin. 'Well, Mark, let us hope so.'

Nevertheless, when he visited America again twenty-six years later, much of the bitterness had died away and he found he was still a very popular writer. Between November 1867 and April 1868 he presented a series of readings of his works to packed auditoriums in several eastern cities, during which he declared, 'If I know anything about my countrymen . . . the English heart is stirred by the fluttering of the Stars and Stripes as it is stirred by no other flag except its own'. Through his travels and his writings, while he is remembered more now in the United States for his descriptions of Victorian England, to his contemporaries the similarities he found in the poverty, squalor and corruption of New York and elsewhere were a real glimpse of the other side of the New World. He always argued that he had castigated his own country's social ills more severely than he had ever done those of the United States, but there is no doubt that he provided a transatlantic incentive to finding a change for the better in the social conditions of the underprivileged.

Washington Irving (1783–1859) was sent to Liverpool in 1815 as a little-known writer to assist in the English branch of his brother's business. Forced to earn his own living when the firm collapsed, he moved to London where, in 1819, he had published in serial form (and as a book in 1820) *The Sketch Book of Geoffrey Crayon*, a set of essays and tales. It was a great success in both Britain and America. In it he wrote: 'The great charm . . . of English scenery is the moral feeling that seems to pervade it. It is associated in the mind with ideas of order, of quiet, of sober well-established principles, of hoary usage and reverend custom. Every thing seems to be the growth of ages of reverend and peaceful existence.' After a spell as an attaché in the American Embassy in Madrid he was posted in 1829 as Legation Secretary in London. During this period he received a gold medal from the Royal Academy of Literature in London and was also awarded an honorary doctorate in Civil Law from Oxford. He finally returned to America in 1832, establishing himself at Tarrytown in the Hudson River valley, where he lived like an English country squire, totally captivated by his exposure to British ways of life.

The title page from Washington Irving's *Sketch Book of Geoffrey Crayon*, 1849 edition.

The authoress of *Little Lord Fauntleroy* and *The Secret Garden*, Frances Hodgson Burnett (1849–1924), was born in Manchester and came to live with relatives in Knoxville, Tennessee, in 1865 when her business-man father died. She had her first story published three years later, but it was *Little Lord Fauntleroy* (1886) that made her reputation. She also wrote a number of best-selling novels about fashionable social life, often set in England, books such as *A Lady of Quality*; and in her subsequent life, both in Britain and in the United States, she emulated the lifestyles she wrote about, wearing exotic clothes, wintering in Bermuda and building a large English-style country house on Long Island.

One of the most familiar and durable American poets on the opposite side of the Atlantic is Henry Wadsworth Longfellow (1807–82), his popularity and influence well demonstrated by his receipt of honorary degrees from both Oxford and Cambridge during the tour he made in 1868 and 1869. Indeed in England he is hardly regarded as American. He was given a private audience by Queen Victoria, who was a great admirer, and his contribution to Anglo-American literature was finally marked by the fact that he is the only American to be honoured with a bust in Poets' Corner, Westminster Abbey.

The bust of Longfellow in Poet's Corner, Westminster Abbey.

The novelist Raymond Chandler (1888–1959) was born in Chicago but his English mother brought him to London where he was educated at Dulwich College. He became naturalized British in 1907 and even worked briefly as an Admiralty Civil Servant. He returned to America in 1912 and, though he remained a naturalized Briton, he regained his American Citizenship in 1955. W. H. Auden paid tribute to him saying: Chandler's thrillers 'were serious studies of a criminal mileau, and his powerful but extremely depressing books should be judged not as escape literature but as works of art'. One of his greatest successes was *The Long Goodbye*, published in 1954.

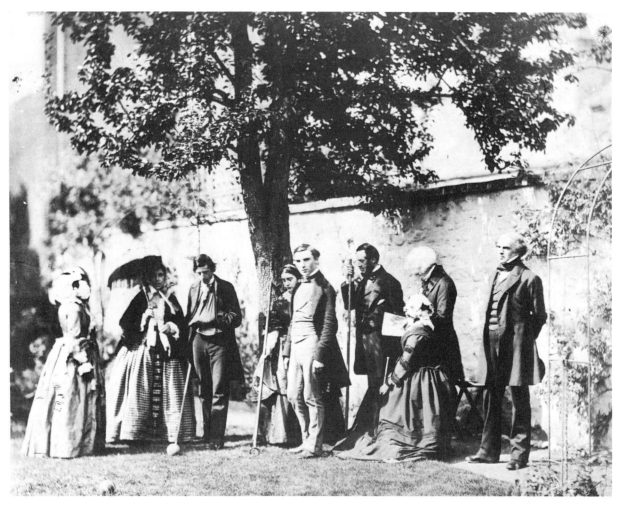

Irving's contemporary, the American writer Nathaniel Hawthorne (1804–64), was strongly influenced by Sir Walter Scott and other British novelists. Hawthorne, who hailed from Salem, Massachusetts, was for four years American Consul in the key emigration city of Liverpool in the years after 1853. He wrote extensively about the English life of the time as seen through American eyes, and is often held to be the most competent and moving of all the American expatriate writers who set out their impressions of the Britain they had come to. His rationale was that 'No author, without a trial, can conceive of the difficulty of writing a romance about a country where there is no shadow, no antiquity, no mystery, no picturesque and gloomy wrong, not anything but a commonplace prosperity, in broad and simple daylight, as is happily the case with my dear native land ... Romance and poetry, ivy, lichens and wallflowers need ruin to make them grow.'

Nathaniel Hawthorne (extreme right) with his friend ex-Mayor Spiers, in an Oxford garden. The group includes Mrs Hawthorne (extreme left) who disliked having her photograph taken and hid her face.

OPPOSITE: Henry James (1843–1916). A sketch for the oil portrait by Sargent.

Surely one of the greatest names in the story of the Rich Tide was the American expatriate, Henry James (1843–1916). James was born in New York City, the second of five children of Henry James, Sr, the Swedenborgian philosopher. In 1862, after spending much of his childhood travelling and attending a variety of schools in Europe, he entered Harvard Law School, but soon abandoned this for his writing. He had already had short stories published in the *Atlantic Monthly* and had written reviews for the *North American Review* and the newly established *Nation* when, in 1869–70, he made his first extended trip to Britain as an adult where he met several leading literary figures including William Morris, Rossetti and Ruskin.

James completed his first important novel, *Roderick Hudson*, in 1875, and from then on he was to bring out a book or more every year. In the autumn of 1875 he settled briefly in Paris but in the following year moved on to London, where, within two years, he had achieved fame on both sides of the Atlantic as the author of *Daisy Miller*. His feelings for his newly adopted land were varied. He was, for example, inspired by the 'great characteristic of English scenery . . . I should call density of feature. There are no waste details; everything in the landscape is something particular – has a history, has played a part, has a value to the imagination.'

By 1889, James had written some of his greatest novels, which frequently dealt with the experiences of the innocent American expatriate in civilized but corrupt Europe. But he failed to match the popular success of *Daisy Miller* and decided to try his luck in the theatre. Between 1890 and 1895 he wrote seven plays, only two of which ever reached the stage – *The American*, which enjoyed a modest run, and *Guy Dornville*, which, on its first night, resulted in James being cruelly booed by the London audience when he stood up to take a bow. After this humiliation he withdrew from London, renting and eventually purchasing Lamb House in Rye, Sussex. It was to be his home for the rest of his life though he later kept rooms at the Reform Club and had a flat in Chelsea. Frustrated by public indifference to his work he began a series of almost autobiographical stories, some with the theme of writers who know that they possess great talent but who are nevertheless unable to satisfy the limited needs of the public and critics. He also began writing his ghost stories or psychological thrillers, including *The Turn of the Screw*, one of the most chilling stories in the English language.

After 1900 James began the most creative period of his life. Returning to international themes, he produced three large novels, *The Ambassadors*, *Wings of a Dove*, and *The Golden Bowl*. In the early 1900s he spent a year in America, his first visit there for

Lamb House in Rye: the front door and (left) garden room where Henry James wrote many of his novels, by Brian Cook.

twenty years, a visit he wrote about in *The American Scene*, one of his great prose works. He later wrote: 'I found my native land, after so many years interesting, formidable, fearsome and fatiguing, and much more difficult to see and deal with in any extended and various ways than I had supposed . . . It is an extraordinary world . . . an immense impression of material and political power; but almost cruelly charmless in effect, and calculated to make one crouch, ever afterwards, as cravenly as possible, at Lamb House, Rye.'

In 1913 the English-speaking world honoured him on his seventieth birthday and efforts were made to get the Nobel Prize for Literature. These failed but his friends and admirers had him sit for a portrait by his fellow American expatriate, John Singer Sargent. During the First World War he supported the British war effort, visiting hospitals and aiding refugees, and in 1915, as a gesture of solidarity with Britain in the war against the Kaiser, and some say as a protest against American tardiness, he became a British citizen. The following year he suffered a stroke and on his deathbed was awarded the Order of Merit. His ashes were brought back to the United States and interred in the family plot in Cambridge, Massachusetts.

The inscription on Henry James's grave says that he was an 'interpreter of his generation·on both sides of the sea'. The fact is that for several years after his death James remained out of favour in America, the prevailing view there being that his work was lifeless. Fellow writers in particular were very cruel about him. Oscar Wilde said that 'Henry James writes fiction as if it were a painful duty', while William Faulkner noted 'Henry James was one of the nicest old ladies I ever met'. The great cynic H. L. Mencken added 'Henry James would have been vastly improved as a novelist by a few whiffs of the Chicago stockyards' to Mark Twain's damning 'I'd rather be condemned to John Bunyan's heaven than read a James novel'. Patriotic Americans resented both his expatriation and his adoption of British citizenship and it was further said of him that by uprooting himself from his native country he had produced rootless art, not realizing that in fact James's roots were in the mid-Atlantic, or the European-American world. In explaining why so many 'fellow Americans of feeling' emigrated, he in return was very cruel about his native land and other Americans generally. 'There is but one word to use in regard to them – vulgar; vulgar, vulgar. Their ignorance – their stingy, grudging, defiant, attitude towards everything European – their perpetual reference of all things to some American standard or precedent . . . On the other hand, we seem a people of character, we seem to have energy, capacity and

OPPOSITE: Henry James revisits America, a cartoon by Max Beerbohm. '. . . So that in fine, let, without further beating about the bush, me make to myself amazed acknowledgement that, but for the certificate of birth which I have – so very indubitably – *on* me, I might, in regarding, and, as it somewhat were, overseeing, *a l'oeil de voyageur*, these dear good people, find hard to swallow, or even take by subconscious injection, the great idea that I am – oh! ever so indigenously! – one of them. . . .' Reproduced by permission of the National Gallery of Victoria, Melbourne. Pencil, pen and coloured wash drawing, 41.9 × 34.9 cm, purchased 1953.

intellectual stuff in ample measure. But . . . it's the absolute and incredible lack of culture that strikes you in common travelling Americans.'

Gradually, however, James's reputation increased and today he is rightly recognized internationally as one of the creators of the modern novel, and, bridging the gap between the morals, men and manners of the New World and the Old, he was certainly the most important American literary figure of his age. It is, however, interesting that one American biographical dictionary persists in giving his brother, the philosopher and psychiatrist, William James, an entry five times longer than his.

*   *   *

We shall not cease from exploration
And the end of all our exploring
Will be to arrive where we started
And know the place for the first time.
T. S. ELIOT, Little Gidding

Another great intellectual emigrant, central to the Rich Tide, was Thomas Stearns Eliot (1888–1965), born and raised in St Louis, Missouri, the son of wealthy Unitarian parents whose roots were in New England. Encouraged by his mother, herself a minor poet, he took an early interest in poetry. He entered Harvard in 1906 and there he specialized in philosophy, editing and contributing poems to a university magazine. In 1914 he came to Europe, studying first in Germany and then, when war broke out, at Oxford. Following his marriage in 1915, he earned a somewhat precarious living, teaching for a time at a boys' school near London, and after that by working as a clerk for Lloyds Bank.

In London Eliot got to know a fellow expatriate, Ezra Pound, who was at that time involved with the Vorticists, a revolutionary art movement with a strong American flavour. As well as Pound its American participants included the sculptor Jacob Epstein and the photographer Alvin Langdon Coburn (both of whom settled in Britain). One of its moving spirits, Wyndham Lewis, had an American father. Eliot himself became involved and his first poems – 'Preludes' and 'Rhapsody on a Windy Night' – were published in 1915 in *Blast*, the literary organ of the movement. Thanks to Pound he got his first major work including 'The Love Song of J. Alfred Prufrock' published in *Poetry* magazine. These two poets with common American roots exerted an immense influence on modern poetry. Eliot acknowledged Pound's influence in his 1917 publication, *Ezra Pound: His Metric and Poetry*, and revealed that his compatriot had helped on the last draft

T. S. Eliot (1888–1965) by D. B. Wyndham Lewis, 1938.

A scene from Eliot's *Murder in the Cathedral*, 1935.

of 'The Waste Land', Eliot's greatest poem which instantly established him as the leading American poet and which was recognized by Pound himself as the chief masterpiece of the modern movement.

In the early 1920s Eliot reached the height of his achievement. As well as producing some of his finest poetry, including 'The Waste Land', he wrote a number of highly influential critical essays and reviews, some of which appeared in the *Criterion*, a quarterly review that Eliot himself edited and helped to found. In 1927 he became a British citizen because, he said, of his interest in the established church. From this point his work – notably his verse drama, *Murder in the Cathedral* (1935) – was increasingly influenced by his Anglicanism or Anglo-Catholicism. In 1948 he received the Nobel Prize for Literature and the Order of Merit. He was to receive further honours from many countries until his death in 1965.

Eliot shaped the whole development of twentieth-century Anglo-American literature, though there is some substance in the accusation of 'out-Englishing the English' in the process as only a foreigner can.

> And youth is cruel and has no remorse,
> And smiles at situations which it cannot see.
> I smile, of course,
> And go on drinking tea.

Eliot's influence, which spread quickly in the 1920s, is still strong today. As a critic he has been called one of the most successful dictators of literary taste in the history of English

Benjamin Britten and Peter Pears. Oil painting by Kenneth Green, 1943, the year after they returned from the United States.

literature, as he had the priceless ability to express clearly and concisely what others often thought and said but struggled to articulate. As a playwright he helped to revive the verse drama, which he increasingly developed after his confirmation in the Anglican church, in the hope of reaching a wider audience. Of his own work and his Anglo-Americanism he said, 'I'd say that my poetry has obviously more in common with my distinguished contemporaries in America, than with anything written in my generation in England. That I'm sure of.' He went on to say of his poetry, 'It wouldn't be what it is, and I imagine it wouldn't be so good; putting it as modestly as I can, it wouldn't be what it is if I'd been born in England, and it wouldn't be what it is if I'd stayed in America. It's a combination of things. But in its sources, in its emotional springs, it comes from America.'

In Stephen Spender's autobiography, *World Within World*, he recalls that while in America his friend, the poet W. H. Auden (1907–73), 'published an essay arguing that the modern creative writer must be international, and probably, celibate; and implying that the literary pilgrimage of Henry James to Europe was now reversed, for today the European writer should come to America'.

Auden of course took this route with Christopher Isherwood (1904–86) as had Aldous Huxley (1885–1963) and Spender himself – four of the brilliant generation of English writers and poets who emerged in the 1930s.

W. H. Auden. Pen and ink drawing by the American artist Don Bachardy, 1967.

Born in York, Auden went to Christ Church, Oxford, where he was much influenced by T. S. Eliot's work. He published his first volume of poems in 1930 and during the next decade emerged as the poetic spokesman of his generation. By 1939 in the face of the rise of fascism, Auden had become disillusioned with the power of poetry to change the world and felt restricted by the English scene and his position as the court poet of the Left. So, in January 1939, he set sail for New York with his friend and collaborator, Christopher Isherwood, vowing never to return to Britain. Many years later Auden gave his reason for emigrating: 'I would say that I felt the situation for me was becoming impossible. I couldn't grow up. That English life is for me a family life, and I love my family but I don't want to live with them.'

Given the timing of their departure, Auden and Isherwood, like Benjamin Britten who came to America shortly afterwards, were widely criticized and accused, by Evelyn Waugh among others, of being cowards. It is not easy to pinpoint the exact reasons for their emigration to America. Auden and Isherwood had been profoundly impressed by New York during a short visit in 1938. Clearly they were drawn to the vitality of the city, and like millions of other emigrants they probably saw America as the land of the future, the land of opportunity. It has been said that Isherwood, who spent much of his time abroad, enjoyed being a foreigner. Rather like Henry James in England, he could get the best of both worlds in the United States. He could live as a foreigner in a country which spoke English and where his work could be commissioned and purchased. Furthermore, he was attracted by the opportunity of film work in Hollywood. And later, writing autobiographically in the third person, Isherwood described the particular attraction of New York as 'a setting in which his public personality would function more freely, more successfully than it could ever have functioned in London'.

Ironically, Isherwood soon left New York and Auden for California. As Spender has written, 'Auden and Isherwood had gone to America together, but, having got there each selected that part of the country to live in which was most suited to his temperament – with the result that they were the whole breadth of the continent apart. Auden chose the fog and humidity and darkness of New York, with its exaggerated contrasts of old buildings and ramshackle tenements, out of which, as from a squalid backyard, skyscrapers rocket like sunflowers towards the higher air filled with the sun. Isherwood, with his love of the bronzed, the sandy and the naked, had made his home at Santa Monica near Los Angeles' (*World Within World*).

In America Auden supported himself mainly through teaching, though his creative talents did not dry up. Some people prefer his earlier English work but in America he executed some of his most famous work, such as the long poem, 'The Age of Anxiety', which won a Pulitzer Prize. As a teacher and a poet he made an impact on a generation of young American poets. Indeed, America's gain was Britain's loss – that is, if Spender was correct when he wrote in 1950 that Auden's 'absence from England was followed by a decline in intellectual effort and technical accomplishment by the younger English poets'. If this was indeed a case of cause and effect, it would have been slightly remedied by Auden's return to Oxford as Professor of Poetry in 1956. In 1971 Oxford awarded him an honorary D.Litt. and the following year, and shortly before his death, he turned his back on New York and returned to live in rooms at his old college. He explained to his friends that, while he was not disillusioned with America, he was 'nervous of being mugged in the streets of New York'. After his death on 28 September 1973 one of his obituaries stated that 'in spite of long residence abroad Auden remained unalterably, unmistakably English'.

Isherwood stayed on in America until his death in January 1986. Many years before, Spender had written: 'In their physical environment and in their philosophical development, the vastness of America had offered Auden and Isherwood each his opportunity. In these two simple facts one learns a great deal about America.'

*   *   *

Two of the most notable Anglo-American painters were, like James and Eliot, American-born but felt the need to go and live in Britain to give full expression to their talents. The first was Benjamin West (1738–1820), born near Springfield, Pennsylvania, of Quaker parents. As a young child he displayed an exceptional talent for drawing, and by the age of sixteen he had received his first commission. In 1760, he left America for Italy to improve his technique, where, armed with letters of introduction and taking advantage of his charm and good looks, he was admitted to the best society. As the first American of note to study art in Italy, he was something of a novelty. (Apparently the blind Cardinal Albani assumed that he was a Red Indian.) West spent three years studying in Rome, Florence, Bologna and Venice. In Rome he came under the influence of the circle of neo-classical history painters, including the Scottish expatriate artist Gavin Hamilton, who was one of its leaders.

West arrived in England in August 1763 for what was intended to be a brief visit. He remained there for 57 years. His plan was to continue his artistic education at the St Martin's Lane Academy before returning to Pennsylvania, but after receiving praise for a full-length portrait of General Robert Monckton he was urged by Joshua Reynolds and the painter Richard Wilson to show the picture with two of his Italian history paintings at the Spring Gardens Exhibition of the Society of Artists in 1765. His work met with a good response from the public and critics, most of whom had not previously encountered an accomplished American artist. Confident that he could live off his art, he decided to stay in England and in 1765 he joined the leading ranks of British painters as a member of the recently founded Incorporated Society of Artists, the forerunner of the Royal Academy.

West was largely preoccupied with painting portraits, the

Self-portrait by Benjamin West, *c.* 1770.

staple of the eighteenth-century artist, but to his pleasure he was commissioned by Archbishop Drummond to depict a historical subject – *The Landing of Agrippina at Brindisi*. The Archbishop was so pleased with the finished work that he introduced West and the picture to George III, and the result was that the King commissioned West to paint *The Final Departure of Regulus from Rome* for the Royal Collection, a picture which appeared, in 1769, at the first exhibition of the Royal Academy, of which West was a founder member. It was the beginning of his long association with the monarch. In 1772 he, an American, was appointed Historical Painter to the King with a handsome salary of £1,000 a year, and thereafter he spent much of his time undertaking commissions – both portraits and historical paintings – for the Crown. There are indeed many of his paintings still in the Royal Collection.

In 1792 he succeeded Sir Joshua Reynolds as the President of the Royal Academy, a position he occupied, with only a single year's break, until 1820. But in the early years of the nineteenth century, he had disagreements with the increasingly insane King, which, to his great personal sadness, eventually deprived him of both his royal patronage and a genuine friend. West himself died in March 1820 only months before George III's own death, and his body lay in state at the Royal Academy before being buried with great honour in the cathedral crypt of St Paul's, near the tomb of Sir Joshua Reynolds.

Despite his rather uncouth accent West was a charming man of immense dignity. Though he liked to see himself as the 'American Raphael', he was not really a great artist, his paintings being both too formal and lacking in vitality. It has been said that he was very fortunate that his work appealed to George III's somewhat limited tastes. Nevertheless, this unknown figure who

The Final Departure of Regulus from Rome by West, *c.* 1767.

The American School (Benjamin West's school in London) by Matthew Pratt. The Metropolitan Museum of Art, gift of Samuel P. Avery, 1897.

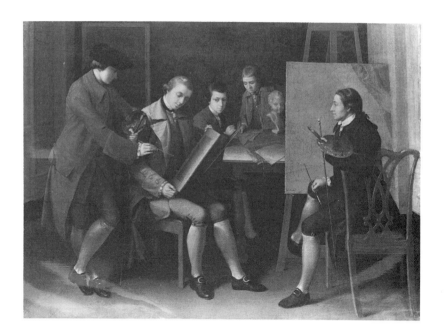

The Death of General Wolfe by Benjamin West.

had come to a London where American artists were not held in high esteem eventually reached the pinnacle of the British art establishment. Although he did not return to America, he did not neglect his native country's art. Three generations of his compatriots not only followed his example by coming to England but also received his hospitality and assistance. Among them, looking for patronage and a market as much as for guidance, were many of the leading American painters of the late eighteenth and early nineteenth centuries such as John Singleton Copley, Ralph Earl, Matthew Pratt, Gilbert Stuart, Charles Willson Peale, Rembrandt Peale, Samuel Morse, Washington Allston, John Trumbull, Thomas Sully, Robert Fulton and Charles R. Leslie (who in his youth worked as a colourist for Alexander Wilson and who painted an enchanting picture of Queen Victoria receiving the Sacrament at her Coronation and another of the Christening of the Princess Royal).

However limited he may have been as an artist, West has an important position in Anglo-American art history. With John Singleton Copley, he effected a revolution in historical painting in Britain and the attitude to it of subsequent generations of painters on both sides of the Atlantic. For example, in 1770 he painted a picture of the death of General Wolfe at Quebec. But instead of depicting his figures in the usual classical robes he broke with convention and gave them contemporary clothes. While George III, Reynolds and others were initially shocked by this innovation, the painting stimulated a movement away from classical subjects to a highly heroic rendering of national history. He did not, however, fully exploit the new genre, and this was left to Copley. Often considered to be the first really great American painter, Copley was born and brought up in or near Boston. Encouraged by Reynolds and West, who had seen the paintings he submitted to the Society of Artists' exhibitions in London between 1766 and 1772, he came to Europe in 1774. After spending a year in Rome studying Raphael, partly under West's Scottish mentor Gavin Hamilton, he settled in London. In America he had developed a highly effective realist 'New England' style of portraiture, but Europe quickly gave him a style acceptable to British tastes, and he soon established himself as a successful historical and portrait painter.

Copley's *Brook Watson and the Shark* exhibited at the Royal Academy in 1778 broke all the accepted rules of history painting, some art historians arguing that it was even more revolutionary than West's *Death of Wolfe*. The hero of the piece, like West's picture, was contemporary not classical, but unlike West's the hero was not a national figure, nor was the action of great

Brook Watson and the Shark by John Singleton Copley, 1765

historical or moral importance. The painting, which, as Ellis Waterhouse has pointed out, relied totally on the dramatic rendering of the subject, looked ahead to the great French romantic painters of the 1820s. That many of Copley's subsequent major paintings dealt with scenes from contemporary national history was in fact largely because the engravings from them sold well to a patriotic public.

That Copley and West modernized British historical painting was probably due more to their New World innocence rather than to any distinct American style. It is certainly remarkable that at the height of the British–American conflict Copley was being made a member of the Royal Academy of which West was President. Both were friends of the King throughout the war – and this all in the age of Reynolds, Allan Ramsay and Gainsborough. As Waterhouse has written, they were like 'forerunners of some of the characters in Henry James's novels: they came to Europe full of eagerness and appreciation but with minds free from the incubus of inherited tradition in the matter of high art'.

Copley himself, in a letter to a friend in 1780, expressed the dilemma. 'Poor America! I hope the best but I fear the worst. Yet certain I am She will finally emerge from her present Callamity and become a Mighty Empire, and it is a pleasing reflection that I shall stand amongst the first of the Artists that shall have led the Country to the knowledge and cultivation of the fine Arts, happy

OPPOSITE: *Boy with a Squirrel* by Copley, probably the first picture painted in America to be publicly exhibited abroad, winning the admiration of the sophisticated London art world at the Spring Gardens exhibition of the Society of Artists in 1766. Joshua Reynolds is reputed to have said that 'he did not know one painter at home who had all the advantages that Europe could give him, that could equal it' and to Copley that he was 'capable of producing such a piece by the mere efforts of your own Genius, with the advantages of the example and instruction which you could have in Europe, that you would be a valuable acquisition to the Art, and one of the first painters in the world, provided you could receive those Aids before it was too late in life, and before your Manner and Taste were corrupted or fixed by working in your little way at Boston.'

Samuel F. B. Morse (1791–1872), one of West's disciples, was born in Charlestown, Massachusetts, and graduated from Yale in 1810. A year later he travelled to England with Allston and and studied with West and at the Royal Academy. During the war with America in the years 1812–15 he became very anti-British, but, despite this, achieved critical acclaim for his portrait painting and his sculpture, winning a gold medal for the latter from the Royal Society of Arts. Lack of funds eventually drove him to return to America where he was to achieve fame as an inventor and pioneer in the telecommunications field with the Morse code and his electromagnetic recording telegraph which he christened with the famous message 'What hath God wrought'.

Self-portrait by Samuel F. B. Morse

in the pleasing reflection that they will one Day shine with a luster not inferior to what they have done in Greece or Rome in my Native Country.'

Later in the nineteenth century, James McNeill Whistler (1834–1903) left his mark on British art. Whistler came from Lowell, Massachusetts, but spent most of his childhood in St Petersburg, where his father, Major George Washington Whistler, was involved in the laying of the railway line to Moscow. As a boy, Whistler had a passion for drawing which was encouraged by his father, who sent him to the Imperial Academy of Fine Arts. In 1848 Whistler came to London with his family to attend the wedding of his sister Deborah to Seymour Hayden, a leading surgeon and accomplished amateur etcher. On a second visit, Whistler was left behind to complete his education first at a school near Bristol, and then in London. But when his father died in 1849 his mother decided to return to the United States. After attending a local school in Connecticut, Whistler was selected for the Military Academy at West Point, but was dismissed for deficiency in chemistry. (He later said, 'Had silicon been a gas, I would have been a major general'.)

J. M. Whistler (1834–1903) by Walter Greaves.

In 1855, following a brief period as a draughtsman for the Coastal Survey, where he learned to etch, he went to Paris to study art. Settling on the bohemian Left Bank, he entered the studio of Charles Gleyre, and published his first set of etchings – *The French Set* – in 1858. These were praised by Parisian artists such as Henri Fantin-Latour, but, despite this recognition, he decided to move on to London, a decision partly prompted by his failure to get his first major painting, *At the Piano*, accepted by the Paris Salon. He moved into a house in Chelsea close to the Thames, where he painted some of the most outstanding and important pictures of the period. But, though his etchings were nearly always well received, his oil paintings, which increasingly defied established artistic convention, provoked controversy. In 1862, his *Symphony in White No. 1: The White Girl*, a painting partly influenced by Rossetti and the Pre-Raphaelites, was rejected by the Royal Academy. It eventually appeared at the Salon de Réfusés in Paris in 1863 where it almost caused as much of a sensation as Manet's famous *Déjeuner sur l'herbe*, and afterwards Whistler wrote his first letter to the press defending his work. It was to be the start of his long and often heated public correspondence with critics and public alike.

Whistler possessed a great talent for design which was recognized by the wealthy shipowner, Frederick Richard Leyland, who commissioned him to produce a series of decorative screens. In 1876, Whistler began work on Leyland's London house in Prince's Gate, where he created his famous Peacock Room. The controversial interior which looked ahead to the Art Nouveau of the 1890s stimulated great publicity but the commission ended in a quarrel and a permanent break between Whistler and his first important patron.

Meanwhile, his oil paintings, especially his experiments in colour harmonies, like *The Nocturnes*, fuelled by his often outrageous behaviour continued to provoke controversy. In 1872, after the Royal Academy had displayed a reluctance to accept his

Whistler's *Symphony in White No 1: the White Girl*, described by the artist to George du Maurier as . . . a woman in a beautiful white cambric dress, standing against a window which filters the lights through a transparent white muslin curtain – but the figure receives a strong light from the right and therefore the picture, barring the red hair, is one gorgeous mass of brilliant white.'

LEFT: A Whistler etching of the Lower Thames.

The Peacock Room by Whistler, originally the dining room in the London mansion of Frederick Leyland, Whistler's most important patron during the 1870s, now in the Freer Gallery of Art at the Smithsonian in Washington.

Arrangement in Grey and Black No. 1: The Artist's Mother, he never again submitted a picture to that institution. When John Ruskin commented, 'I have seen and heard much of cockney impudence before now but never expected to hear a coxcomb ask two hundred guineas for flinging a pot of paint in the public's face' by producing the painting entitled *Nocturne in Black and Gold: The Falling Rocket* (*c*.1874), Whistler took Ruskin to court on a charge of libel. He won the case but, as much for his caustic behaviour in the witness box as for the triviality of the case in the eyes of the law, was awarded only a farthing's damages. The affair, described in his *The Gentle Art of Making Enemies* (in which his famous phrase, 'I'm not arguing with you: I'm telling you', appears), confirmed his reckless reputation, but also provided him with a stage to air his views on art to the British public. He thereby made himself known as the chief protagonist of 'art for art's sake', as opposed to the prevailing Victorian view, articulated by Ruskin, which emphasized the moral responsibilities of the artist. (Ruskin's own view of America was to the point: 'Though I have kind invitations enough to visit America, I could not, even for a couple of months, live in a country so miserable as to possess no castles.')

Despite his victory, the trial put a severe strain on Whistler's financial resources, and in May 1879 he was declared bankrupt. He lost his house, and many of his works were dispersed at auction. However, that same year he was commissioned by the Fine Art Society to produce a series of etchings of Venice, which were successfully exhibited in London in the 1880s and, to great acclaim, he held his first large exhibition of watercolours. The following year he delivered his famous *Ten O'Clock Lecture* at which he argued his aesthetic credo, and re-established his reputation.

Gradually Whistler received more and more recognition for his work. He was elected President of the Society of British Artists, and quickly increased the prestige of that institution. In 1889, the year of his marriage, he held a large and successful exhibition in New York. Growing recognition of his ability was reflected by the flood of commissions that came in, and by the high prices his earlier works, once shunned by the public and press, now fetched. It was a period when modesty was not his strong-point. A newly introduced female enthusiast is reputed to have said to him, 'I only know of two painters in the world, yourself and Velasquez.' 'Why,' answered Whistler in dulcet tones, 'why drag in Velasquez?' And in answer to a lady who said that a landscape reminded her of his work he replied, 'Yes, madam, Nature is creeping up'. In 1893–4 he also began a series of portraits. But few were finished when his wife, afflicted by chronic illness, eventually died in 1896. Whistler was too distracted and upset to complete his commissions, but he still kept his wit: 'I'm lonesome. They've all died off. I have hardly a warm personal enemy left.' In the last years of the century his own health declined, and after trips to Corsica and Algeria failed to improve it he returned to London where he died on 17 July 1903.

Whistler remains an enigma. Like the other American expatriates he is hard to categorize. How much the individuality of their work has to do with their American backgrounds is difficult to assess, but they probably benefited from coming from a country that lacked a strong literary and artistic tradition. Whistler, unlike West and Copley, was not an innocent from the New World, but a true cosmopolitan. His broad upbringing put him in touch with European culture at an early age and at the same time gave him the wider outlook which enabled him to draw from a more diverse range of experiences than most other artists of his time, whether American or European. The problems in categoriz-

'Afternoon Swimming' by David
Hockney. Lithograph in colours,
1979.

OPPOSITE: *Nocturne in Blue and Gold*
by James McNeill Whistler.

ing Whistler have often led to him being described as a mid-
Atlantic artist. In reality, he was just Whistler.

Since the Second World War the artistic pilgrimages of West,
Copley and Whistler from America to Europe have arguably been
reversed. For many British and European artists the United States
has become the centre of creative vitality. Attracted by its vibrant
popular culture (and by the images presented by that culture –
Hollywood movies, rock and roll, etc.), by the innovations of
American artists such as Jackson Pollock or Roy Lichtenstein, and
no doubt by the lure of the dollar, several British artists have lived,
worked, exhibited or visited the United States during the last forty
or so years.

In 1963 the Yorkshire-born painter David Hockney (b.1937)
moved to California and has since become one of the leading
figures in the Anglo-American art world. Born in Bradford, he
studied at Bradford College of Art and then at the Royal College of
Art where the work and views of his fellow student, the American
R. B. Kitaj, made a strong impression. Hockney visited New York
for the first time in 1961 and instantly fell in love with America.
Two years later, seeking a more uninhibited and hedonistic
lifestyle than he had been able to find in London, and inspired by
the images he had seen of California in books, magazines and
photographs, he decided to move to Los Angeles.

Later he described how he was immediately captivated by the city: 'In Los Angeles, there were no ghosts; there were no paintings of Los Angeles. People then didn't even know what it looked like. And when I was there, they were still finishing some of the big freeways. I remember seeing, within the first week, a ramp of freeway going into the air, and I suddenly thought: ''My God, this place needs its Piranesi; Los Angeles could have a Piranesi, so here I am!'' ' (interview published in *The Listener*, 22 May 1975). He soon achieved this aim. In his paintings of the city's buildings, its domestic interiors and swimming pools he has presented us with a strong image of Los Angeles that few if any native American artists have been able to equal.

Like many modern members of the Rich Tide, Hockney has not neglected his native country. He has returned to live in London on more than one occasion and he has always been a frequent visitor. He is an English artist but one for whom America has been a constant source of inspiration.

*   *   *

Dickens, James, West, Copley, Eliot, Hockney and the rest are exemplars of the artistic and literary talent that, irrespective of origin, has contributed much to Western culture. Some men thrive in their own environment; others need to escape or have the impetus of the strange and unfamiliar to bring out their best. Paris, Rome, Venice have long attracted the emigrant, English-speaking muse, but that has tended to be a by-way for them. The richness that has come from the American exile in Britain, and from the British exile in America, has added a special dimension to the culture of both peoples, and has been more deeply lasting.

OPPOSITE: *Ellen Terry as Lady Macbeth.* Oil painting by John Singer Sargent. 'My portrait as Lady Macbeth by Sargent used to hang in the alcove in the Beefsteak Room when it was not away at some exhibition, and the artist and I have often supped beneath it. I have always loved the picture and think it is far more like me than any other.' *(see page 272)*

CHAPTER NINE

From Drury Lane to Tinseltown

But England, not Spain or France, gained control of most of the North American continent, and the theatre when it came like nearly everything else in the new land was wholly English in origins.

BARNARD HEWITT, *Theatre USA*

During the early nineteenth century the American theatre was largely dominated by British actors and actresses some of whom toured as established stars, while others had emigrated to the United States, often after failure or involvement in scandal in their native country. These performers brought the wonders of the London stage to American audiences and had an important long-term impact on the development of American drama, setting the standards which native American players had to match.

The first notable English actor to come to America was the eccentric dipsomaniac and strolling player, George Frederick Cooke (1756–1812), who sailed for the United States after twenty years as a lead at Covent Garden. He was the first of the proponents of the so-called 'star system', an important feature of nineteenth-century American theatre, whereby a noted actor or actress would tour cities nationwide, performing the parts by which they were best known – in Cooke's case, Richard III – and supported by members of the local theatrical company. Cooke was followed by actors and actresses of the calibre of Edmund Kean, Junius Brutus Booth, William Charles Macready, and Fanny and Charles Kemble.

The eccentric genius and tragedian, Junius Brutus Booth (1796–1852), was born in St Pancras, child of a London theatrical family. In a career that began in Drury Lane when he was only seventeen, he became a well-known rival of the great Edmund Kean. But, after abandoning his wife for a Bond Street flower girl – something that, at that time, even actors could not do – he left in disgrace for America, but there rapidly picked his career up again, making his New York début as Richard III at the Park Theatre in

OPPOSITE: George Frederick Cooke as Richard III. Oil painting by Thomas Sully, during Cooke's American tour.

1821. From then on he played almost entirely in the United States. Successful though he was, his memory is largely obscured by the famous and infamous exploits of two of his three actor sons. One, Edwin Booth, became one of America's first great tragedians and one of the first to make an impression on the London stage. Another, John Wilkes Booth, who inherited his father's instability but not his acting ability, cast himself as Lincoln's real-life assassin during a performance of *Our American Cousins* (produced by the English actress Laura Keene) at Ford's Theatre, Washington, on the evening of 14 April 1865. He shouted as he jumped from Lincoln's box to the stage: 'Sic semper tyrannis! The South is avenged!' (The fact that Booth declared in Latin later convinced the cynical Matthew Arnold that there was still hope for America.) Booth was killed two weeks later when troops surrounded and burned down the Virginia barn in which he was hiding.

Also more directly involved in real tragedy was the first American-born tragedian to achieve stardom, and media notoriety, on both sides of the Atlantic, Edwin Forrest (1806–72). Forrest was born in Philadelphia, the poor son of a runaway scion of a landed Scottish family. Although he is often remembered for his at times bullish anglophobia, his rise to the top of the American theatre owed much to the Rich Tide. He finally established himself in New Orleans at the theatre of the English-born impresario, James H. Caldwell. And when Forrest came to the Albany Theatre in New York in the autumn of 1825 he was given the opportunity to play seconds to Edmund Kean's leads: Titus to the great Englishman's Brutus; Richmond to his Richard; Iago to his Othello. The experience was to be one of the major formative influences on the American's career. According to one commentator Forrest's romantic and passionate but realistic style was inspired by Kean's performances. Kean encouraged Forrest to experiment and so impressed was he by Forrest's reading of Iago that he asked him: 'In the name of God, boy, where did you get that?' Forrest replied humbly but proudly: 'It is something of my own.' 'Well,' said Kean, 'everybody who speaks the part thereafter must do it just so.' Later at a banquet Kean exclaimed, 'I have met one actor in this country, a young man named Edwin Forrest, who gave proofs of a decided genius for his profession, and will, I believe, rise to a great eminence'.

The English actor's pronouncement was as prophetic as it was sincere, as Forrest soon became one of the most popular figures on the American stage, especially with the less refined theatregoers. He was a dark-haired, handsome man who always tended to choose strong, masculine roles which he played vigorously in a

Edwin Forrest as Metamora. Oil painting by Frederick Styles Agate, 1830.

deep, stentorian voice. Against the background of his humble beginnings, he was often accused of playing to the masses with a deliberate flaunting of his fine physique and use of an uneducated style of speech.

Finding, in consequence, many of the standard roles too limited, Forrest encouraged the writing of new plays, particularly with an American theme, that would suit his vibrant style of acting. In 1829 he offered 'a prize for the best tragedy in five acts of which the hero . . . shall be an aboriginal of this country'. The first prize was awarded to John Augustus Stone for *Metamora*, which was premièred in New York in December 1829. Forrest was to play the leading role in it for nearly forty years thereafter.

A contemporary English actor, George Vandenhoff, described his performance thus:

> His voice surged and roared like the angry sea, lashed into fury by a storm; till, as it reached its boiling, seething climax, in which the serpent hiss of hate was heard, at intervals, amidst its louder, deeper, hoarser tones, it was like the falls of Niagara, in its tremendous downsweeping cadence: it was a whirlwind, a tornado, a cataract of illimitable rage.

Forrest's popularity increased rapidly and in 1836–7 he toured England with great success. He played thirty-two nights at Drury Lane. 'The approbation of my Shakespeare parts gives me peculiar pleasure,' he wrote to a friend, 'as it refutes the opinions very confidently expressed by a certain *clique* at home that I would fail in those characters before a London audience.' Forrest reached the peak of his popularity in the late 1840s, but his reputation was severely damaged by the horrific and infamous events that became known as the Astor Place Riot of 1849. The riot was the product of the rivalry which had built up over the years between Forrest and the British tragedian William Charles Macready (1793–1873).

This conflict was part and parcel of Forrest's catering to the masses in theatres like the Bowery and the National. New York's gentry, by contrast, patronized the Park or Burton's and their many foreign, particularly British, actors. Macready, the son of a provincial English manager had made his début in the Covent Garden Theatre in 1816 and had established himself as one of the great rivals of Edmund Kean. A proud man, in total contrast to Forrest, he always played the gentleman's role and had gained success in tours of the States in 1826 and 1843. During Forrest's first British tour he had written of Macready's 'native kindness' and 'great refinement and good breeding'. However, professional rivalry between the two men grew into personal bitterness when, after Forrest's later tour of Britain in 1845, he blamed the lack of acclaim from London and Edinburgh critics (he was hissed by an Edinburgh audience for his Hamlet) on the machinations by Macready. While the latter denied this, Forrest held a deep grudge and thus, when Macready was billed to play at the Astor Place Opera House, the New York masses rallied to demonstrate against their hero. Meanwhile the gentry flocked to hear the distinguished visiting actor.

On the night itself, the house was packed and the gallery was also packed, but by – it was alleged – paid supporters of Forrest. When Macready appeared on stage he was shouted down, missiles were thrown at him and the performance was abandoned.

Mr MACREADY as SHYLOCK,

MERCHANT OF VENICE,

ACT I SCENE 3

Persuaded against his will by, among others, Washington Irving, Macready again appeared on stage on 10 May 1849 at the Opera House. While he again was hissed and booed, more ominously, a huge crowd gathered outside and, when they tried to storm the building, the cavalry and the militia were called in; there was firing, riot and panic ending with several dead and many seriously injured.

As a result, Forrest, though criticized by the authorities, became even more the darling of the masses, who, to quote one assessment, 'looked upon him as their champion against the tyranny of the English'. Macready himself wisely decided never to appear in America again. Forrest's long-term popularity suffered, however, though he continued to get the support of the occupants of the cheaper seats. He continued to perform until shortly before his death in December 1872. What he had achieved was, with Edwin Booth, to end the monopoly by British actors and actresses of the leading roles in the American theatre. At the same time, on his British tours, he brought the American style of romantic acting to Britain, laying a path for other American actors and actresses such as John and Ethel Barrymore and Walter Hampden to follow his example and become stars of the English stage.

Despite the emergence of native-born stars like Forrest, visiting English players continued to exert a considerable influence on American drama. In the late nineteenth century, American theatre was, for example, enriched by the frequent tours of two of Britain's greatest thespians – the actor-manager, Henry Irving (1838–1905), and his legendary leading lady, Ellen Terry (1847–1928).

Ellen Terry, the grandmother of John Gielgud, was the most beautiful and talented English actress of her time. Born in Coventry on 27 February 1847, the third of eleven children of actor parents, she made her first stage appearance at the age of nine in *The Winter's Tale* for the company of Edmund Kean's son, Charles, at the Princess's Theatre in London. In 1861, after a spell in the English provinces, she joined the Haymarket Theatre company and established herself as a leading lady, but in 1864 she created a great scandal when she left in the middle of a run to marry the artist George Frederick Watts, who was twenty-seven years her senior. It was a poor match and after only ten months they parted company, and Terry made a brief return to the theatre before quitting once again to go off and live in the country with Edward Godwin, by whom she had a son and a daughter.

In 1874, prompted by her considerable debts, she made a brilliant comeback on the London stage in Charles Reade's *The*

Henry Irving 'his face . . . alive with raffish humour and mischief' by J. P. Lapage. Ellen Terry called this portrait 'Irving at play'.

Wandering Heir. From there she went from strength to strength, giving many notable performances including one as Portia. In 1877, after divorcing Watts, she made another brief and unsuccessful marriage before the actor-manager Henry Irving, who had just obtained the tenancy of the Lyceum, took her on as his leading lady in 1878.

Irving, born John Henry Brodribb, had made his début on the London stage in 1866 after a long apprenticeship in the provinces. In 1870 he was engaged as the leading man of the old Lyceum by the American H. L. ('Colonel') Bateman, who had taken over the theatre in order to launch his daughter Isabel's theatrical career. Irving soon established himself as one of the major stars of the London stage, his 1874 Hamlet causing a sensation. His 200 consecutive performances doubled the record that had been set in New York ten years earlier by Edwin Booth. When Bateman died, Irving took over the management of the Lyceum and, with Terry to help him, dominated the London theatrical scene for the next twenty-five years.

Under Irving's guidance, Terry played the parts which established her reputation as one of the greats of the English stage –

Henry Irving and Ellen Terry in Goldsmith's *The Vicar of Wakefield*.

Beatrice and Portia, Olivia and Viola – and in 1883 she was the star of Irving's sensational first American tour, making her début as Queen Henrietta in *Charles I* at the Star Theatre, New York, on 31 October. It was the first of seven major tours of the United States which they made together playing all their famous roles, and the first time an actor-manager had brought with him a complete company equipped with scenery and costumes. Irving also brought to America the innovations in staging and production which he had introduced at the Lyceum. Of their novelty, Ellen Terry later remarked: 'We were pioneers, and we were *new*; to be new is everything in America.'

Their appearance in the United States was an auspicious

occasion for the American theatre, and their first nights in New York at the Star Theatre were greeted with tremendous enthusiasm. Tickets for the performances were touted for up to five times their face value. As in England, Irving's unique acting style divided the critics. No one, however, could doubt that he had his audiences in America completely under his spell. As one American critic put it: 'His success with the public last night was most emphatic. He was not only applauded, but he was cheered and called before the curtain again and again . . .' It is simply a matter of fact that Mr Irving held his audience under complete control whenever he was upon the stage.' The crowds were equally enthusiastic about Ellen Terry, and she soon became as popular a figure in America as she was in Britain. Of her Portia the eminent American theatre critic, William Winter, wrote: 'Ellen Terry embodied Portia . . . the essential womanliness of that character was for the first time in the modern theatre adequately interpreted and portrayed. Upon many play-going observers indeed the wonderful wealth of beauty that is in the part came like a noble and passionate surprise.'

While Irving retired in 1902, this did not stop Ellen Terry successfully touring America five years later as Lady Cecily Wayneflete in *Captain Brassbound's Conversion*, a part specially written for her by George Bernard Shaw. In the same year she married a young American actor, James Carew, a union which, again unsuccessful, ended after three years. Later, after retiring as a full-time actress, she made further tours of America as a lecturer on Shakespeare. All in all she spent nearly five years in the United States and at one point said, 'I often feel that I am half-American'.

Terry's acting prowess was officially, if belatedly, recognized in 1925 when she was made Dame Ellen Terry, the first actress to receive this accolade, just as Irving had been the first actor to be knighted.

When she died in July 1928, tributes poured in from all over America. A newspaper in Albany, New York, remarked: 'In Ellen Terry was something more than an exceedingly competent actress. She was a glowing personality; someone who was at the same time, queenly and most human. She was romance, grace, humor. She conjured a high mood of beauty in those who saw and heard her. She dominated an age.' It was this truth, above all, that qualifies Ellen Terry, with Henry Irving, for inclusion in the Rich Tide. Gone were the times when actors and actresses were confined to the stages of one nation alone. Just as film and later television were to have their stars whose reputations knew no frontiers, so Ellen Terry was, above all, a pre-eminent actress of the truly Anglo-American stage.

Lawrence Olivier in 1930.

There have been many other British actors who have made a great impression on the American stage, such as Herbert Beerbohm Tree (1853–1917), Johnston Forbes-Robertson (1853–1937) and, more recently, John Gielgud (b.1904) and Laurence Olivier (b.1907). Gielgud made his American début as the Grand Duke Alexander in *The Patriot* at the Majestic Theatre, New York, on 19 January 1928, while his Hamlet, performed at the Empire Theatre there in 1936, was his first real triumph on the American stage. Olivier made his American debut a year later than Gielgud in 1929 at the Eltinge Theatre, New York City, but did not receive wide recognition until 1946 when, with Ralph Richardson (1902–84) he led the Old Vic Company on an enormously successful repertory tour. He, too, was later to become much more widely known through his Hollywood movie roles.

As William C. Young wrote:

Laurence Olivier bestrides the mid-twentieth century stage in both America and England like a colossus. He has been called the greatest actor of the twentieth century and few critics would dispute that claim, for he is one of those rare actors who can actually create a character by changing his appearance, his voice, and his mannerisms.

(*Famous Actors and Actresses on the American Stage*, Vol. 2)

The most popular of American duos were Alfred Lunt (1882–1977) and Lynn Fontanne (1887–1983). Lunt made his début in Boston in 1912 and in 1922 married Lynn, who was born

Alfred Lunt and Lynn Fontanne with Noel Coward in *Design for Living*.

in England, had studied with Ellen Terry and who had already appeared on the New York and London stage. They first appeared together in 1923 and from then on were constantly seen in London in plays such as Shaw's *Pygmalion* and Coward's *Design for Living*. Their last West End appearance was at the opening of the new Royalty Theatre in 1960.

The Barrymore family – 'the Royal Family of American Stage' – was perhaps the greatest of the age. John (1882–1942), Ethel (1879–1959) and Lionel (1878–1954) were all descended from Maurice (1847–1905), who was born Herbert Blythe in India of

Mrs Drew in one of her best-known roles, Mrs Malaprop in Sheridan's *The Rivals*.

'Miss Ethel Barrymore, now appearing in *Peter the Great* at the Lyceum.'

RIGHT: John Barrymore as Hamlet in his own production (1925), on his first British appearance. With Constance Collier as Gertrude.

British parents. He came to the United States in 1875, and married Georgina, daughter of John and Louisa Drew. John Barrymore stunned New York and London with his brilliant Hamlet, playing for a record-breaking number of performances in both cities, before turning in the 1920s to concentrate on his film career. His sister Ethel was equally distinguished on both sides of the Atlantic, acting opposite Henry Irving at the Lyceum in London in

1898, while his brother Lionel also had many successful stage roles before turning to more celebrated successes on the screen.

No account of the theatrical relationship would be complete without mention of the great showmen, Sir C. B. Cochran (1872–1951) and P. T. Barnum (1810–91). Cochran, born and bred in Brighton, went to America in 1891 but, failing to make an impression as an actor, moved into theatrical management and in the 1890s opened, with E. J. Henley, a school of acting in New York. After working with the actor-manager Richard Mansfield, he returned to Britain where he set himself up as a theatrical agent and earned his success through the promotion of boxing, wrestling, circuses, revues, music-hall, theatre and ballet, and managing many great acts such as Houdini. He had equal success in the United States taking many Noël Coward plays to Broadway, often with Gertrude Lawrence in the starring role.

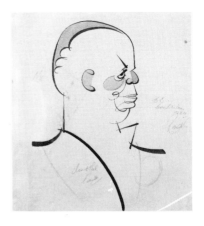

C. B. Cochran. Drawing by R. S. Sherriffs, 1934.

The Connecticut-born Phineas Taylor Barnum, known in his day as 'the great American showman' or 'the prince of hoax and humbug', made three celebrated trips to Britain. In 1844 he brought General Tom Thumb, the dwarf, and several other curiosities to England (and exhibited the famous midget to Queen Victoria and her young family), one of the earliest examples of American showmanship arriving to woo British popular audiences. Fourteen years later Barnum delivered a highly amusing lecture, 'The Science of Money-Making and the Philosophy of Humbug', to a delighted London audience. In 1889 he rounded off his long career by going to London in partnership with his partner Bailey where their circus show performed at Olympia.

American influence in the popular theatre had, by the beginning of this century, extended well beyond the role of individuals. In 1902, for example, Americans controlled no fewer than eight London theatres, and their imported popular entertainment, including many groups such as Wild West and Buffalo Bill shows, were huge favourites. The first purely American performer to bring to Britain a musical art form that was not of British origin had been Thomas Dartmouth (Daddy) Rice (1808–60) and, ironically, that form was 'blackface' or 'nigger minstrel' comedy. He was followed by another group, the Virginia Minstrels, in 1844.

Mr P. T. Barnum and General Tom Thumb.

The advent of modern dance steps and especially ragtime, along with popular songs (eleven of the top sixteen songs in Britain during the twenties were said to be American), together with other American popular cultural traits, set the scene for the coming of the cinema. On the silver screen, while much individual talent moved from Britain to America, there is no doubt in which way the output flowed. It has been estimated that around

Buffalo Bill's Wild West show – a programme cover from a show at Earl's Court, July 1892.

OPPOSITE: Jim Crow as sung by Mr Thomas Dartmouth ('Daddy') Rice (1808–60).

three-quarters of the films shown in British cinemas in the decade up to the beginning of the First World War were American – in a Britain where the weekly cinema audience in 1914 was around seven million. No wonder that the British image of America was a spectacular one and, particularly after the advent of the talkies, was never really to wane right up to the present day.

* * *

The only authorized Edition.

JIM CROW.

Dear Sir.

Enclosed you will find a copy of my Song "Jim Crow"
you have my full permission to Publish it
Yours Resp.t

AS SUNG BY

MR. T. D. RICE,

AT THE

Theatre Royal, Adelphi.

In the popular Drama of a

FLIGHT TO AMERICA

Arranged with appropiate Symphonies & Accompaniments by

J. BLEWITT.

by permission of Mr Rice.

Ent. Sta. Hall.   Price 2/-

LONDON.
Charles Jefferys & Co. Frith Street.

*I remain just one thing, and one thing only – and that is a
clown. It places me on a far higher plane than any politician.*
CHARLIE CHAPLIN

When the British-born Bob Hope said, 'There'll always be an
England, even though it's only in Hollywood,' he was presumably
thinking in part of the Hollywood image of that country. But
equally the list of British-born exiles among the 'tinseltown
greats', in addition to Hope himself, is impressive: Charlie
Chaplin, Stan Laurel, Charles Laughton, Boris Karloff, Ronald
Colman, Cary Grant, James Mason, Stewart Granger (born,
confusingly, James Stewart) and his wife Jean Simmons, Greer
Garson, Olivia de Havilland and her sister Joan Fontaine,
Deborah Kerr, James Mason, David Niven (the archetypal
Englishman, but in fact a Scot from Kirriemuir), C. Aubrey Smith,
and a host of closer contemporaries: Rex Harrison, Elizabeth
Taylor, Richard Burton, Michael Caine, Dudley Moore, Sean
Connery, Joan Collins and many more.

Pre-eminent was Charles Chaplin (1889–1977), born on 16
April 1889 in the slums of Walworth, South London, the son of
music-hall performers who separated when he was only one year
old. At the age of five he made his first stage appearance when his
mother lost her voice in the middle of a singing performance and
he went on stage to keep the audience happy – singing songs and
imitating parts of his mother's repertoire. But, as Chaplin later
remarked, the night of his first appearance on the stage was also
his mother's last. His father died of alcoholism at about the same
time; his mother was unable to cope, and consequently Charles
and his elder half-brother, Sydney, were taken in by an orphan-
age for destitute children. This did not prevent him, at the age of
seven, from returning to the stage as a member of a troupe of child
performers, 'the Eight Lancashire Lads', from where he went on
to play juvenile parts in several London theatre productions.

When he was seventeen Chaplin joined Sydney in the Fred
Karno Company. Karno (1866–1941), an itinerant glazier, ex-
circus hand and acrobat, had built up a number of troupes which
performed comedy routines in Britain and abroad. With Karno,
Chaplin (like another famous member of the company, Stan
Laurel) learned the rudiments of his comic style. As Laurel later
said, 'Fred Karno didn't teach Charlie and me all we know about
comedy. He just taught us most of it.' As one commentator wrote,
'Fred Karno . . . brought pantomime slapstick to the region of

Charlie Chaplin watched by a crowd of actors and sightseers while making *Kid Auto Races*, 1914.

high art. He took the conventional English pantomime with its somewhat arcane British orientations and made it universal.' Chaplin himself always admitted that Karno gave him the solid foundation for his future film-comedy success. Later, Karno with Chaplin and Laurel's help tried to make it in Hollywood, but failed to make an impression. It has been said that he was twenty years too late, but it was due more to his inability to let American directors take any credit for routines which he had pioneered. In consequence, Karno made no films and only enemies in the United States, and soon returned to England and bankruptcy. However, the Hollywood slapstick tradition usually associated with Mack Sennett and others owed much to Karno's influence, as transmitted through Chaplin and Laurel and the company's American tours.

Chaplin, along with his room-mate Laurel, toured America in 1910. On a second tour in 1912–13 Chaplin was recruited by the Keystone Studios after Mack Sennett had seen him brilliantly portraying a drunken party-goer in the show *A Night in a London Music Hall*. Starting on a salary of $150 a week, Chaplin made a slightly disappointing film début as a smooth, debonair villain in *Making a Living*. In his next film, *Kid Auto Races at Venice*, he gave his first performance as the famous Tramp, complete with baggy trousers, small bushy moustache, bowler and cane. In subsequent movies he developed the Tramp's character, the down-at-heel

Charlie Chaplin in *The Gold Rush*, 1924.

little dandy with the waddling walk, the ever-present courtesy to beautiful women, and the unconquerable, if pathetic, attitude to evil. Soon Chaplin established himself as the cinema's leading comedian and in a mere year at Keystone he made 35 films, many of which he also wrote and directed himself. In January 1915 he went to the Essanay Studios for the magnificent salary of $1,250 a week. After a year there he joined Mutual, who guaranteed him a staggering $670,000 a year. Two years later he signed a contract with First National to make 8 films for over $1 million. His fame at this point can also be gauged by the fact that there were numerous Chaplin imitators, a situation which prompted him to preface his films with the words: 'None genuine without his signature.'

In 1919, Chaplin founded United Artists with Mary Pickford, Douglas Fairbanks and D. W. Griffith, and three years later returned triumphantly to Europe shortly after the phenomenal success of his first feature film *The Kid*. By this time he was internationally famous but he was still amazed and delighted with the extent of his popularity. In 1925 he made and starred in the *Gold Rush*, a movie which many critics consider to be his best work.

The emergence of the 'talkie' presented an obvious problem for Chaplin. At first he decided to ignore it, and his next two films seemed to support this decision since *City Lights* (1931) and *Modern Times* (1936) were both silent (apart from some sound effects) yet had great commercial and critical success. It was only in 1940 that he made his first feature with spoken dialogue – *The Great Dictator*, a satirical attack on Hitler and fascism. In the film this English-American genius gave his last performance as the Tramp, thus marking the end of an epoch in film comedy.

Charlie Chaplin with D. W. Griffith, Mary Pickford, and Douglas Fairbanks Snr., at the historic formation of United Artists.

From his earliest days in Hollywood Chaplin's fame was to be accompanied by controversy. During the First World War he was unfairly criticized for not returning to Britain for military service, though in fact he did volunteer but was rejected for medical reasons. Again, moral purists were shocked by his marital affairs and his liking for beautiful young girls. In 1918 he married Mildred Harris, a sixteen-year-old film extra, and after their divorce two years later he married another sixteen-year-old, Lillita McMurray (Lita Grey). This marriage produced two sons but ended in a legal separation after three years. In 1936, when Chaplin was in his late forties, he secretly married for a third time – on this occasion, the 25-year-old Paulette Goddard. Their marriage was not revealed for some time, but ended after six years, in 1942. Just before their separation, a paternity suit was brought against Chaplin by a young actress, Joan Barry. While he was cleared of another charge of transporting another minor across state lines for immoral purposes, he was ruled the father of the child. Meanwhile he had met and married Oona O'Neill, the eighteen-year-old-daughter of the American playright, Eugene O'Neill.

On other fronts, conservative elements in America were

Charlie Chaplin in *The Great Dictator*, 1940.

offended by Chaplin's satire on capitalism and the assembly line, in his 1936 film, *Modern Times*. During the Second World War when he was one of the first to advocate opening a second front, rumours circulated that he was a communist. After the release of his pacifist film *Monsieur Verdoux* in 1947 some American right-wingers, fuelled by the 'reds under the bed' paranoia of the McCarthy era, led a vicious smear campaign against Chaplin, who was subpoena'd by the House Un-American Activities Committee to testify on his alleged communist affiliations. Despite a guaran-tee from Chaplin that he was not a communist or a member, at any time, of any political party or organization, the accusations and demands for his deportation did not abate. In 1952 when Chaplin and his wife were sailing to England for the London

Chaplin arriving with his wife and family for a premiere of *A Countess from Hong Kong*, at the Carlton Cinema, London, 1967.

première of *Limelight*, he learned that on his return to America he would be denied a re-entry visa unless he submitted to an inquiry to prove his moral worth. Incensed, Chaplin vowed never to return to the United States, deciding to settle with his large family in Switzerland.

He made two disappointing films in England – *A King in New York*, a bitter attack on America, and *The Countess from Hong Kong*, ironically made with American money. Both films failed critically and at the box office. In 1972, twenty years after his break with America, Chaplin returned to accept a special Academy Award for the 'incalculable effect he has had on making motion pictures the art form of this century'. He was rapturously received at the Oscar ceremony and everywhere else he went; an enormous party was given in his honour at New York's Philharmonic Hall, at which he said: 'This is my renaissance. I'm being born again.' He had made his peace with Hollywood. Three years later, and two years before his death in Switzerland, he was honoured with a knighthood by his native country.

Chaplin, a pauper from the slums of South London, rose to become one of Hollywood's immortal heroes. An enigmatic character, he made an enormous impact on the development of the cinema on both sides of the Atlantic and on the screens of the wider world. He did it, not only on the back of the opportunities which the new Hollywood offered, but also using much of the Karno-style training and essentially English elements of comedy and slapstick. Thus, again, contributions of inheritance from the old and incentive from the new made Chaplin a true figure of the Rich Tide. In the words of J. B. Priestley, Chaplin 'had an image that conquered the world – but the man could not ever conquer himself. He was an insecure man, posturing, sensitive to jokes at his own expense, who had a Dickensian nostalgia for all things English . . .'

Stan Laurel (1890–1965) (left), another of Fred Karno's troupe, was born as Arthur Stanley Jefferson into a theatrical family Ulverston, Lancashire. He first appeared with Karno in 1910. On a later tour of America he decided to stay on and try his luck in films. He made his first film, *Nuts of May*, in 1917. Nine years later he established his partnership with Oliver Hardy in the film *Putting Pants on Philip*, and together they went on to make over two hundred films. Laurel died at Santa Nonica in 1965, retaining his British citizenship to the end.

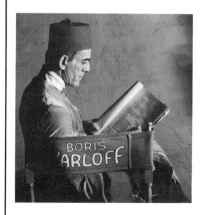

The name of William Henry Pratt is hardly a familiar one, but this son of a British Civil Servant from Dulwich who fled from his family who wanted him to join the Consular Service, was transmogrified into the monster actor, Boris Karloff (1887–1969), who, at Universal Studios, played in films that included *Frankenstein* (1931), *The Mummy* (1932), *The Black Cat* (1934) and *The Body Snatcher* (1945). He was also the villainous brother in the Broadway and film versions of *Arsenic and Old Lace*. Regretting always his evil typecast, he returned to Britain in 1955 and went to America only to work. In Hollywood, very much the Englishman, 'he read *Wisden* (the Cricketers' Almanac) and never yielded his lugubrious articulation'. He died in Middleton, Sussex, in 1969.

Karloff was far from being the only Hollywood cricketer. C. Aubrey Smith started the Hollywood Cricket Club with Herbert Marshall, Clive Brook and Ronald Colman (1891–1958). C. Aubrey Smith (1863–1948), after a long career on the stage, made his first Hollywood film in 1915. Cast always as the officer or the aristocrat, he appeared in numerous movies until his death at the age of eighty-five. Colman was born in Richmond, Surrey, and served in the First World War before moving to the States in 1920. One of his first roles there was to play with Lillian Gish in *The White Sister* in 1923. He signed up with MGM and soon established himself as a romantic star, playing in *A Tale of Two Cities* (1935), *Lost Horizon* (1937), *The Prisoner of Zenda* (1937) and *Random Harvest* (1942). He won an Oscar for Best Actor for his role in *Double Life* (1948). He, unlike many of his compatriots, always kept his British citizenship, declaring that 'a British passport is still the best in the world'.

Many writers were wooed by a Hollywood that believed Britain still had most of the literary talent and the scholarship. Paramount, as one example, bought up job lots of the works of J. M. Barrie, Arnold Bennett, H. G. Wells and Compton Mackenzie. One of the most famous and successful scriptwriters was tax-exile and failed British parliamentary candidate for Blackpool, Edgar Wallace, whose bucolic and horserace-betting lifestyle still allowed him time to write for films as well as his books. One of his best known was *King Kong*. Bernard Shaw was one of the few who resisted Hollywood's blandishments to the end.

And where the writers were, so were the British directors from Chaplin himself to Alfred Hitchcock. Hitchcock (1899–1980), the son of a London poultry dealer and fruit and vegetable importer, was educated by Jesuits before studying at the London School of Engineering and Navigation. Aged nineteen, he started to work as a technician for a telegraph company, but at the same time attended art lessons which enabled him to transfer to the

company's advertising department. In 1920 he made his entry into films at the newly established Islington branch of Hollywood's Famous-Players Studios, which later became Paramount. His job was to letter and design the backgrounds for silent film titles, and soon he was head of the title department, though on occasions he was given the opportunity to direct an occasional unimportant scene. When the Studios were taken over by a British production company set up by Michael Balcon, Hitchcock

Alfred Hitchcock (1899–1980) in 1946

was kept on as an assistant director and before long he was also working as an art director and scriptwriter.

In 1925 he directed his first feature film, *The Pleasure Garden*, though he himself considered *The Lodger* (known in the United States as *The Case of Jonathan Drew*) as his first proper film. A story about a landlady who believes that her new tenant is Jack the Ripper, the film contains many of the ingredients that were to mark Hitchcock's style – bold and imaginative cinematic effects with the theme of the innocent man cruelly caught up in a web of extraordinary events. Needing another extra, Hitchcock himself appears in the film, and subsequently his cameo appearances in his own films became an almost obligatory part of any Hitchcock film.

In 1926 he married Alma Reville, a film editor and scriptgirl who had worked with him for years and who was to script many of his subsequent films. In 1929 Hitchcock directed the first British feature film with synchronous sound, *Blackmail*.

For some years thereafter, Hitchcock directed a number of largely uninspired adaptations of novels and plays, but, commencing with *The Man Who Knew Too Much*, in 1934, he made a series of films which established his reputation as the master of the suspense genre – *The Thirty-Nine Steps* (1935), *Sabotage* (1936) and *The Lady Vanishes* (1938) which won him the best director award from the New York film critics. Shortly after this he was signed up by the top American producer David O. Selznick to come to Hollywood. Somewhat ironically, Hitchcock's first film in America was on a British theme, an adaptation of Daphne du Maurier's romantic mystery *Rebecca*, with an all-British cast which included Laurence Olivier and Joan Fontaine. The film was a critical and popular success, winning the Academy Award for Best Picture in 1940, Hitchcock a nomination for Best Director, and grossing more at the box-office than any previous film apart from Selznick's previous production *Gone with the Wind*.

Hitchcock's next major film, *Suspicion* (1941), marked the beginning of his fruitful collaboration with Cary Grant, an actor whose presence in a sense had tended, it was said, to weaken the plot since it was known that the studios insisted that a star of Grant's standing should not be allowed to portray a murderer. During the 1940s Hitchcock's career went through some bad patches, though there were still one or two memorable films such as *Notorious* (1946). With *Rope*, his first colour film, he became his own producer, and his reputation was re-established in 1951 with *Strangers on a Train*. Over the next few years his work arguably reached full maturity with movies such as *Rear Window* (1954), *The Wrong Man* (1957), *Vertigo* (1958) and *Psycho* (1960), his

Alfred Hitchcock in 1976, when he celebrated fifty years of making films with *Family Plot*, his 53rd motion picture.

biggest-ever hit which made over $15 million on its first run.

From then until his death in 1980, he made six more films including *The Birds* (1963), but he never matched the success of the 1950s. He also produced and hosted, between 1955 and 1965, two anthology mystery series for television – *Alfred Hitchcock Presents*. In 1979 he received the American Film Institute's Life Achievement Award, while shortly before his death he, like Chaplin, was knighted by his native country.

In a career spanning over 50 years Hitchcock completed over 50 feature films (23 in his British period, and 30 in his American period) and consequently exerted a considerable influence on the development of the motion picture on both sides of the Atlantic through his sense of the visually dramatic and his technical inventiveness. Few directors have given so much to the cinema as

OPPOSITE: Cary Grant with Noel Coward and Mae West.

an art form and at the same time entertained so many people, and it has been argued that no other director has been able to manipulate the emotions of his audience so consistently and well.

Of Hitchcock's many leading men, his favourite undoubtedly was Cary Grant, who was born Archibald Alexander Leach in January 1904 in Bristol. At thirteen Grant ran away from home to join a troupe of acrobats as a song and dance artist and juggler, coming to New York with the troupe in 1920. Deciding to stay on after the end of the tour he worked as a lifeguard on Coney Island, and during the winter months when he was not doing one-night stands as a song and dance performer he worked as a sandwich-board man on stilts.

In 1923 Grant came back to Britain and got a certain amount of stage work in musical comedies. Noticed by Arthur Hammerstein he was invited back to New York to appear in the musical *Golden Dawn* and this was followed by other Broadway appearances. In the early 1930s he came to Hollywood, signing a contract with Paramount, and making his début in *This Is the Night* in 1932. He appeared as a supporting actor in many other films before being cast in a major role, with Marlene Dietrich, in Von Sternberg's *Blonde Venus*, and making his first real impression on cinema-goers with his next film, *She Done Him Wrong* (1933), in which he co-starred with Mae West. Soon he became one of Hollywood's most sought-after leading men. In 1937–8, working for RKO and Columbia, Grant broadened his screen personality with several comic performances in such films as *Topper* (1937), *The Awful Truth* (1937) and *Bringing Up Baby* (1938). In these films he developed his highly sophisticated, witty, nonchalant, quizzical style – the 'debonair man-about-town at odds with an upside-down world'. It has been said that Grant was limited as an actor – and certainly no one expected him to turn up at the Old Vic as King Lear – but whatever he was asked to do in films he carried off with sublime style.

In recent years, the power of the American cinema as an arbiter of taste and, indeed, craze has become greater than ever – two men, George Lucas and Steven Spielberg, almost exclusively determining the direction of family entertainment for a decade. George Lucas created the *Star Wars* trilogy, and Steven Spielberg, both *Jaws* and *E.T.* When they chose to combine forces the result was *Raiders of the Lost Ark*. Sir Richard Attenborough with *Gandhi* and David Puttnam with *Chariots of Fire* made their impact on Hollywood and have the Oscars to prove it, but theirs were essentially individual contributions that could not by definition spawn an industry or even a sequel.

*　　*　　*

Cecil Sharp (1859–1924). Drawing by E. B. Mackinnon, 1921.

Music is one of the most truly international cultural forms and, therefore, to claim a purely bilateral Anglo-American connection could be misleading. This said, however, there are many direct musical links such as that provided by folk songs as they travelled from England, Scotland, Wales and Ulster to the New World. How little they changed when they emigrated was illustrated by the researches of scholars such as the Bostonian, James Child (1825–96), who collected and compared every ballad he could find. Child was more interested in the words but his follower, the Englishman Cecil J. Sharp (1859–1924), a collector of British ballads and songs, drew attention to the fact that they stayed very much alive and unchanged in the United States. His researches in the Appalachians in 1916 led to his finding many unaltered or modified British folk songs there.

Songs like 'The Maid Freed from the Gallows' had survived the transatlantic crossing almost untouched:

O true love, O true love, have you got any gold for me?
Or silver to pay my fee?
They say I've stoled a silver cup
And hanged I must be.

Yes, true love, I have gold for you
And silver to pay your fee.
I've come here to win your neck
From yon high gallows tree.

(Sung by Mr T. Jeff Stockton at Flag Pond, Tennessee, 4 September 1916.)

Such traditional songs and ballads with their Irish counterparts were the forerunners of the purely American hillbilly and country and western music, which, along with music that stemmed from Afro-American influences – the negro spiritual, gospel singing, ragtime and the whole jazz ethic – was to flow strongly into the British musical world.

The first songs published in America were concert and so-called 'pleasure garden' songs that were performed in a lively British style. Many were traditional tunes adapted for stage or parlour singing, and incorporating lots of nostalgia – the best-loved songs in the nineteenth-century United States tended to be identical to those in Britain – 'The Minstrel Boy', 'The Last Rose of Summer' and Robert Burns's adaptations such as 'Auld Lang Syne' and 'Coming Through the Rye'.

The Americans also imported opera, often adapted and translated from the Italian by the British composer Sir Henry Bishop (1786–1855). (The first recorded operatic production of a Mozart

OPPOSITE: 'Home Sweet Home' by Sir Henry Bishop. A song sheet of 1823.

RANSFORD'S EDITION.

as Sung by

MADAME ADELINA PATTI.

HOME, SWEET HOME!

Ballad,

WRITTEN BY J. H. PAYNE, ESQ.RE

Composed by

SIR H. R. BISHOP.

Ent. Sta. Hall.   *Price 2s/.*

London,
RANSFORD & SON,
2, Princes Street, Oxford Circus.
WHERE MAY BE HAD
RANSFORD & SON'S COLLECTION OF THE SONGS OF SCOTLAND,
... COMPRISING TWENTY-FOUR IN NUMBER OF THE MOST POPULAR SCOTCH SONGS & BALLADS.
as sung by all the London Vocalists.

One of Wales's leading musical talents, Joseph Parry (1841 –1903), emigrated with his family to America in 1854 and won many prizes and awards both in America and in his native land, while Jules Styne (b. 1905), born in London, was a musical prodigy whose début as solo pianist with the Chicago Symphony was at the age of nine. In the 1920s he turned to popular music, coaching singers in New York and Hollywood and, with Sammy Cahn, writing songs for Bing Crosby and Frank Sinatra. He also wrote the scores for *Gentlemen Prefer Blondes* and *Funny Girl*. Ivor Novello, librettist and actor, talent-spotted while dining at the Savoy by D. W. Griffith, was heralded as the Adonis or Valentino of Britain. He wrote many hits such as 'Keep the Home Fires Burning'.

The American composer Nat Ayer (1887–1952), who was born in Boston, came to England with a group called the American Ragtime Quartet and stayed on to become an established song-writer with titles such as 'If You Were the Only Girl'. Jerome Kern (1885–1945) also spent some time in Britain, particularly studying musical theatre and contributing to London musicals. He worked with P. G. Wodehouse (1881–1975), the Guildford-born author and creator of Jeeves who had gone to America in 1909. Among their best-known songs were 'Bill', 'The Siren's Song' and 'You Never Know About Men'. Wodehouse, humorous writer of eighty novels, became an American citizen in 1955. He spent several controversial years in France during the Second World War, but eventually received the accolade of knighthood in 1975 at the age of ninety-three.

TOP: Jerome Kern in the 1920s.

CENTRE: Jule Styne

RIGHT: Nat Ayer at the Ambassador Theatre, 1916.

adaptation was Bishop's *The Libertine* – an anglicized version of *Don Giovanni* – at the Park Theatre, New York, in November 1817.) Bishop's 'Home Sweet Home' was the most popular song in America throughout the entire nineteenth century – as it was in the entire English-speaking world. There were many immigrant songwriters like Benjamin Carr (1768–1831) who came to America in 1793 and published many popular songs, including 'The Little Sailor Boy'; and William Selby (1738–98) who came to Massachusetts writing dozens of published songs in the years after the Revolution.

Louis Armstrong (1900–71)

In April 1919 five young white musicians from America, the Original Dixieland Jazz Band, came to London and set the clubs and music-halls alight with their exciting rhythms and improvization. Nothing quite like them had been heard or seen in England before. To some they went beyond the accepted standards of musical taste; but to others they were a revelation. Public prejudice against the Americans was largely overcome when George V attended a Royal Command Performance by the band. After several months they returned triumphant to America having completed the first great musical conquest by their country over Britain, a conquest reinforced by the subsequent tours of such legendary black musicians as Sidney Bechet, Louis Armstrong and Duke Ellington. British musicians quickly caught the jazz bug and tried to emulate their American heroes. One of the first important British jazzmen, the bass player Spike Hughes, achieved his life's ambition in 1933 when he went to New York to cut a record with a leading black orchestra. After the war British jazz was heavily influenced by the brilliance of Americans such as Charlie Parker, Dizzy Gillespie and Miles Davis.

And so on to contemporary musical culture. Here it begins to be almost impossible to define what is purely British or purely American. Of course the Beatles, in their first appearance on the 'Ed Sullivan Show' in February 1964, were very obviously ethnic Liverpudlian. But what they were doing was bringing back to the States their version of rock and roll – which they always claimed was the hallmark of their style. Before and since, with Elvis Presley, Chuck Berry and Fats Domino through to Joan Baez and Bob Dylan, on to the Rolling Stones, Michael Jackson, The Who, Elton John and Bruce Springsteen, sounds have crossed and recrossed the Atlantic, feeding on each other and catering to an increasingly erratic and volatile mid-Atlantic taste. It is relatively rare that one country's current hits do not feature somewhere on the other's 'Top Twenty' list. The mood and the background are musical but the transatlantic influence stretches to every item of popular cultural taste, fashion, hairstyles, on to what has been called the drug culture.

*   *   *

The so-called intellectuals of the country are simply weather-vanes blown constantly by foreign winds, usually but not always English.

H. L. MENCKEN

What was true is often still held to be so. The banner headlines of Hollywood sometimes proclaim that the British are getting more than their fair share, just as Fleet Street sometimes complains that the West End theatres are dominated by American hits. The truth is that what was once a great, almost irreversible step into the unknown for figures from all walks of life when they left their native land to become expatriates is now a commonplace of the masses, a gesture achieved or reversed by the simple purchase of an airline ticket. For the early cultural flotsam on the Rich Tide the die was cast with a strength that was significant because it was of lasting duration. Now the talent is largely transient, as long as a concert lasts, or the time it takes to shoot a film. Real cultural talent, real fame now requires that one is as at home in Tinseltown as in Drury Lane, in the galleries of Manhattan or Bond Street. We are all one culture now.

Or are we?

CHAPTER TEN

In All Walks of Life

Here [in America] was the bigot, the fanatic, the dreamer, the utopian, the misfit, the adventurer. By the middle of the eighteenth century, the phrase was already current: He has skipped to America. THORNTON WILDER (1952)

All I ask of Americans is that you go on being yourselves – valiant without being fanatical, individualistic without being foolhardy, skeptical without being cynical, open-minded without being indecisive, generous without being naive, patriotic without being nationalistic, and good without being perfect. PETER JAY (1977)

The English themselves hardly conceived their mind was either economical, sharp, or direct; but the defect that most struck an American was its enormous waste in eccentricity. Americans needed and used their whole energy, and applied it with close economy; but English society was eccentric by law and for the sake of eccentricity itself . . . Eccentricity was so general as to become hereditary distinction. It made the chief charm of English society as well as its chief terror. HENRY ADAMS

Americans and British have long had something of a love–hate relationship with one another, and for every Joseph P. Kennedy (the American Ambassador to London at the beginning of the war) who said, 'I do not want to see this country go to war under any conditions whatsoever unless we are attacked . . . England is not fighting our battle. This is not our war,' there are a thousand who echo Roosevelt speaking in the same year: 'The best immediate defence of the United States is the success of Great Britain defending itself.'

Each is adept at being rude about the other, and they often get it right. For example:

Let us pause to consider the English,
Who when they pause to consider themselves they get all
   reticently thrilled and tinglish,
Because every Englishman is convinced of one thing, viz:
That to be an Englishman is to belong to the most exclusive
   club there is . . .   OGDEN NASH

Or again . . .

Kelvil: I am afraid you don't appreciate America, Lord Illingworth. It is a very remarkable country, especially considering its youth.
Lord Illingworth: The youth of America is their oldest tradition. It has been going on now for three hundred years. To
hear them talk one would imagine they were in their first
childhood. As far as civilisation goes, they are in their
second.   OSCAR WILDE, *A Woman of No Importance*

Or, more aggressively:

Every time Europe looks across the Atlantic to see the
American eagle, it observes only the rear end of an ostrich.
        H. G. WELLS

and

The English are mentioned in the Bible: 'Blessed are the
meek, for they shall inherit the earth.'   MARK TWAIN

Such insults apart, in all conditions, Britons and Americans of
various strange callings have had a profound effect on each other
and their ways of life. Many have an obvious place in the Rich
Tide, but there are others whose influence, for good or ill, has
been less noticeable but of an unexpected and often important
variety. They all add to the richness of the process.

One such figure was John Paul Jones (1747–92) from Kirk-
bean in Scotland, to whom goes the credit for founding the United
States Navy. The son of a local landscape gardener, he was
apprenticed to a merchant-shipper, making his first voyage to
Virginia as a cabin boy at the age of twelve. Later, in 1766, he
received his commission as a midshipman in the British Navy, but
it was uncertain whether he ever took up the position, since, in
that same year, he was heard of serving in a slave ship in the
Caribbean. A turbulent few years elapsed during which, as the
master of a brigantine bound for Scotland, he was charged, in
1770, with murdering his ship's carpenter by flogging him to
death for alleged laziness. Released on bail, he ended up in Tobago
in the West Indies where, in 1773, he made 'the great misfortune

John Paul Jones (1747–92). Oil painting by Charles Willson Peale, 1781.

of my life' by also killing the ringleader of a mutinous crew. As a result he had to flee Tobago and was next heard of in Fredericksburg, Virginia, in 1773 where he added Jones to his name. Arriving in Philadelphia at the start of the Revolution, by 1775 he was commissioned and serving in *Alfred*, the very first ship to fly the Continental flag. Following a number of distinguished actions against the British in the following year, he was given command of *Providence* and was sent to France where, from his base at Brest, he raided English ports and shipping. In February 1779 the French king placed under his command a former East Indiaman, *Duc de Duras*, which Jones renamed *Bonhomme Richard*, and at the

John Paul Jones in action.

head of a squadron of American ships he went prize-fighting his way round the coasts of Scotland and Ireland.

'I was, indeed, born in Britain,' Jones once said, 'but I do not inherit the degenerate spirit of that fallen nation, which I at once lament and despise.'

On one earlier engagement he had raided St Mary's Island on the Solway Firth, very close to his birthplace, with the intention of seizing Lord Selkirk and holding him hostage. Failing to do this, his crew, instead, took the Selkirk family silver, which Jones in a strange act of penance was later to redeem and return to Lady Selkirk along with a letter of apology.

Jones's most notable battle was achieving the surrender of the 44-gun British ship, HMS *Serapis*, which was leading a British Baltic convoy, in a battle off Flamborough Head, Yorkshire, in September 1779. *Bonhomme Richard* actually sank, but Jones commandeered *Serapis* and sailed her back to France. This and his famous reply when Captain Pearson of *Serapis* asked him if he was ready to surrender – 'I have not yet begun to fight!' – made him a folk hero, both in France and in the United States. Briefly returning to Philadelphia in 1781, he was, only two years later, re-despatched to France as an agent for the American Government.

In later life, Jones always argued that he was no mercenary: 'I have not drawn my sword in our glorious cause for hire, but in

Jones commanding the *Bon Homme Richard* against HMS *Serapis* off Flamborough Head.

support of the dignity of human nature and the divine feelings of philanthropy. I hoisted with my own hands the flag of freedom the first time it was displayed on board the *Alfred* in the Delaware; [it was in fact the 'Grand Union Stripes' – the Union Jack and stripes that symbolized resistance to tyranny but loyalty to the Crown], and I have attended it ever since with veneration on the ocean.' But this sailor of fortune, having been awarded a gold medal for his services by the United States Congress, also actually went on to serve as a Rear-Admiral with the Imperial Russian Navy and fought successfully against the Turks before returning to Paris in 1789. Embittered and broken because he felt his later achievements were largely unrecognized, he died there in 1790 and was buried in an unmarked grave. It was to be more than a century before his body was identified and returned to America, where his crypt at the naval chapel at Annapolis is now an object of veneration.

One picaresque character who is particularly hard to place in any one place in this book is the soldier, government official, philanthropist, Bavarian count, inventor and scientist, Benjamin Thompson (1753–1814). He was born in North Woburn, Massachusetts, a descendant of James Thompson who had accompanied John Winthrop to New England in 1630. At the age of nineteen he married one of New Hampshire's richest widows, and through her connections was given a major's commission in one of the colony's regiments. But in 1775 he was imprisoned for his 'lack of enthusiasm' for the cause of American liberty. After his release he left for Boston where he remained with the British garrison until the capitulation, when he sailed for England, carrying with him some important despatches from General Gage to Lord George Germain, the Secretary of State for the American Colonies. Lord Germain was impressed enough by the young American to appoint him Secretary for Georgia and to a position in the Colonial Office. After a spell as an under-secretary, Thompson returned to America in about 1781 as a lieutenant-colonel in the British army. In September 1783 he left the army on half pay and went on a tour of Europe.

In Strasbourg he befriended Duke Maximilian, the nephew of the Elector of Bavaria, and entered his service in 1784. Thompson's strange Bavarian period lies beyond the scope of this book but it is worth mentioning that he effected several radical reforms in the Elector's army and civil government. In 1795 he returned to England in order to deliver some papers to the Royal Society, of which he was a fellow, and to publish the first volume of his *Essays, Political, Economical and Philosophical*. He also visited Ireland where he installed important improvements to Dublin's

Benjamin Thompson, Count Rumford, (1753–1814). Oil painting by Rembrandt Peale.

OPPOSITE: Thompson's plans of Baron de Lerchenfeld's kitchen, and his designs for a portable furnace, the Rumford Roaster.

workhouses and hospitals. In England his improvements in heating and cooking equipment aroused a lot of interest, while his 'non-smoking fireplaces' were installed in over one hundred and fifty London homes, and his Rumford Roasters became widely used in both Britain and the United States.

Thompson, or Count Rumford as he became known after 1791, also devoted a lot of attention to pure science and is acknowledged as the first person to determine that heat was a mode of motion. He is probably best remembered in Britain as one of the founders, in 1799/1800, of the Royal Institution, a body he hoped would bridge the gap between science in the laboratory and industry in the factory. Thompson left England for good in

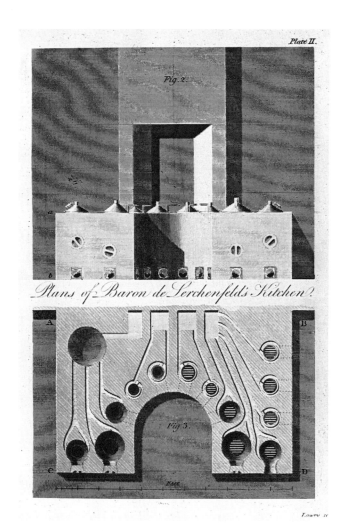

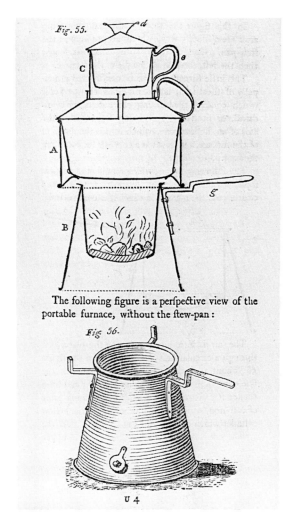

The following figure is a perspective view of the portable furnace, without the stew-pan:

1801 and settled in France where he was married for a time to Lavoisier's widow.

But not all those who properly figure in the Rich Tide have made positive contributions to the Anglo-American relationship. Some have done it positive disservice. One of the most controversial characters was the fourth-generation New Englander, Benedict Arnold (1741–1801), whose biography must describe him as both general and traitor. He had a wayward childhood, deserting from the army in his teens whilst in the middle of an expedition against the French. But he then moved on to have a distinguished career in the War of Independence, playing a major role in the invasion of Canada, and in 1777 was promoted to

John Trumbull's *The Declaration of Independence*, 4th July 1776.

major-general after his successful attack on the British at Ridgefield, Connecticut. As a result of this and his leading part in the Saratoga campaign, George Washington befriended him and appointed him to command Philadelphia when it was relinquished by the British. A flamboyant and extravagant character who entertained lavishly, Arnold soon became angered and embittered by being referred to court martial after a row with the Pennsylvania Civil Authorities (one of many conflicts Arnold had with authority over the years, usually as a result of his alleged misconduct).

He consequently entered into secret correspondence with General Sir Henry Clinton, the British Commander-in-Chief, with a view to defecting to Britain. Despite the fact that the court martial found him innocent, and even though his friend Washington subsequently appointed him, at his request, as Commander of West Point, the fort that was the key to the Hudson River Valley, Arnold had further secret negotiations with Clinton to surrender the fort to the British Army, for which treachery he was to receive £20,000. All this was negotiated between Arnold and Clinton's adjutant-general, Major John André, at Stony Point on the night of 21 September 1780. Unfortunately, André was caught two days later in possession of incriminating papers and was quickly court martialled and hanged. But the officer who had arrested André unsuspectingly reported the matter direct to Benedict Arnold himself, who consequently had time to flee to New York. Once there, commissioned a brigadier-general in the British Army and in receipt of a large sum in compensation for the loss of his property, he fought on the British side in many successfully daring but brutal raids on American forces in Virginia and even in his native Connecticut.

Eventually he left to settle in England, where, for a time he

Bened. Arnold

Plan of the defeat of the American Fleet, under Benedict Arnold, on Lake Champlain, October 11th, 1776.

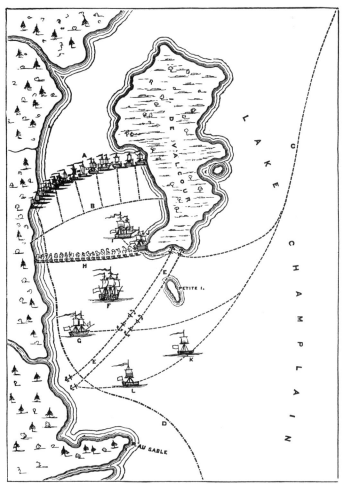

PLAN OF THE DEFEAT OF THE AMERICAN FLEET, UNDER BENEDICT ARNOLD, ON LAKE CHAMPLAIN, OCT. 11, 1776.

A. American fleet of fifteen vessels.
B. American line during the attack.
C. Course of the British fleet from St. John.
D. Track of American ships which escaped to Ticonderoga.
E. Position in which the British fleet anchored during the night.
F. Inflexible.
G. Schooner Maria.
H. Twenty gun-boats.
I. Schooner Carleton.
J. The Royal Savage on shore.
K. Thunderer.
L. Gondola Loyal Convert.

advised the King and Government on American affairs. Eventually his usefulness ran out and he died, as he had lived, stubborn, embittered and alone. At the height of his fame in the Saratoga campaign he had been seriously wounded in the leg and the monument that had been erected to his heroism at that time was in the form of a booted leg with a bullet hole in it. As an enduring mark of his treachery, the monument no longer bears any name upon it (though it does call its now nameless subject 'the most brilliant soldier in the Continental Army').

Another fugitive from justice, in this case British, ended up with a very different worldwide reputation. The man who invented the term 'Private Eye' from his trademark of an open eye and his slogan 'We never sleep', Allan Pinkerton (1819–84), was born in the poverty of Glasgow's worst slums, the Gorbals. Son of a former blacksmith and part-time policeman, when his father was killed in a political riot, he himself, while working out his apprenticeship as a cooper, became a convert to the Chartist, or working-men's, cause. His subsequent political activities attracted the attention and then opprobrium of Sir Robert Peel's government (Peel was responsible for the formation of Britain's national police force), and in 1842 he only narrowly escaped arrest by the authorities through escaping on board a ship bound for Nova Scotia.

Arriving in the Scottish settlement of Dundee in Kane County, Illinois, Pinkerton became a prosperous cooper, at the same time winning popular neighbourhood acclaim by helping the local sheriff to arrest a gang of counterfeiters. Promoted part-time deputy sheriff, he then moved on to Chicago where he became the first and only detective of that city's newly formed police force. There he successfully solved a spate of railroad robberies, and his Pinkerton's National Agency, set up around 1852, was the inevitable next step. Pinkerton himself became known as 'The Eye', feared and respected as provider to the law-abiding of everything from security for Presidents, to a nationwide network of detective agencies. Some of his most notable successes were the capture of the leaders of the thieves who stole $700,000 from the Adams Express Company 1859–60 and the uncovering of a plot to assassinate President-elect Lincoln in Baltimore in February 1861. In that same year, Pinkerton organized an intelligence operation to get hold of military in-

Allan Pinkerton, (seated right) in a group of secret service men at HQ Army of the Potomac, October 4th, 1862.

formation in the Confederate States, an organization that was later to be developed into the Federal Secret Service, and his detectives were also instrumental in breaking up the infamous Irish-American criminal secret society, the Molly Maguires, over the years 1873–7. But as a former Chartist his organization's reputation with American unions was unhappily different. In the many famous industrial disputes and strikes, Pinkerton's men were notorious as industrial police and strikebreakers for the kings of industry.

*　　*　　*

Folding my map, I shouldered my little bag and plant press and strode away among the old Kentucky oaks, rejoicing in splendid visions of pines and palms and tropic flowers in glorious array, not, however, without a few cold shadows of loneliness, although the great oaks seemed to spread their arms in welcome.

JOHN MUIR. *A Thousand-Mile Walk to the Gulf* (1916)

John Muir (1838–1914). Oil painting by Orlando Rouland.

In more peaceful vein, one outstanding representative of the Rich Tide who did much for future generations of Americans in his campaigning for and development of a National Parks system was the Scottish-born naturalist, explorer and conservationist, John Muir (1838–1914). Born in Dunbar, Scotland, he was brought to America in 1849, and settled with his family in Wisconsin. His childhood in Scotland and Dunbar is delightfully told in his book *The Story of My Boyhood and Youth* (1913). He attended the University of Wisconsin, travelled widely on foot through the Mid-West, and eventually arrived in California in 1868, where he spent six years studying and exploring the Yosemite Valley. It was an accident which made him believe that his eyes would be 'closed for ever to all God's beauty' that prompted him in his wanderings which he later described in *A Thousand-Mile Walk to the Gulf* (1916), and other books. He was constantly extolling the natural beauties of the continent. Thus: 'The forests of America, however slighted by man, must have been a delight to God, because they were the best he ever planted.'

Later Muir travelled and did equivalent work in Nevada, Utah, the North-West and in Alaska. On all his journeys he made extensive scientific notes and sketches of his observations. He married in 1880, and settled in California, who he rented and later bought a part of his father-in-law's fruit ranch. By 1890 this was providing him with sufficient money to devote himself once again to travel and study, and he returned to his principal

Yosemite Valley: The Three
Brothers, from an early photograph.

interests, which were in glaciers and forests. He was the first to
demonstrate that the origin of the Yosemite Valley lay in glacial
erosion and he also described several glaciers in Alaska, one of
which was named after him. Along with Robert U. Johnson, he
started a vigorous campaign to conserve the Yosemite Valley, and,
largely as a result of their propaganda, the Yosemite National Park
was founded by Congress in October 1890.

The following year, Congress passed an act empowering the
President to create forest reserves, thus implementing a measure
for which Muir had been pressing for over fifteen years. In 1897
President Cleveland created thirteen forest reservations comprising more than 21 million acres, and when private interests sought
to get Congress to nullify the reserves Muir led a successful
propaganda campaign in the press to stop or revoke this action.
Out of the dispute Muir emerged as the recognized leader of the
forest conservation movement in America. His views on conservation were strongly supported by President Theodore
Roosevelt, who set aside 148 million acres of additional forest
reserves, established six national monuments, and doubled the
number of national parks. Muir's contribution to the conservation of America's natural heritage thus is second to none. Yet he

remained to the end a modest man, and his own finances were the least of his concerns. On one occasion he said of one great contemporary millionaire, E. H. Hanniman: 'I have all the money I want and he hasn't.' By Yosemite standards a very modest country park in Dunbar, Scotland, is his homeland's memorial to him where, as so often happens, his name is much less well-known than in the country of his adoption.

One of the great landmarks of New York City is Central Park, the design and lay-out of which were the work of Calvert Vaux (1824 –95), the English-born landscape gardener and architect. He came to the United States at the age of twenty-six, and with the American landscape architect F. L. Olmstead he laid out many public parks in various other cities including Boston and Buffalo. He also designed and built many notable American country houses on great estates along the Hudson.

When the first British colonists arrived, they brought with them not only their language, their skills, their religion, but also their sports and recreations. Equestrian and hunting skills, games with bat, racket and ball as well as indoor games – chess, cards and family pastimes. In later generations, the newer sports of football, golf, tennis, rounders, and even cricket, were introduced into the New World where they sometimes took new forms, such as baseball and American varieties of football, and were always given a new impetus and vitality. At least two games came in the other direction: basketball and lacrosse, the latter originating with the North American Indians.

The game the British consider the most American of all, baseball, most experts now agree evolved directly from the English game of rounders. In colonial America the game was often known as 'town ball', though the name 'base ball' appears in print in the early eighteenth century, and there consequently seems little truth behind the popular story that it was spon-

Lacrosse at Hurlingham, London, June 1876.

taneously invented by the young civil servant, Abner Doubleday, in Cooperstown, New York, in the summer of 1839. (The story that Doubleday invented it was undoubtedly propagated in the early twentieth century by a group of distinguished and patriotic administrators of the game in order to kill the suggestion that it was of purely English origin.) Historians of the sport have now additionally shown that the rules of the game, as attributed to Doubleday, were exactly the same as those in a rule book for

Grand match for the baseball
championship at Elysian Fields,
Hoboken, New Jersey, 1866.

RIGHT: Floyd 'Babe' Herman, star of
the Brooklyn Dodgers in the 1920s.

English rounders published in London some twelve years earlier. In this book, the British author remarked that many people, especially Americans, called rounders by its new name 'base ball', but that many Britons also used that term.

The greatest claim to be the father of modern baseball is held by the American, Alexander Joy Cartwright, of the New York Knickerbockers, but one of the other founding fathers was Harry Wright (1835–95) from Sheffield, England, who organized the first fully professional baseball team, the Cincinnati Red Stockings. As a young man, Wright had excelled in athletics, and in 1856 he became a professional cricketer for the St George Cricket Club on Staten Island, at the same time starting to play for the Knickerbocker Baseball Club. Proving that the two games were not exclusive, be became their coach in 1866, at the same time captaining the Cincinnati Baseball Club, but continued to bowl for the Union Cricket Club of that city. Three years later, under the captaincy and management of Wright, the Cincinnati Red Stockings became the first full team of professionals. In 1874, he returned to England with a baseball team, which played both the American game and also cricket. His subsequent distinguished managerial career took him to Boston and Philadelphia, one of the outstanding figures of American sporting history.

Harry Wright's brother George, also a cricketer, was one of baseball's first stars, while another pioneer of the game, and no mean cricketer, was Henry Chadwick (1824–1908), who was also one of the first sports writers in America. Born in Exeter, England, he came to America at the age of thirteen, settling with his family in Boston. He wrote for a number of newspapers and, in 1869, founded an annual baseball guidebook which later became *Spalding's Official Baseball Guide*, the baseball equivalent of *Wisden*. He was also to become the chairman and mentor of the Rules Committee of the first National Association. But, like many other earlier baseball players, he never lost his passion for cricket.

For many decades throughout the nineteenth century, cricket and baseball were played fairly widely in the United States, while, in a contrary move, a group of American promoters sent two American baseball champion teams, the Boston champions of 1874 and their nearest rivals, the Athletics of Philadelphia, to Britain to further the game there where they played before enthusiastic crowds. They, too, played cricket, including games against an MCC XI, though admittedly they were allowed to use eighteen men. The Americans, it is only fair to report, won every cricket match they played, to the generous praise of English sportswriters.

English cricket teams also travelled to the States and the

benefits and merits of both games were widely debated – with the faster baseball in the end winning out decisively in the United States. Cricket continued to be played, however, as in New York by the St George's Cricket Club, founded in 1840, which even played international matches against Canadian sides from Montreal and Toronto. Immigrant English factory workers also played a great deal in the districts around Philadelphia, the pioneer club there being the Union Cricket Club, which was very active during the 1840s and 1850s. Almost all these clubs relied heavily on a nucleus of newly arrived English expatriate support, though the Young America Cricket Club of Germantown only allowed native-born Americans to play.

*   *   *

It is a difficult task establishing the origins of golf in America, though it is known that Scottish officers played golf in New York as early as the 1770s, and in 1786 the South Carolina Golf Club was founded at Charleston with other clubs coming into existence in the southern States about the same time. But the game did not catch on and declined until it was revived almost a century later with the foundation of the Oakhurst Club in West Virginia. In the history of that sport, the name of John Reid is pre-eminent. This Scots immigrant, the story goes, unveiled his set of golf clubs to a group of friends in Yonkers in February 1888. These friends started playing together and so popular did the game become locally that by November of that year Reid proposed the formation of what is widely claimed as America's first fully established golf club – the St Andrews Club of Yonkers. After several moves, the club made a final transfer to Mount Hope where the first full eighteen-hole course was constructed.

By 1891, William K. Vanderbilt was employing Willie Dunn, a leading Scottish golfer, to design the first professionally laid-out links at Shinnecock Hills, Southampton, Long Island. The golf revolution had begun, catching the interest of the wealthy in Boston, New York and other cities, who brought in many other Scottish golfers to teach the skills of the game, and adopted the British custom of holding open tournaments. These early years of the sport in America long continued to be dominated by immigrant and touring Scottish and, to a lesser extent, English players such as the leading professional Harry Vardon, who came on an exhibition tour in 1900. It was only in 1913 that a native-born amateur, Francis Ouimet (1893–1967), defeated Vardon and another leading British professional, Edward Ray, to win the American Open Championship. Ouimet's victory generated an

'The Golfers', St Andrews, 1847.

enormous amount of interest in golf which was to lead to eventual American pre-eminence in the game.

Successive American golfers of the class of Bobby Jones, Arnold Palmer and Jack Nicklaus have come to Britain and beaten the natives at their own game. Moreover, despite the fact that golfing enthusiasts from the United States still flock to St Andrews and other golfing shrines, American-style courses designed by Americans are now being set up in Britain, the results of the Ryder Cup underlining their domination. Many of the designers of such courses are current or former professional golfers represented by Mark McCormack whose International Management Group has helped to transform the power and financial clout of professional sportsmen over the past twenty years, beginning with an experimental offer of assistance from McCormack, a lawyer, to his friend, the aforementioned Arnold Parlmer, in Cleveland, Ohio.

*   *   *

Scottish influence was also considerable in the development of an American interest in field and track athletics. The co-founder of the New York Athletic Club (1868), William B. Curtis, was as much impressed by the highly popular American–Scottish Highland Games as he was by the zeal with which the English were developing track and field events. Of course distance and endurance races, some of them professional, were popular throughout early nineteenth-century America, and a number of professional runners came from Britain to compete for the high financial stakes that were offered in the United States.

In November 1844, at the Beacon course, Hoboken, the

Jack Nicklaus, 'the Golden Bear', after winning the Open.

ABOVE: 'Deerfoot'

RIGHT: America wins back the Wightman Lawn Tennis cup from Britain. Mrs Covell presenting the Cup to Mrs Wightman at Forest Hills, New York, 1929.

English runner John Barlow won the first prize of $700 for running a set ten-mile course in 54 minutes and 21 seconds. American runners came to Britain in return, including Louis Bennett who was half Scots and half Seneca Indian and called himself Deerfoot. He dressed in breechcloth and moccasins and, wearing a feather in his hair, won his first great cash race in 1835, but was still a top runner when he came to England in the 1860s, as he proved by beating most of the top British names there over the favoured ten-mile course. It was not until the turn of the century, however, that the United States started on what was to become its pre-eminent role in the field of athletics – first winning substantial numbers of medals in the 1908 and 1912 Olympics.

The origins of tennis-playing in the United States are as obscure as those of golf. From the earliest days, people had played games with bat and ball, but one claim for introducing lawn tennis goes to Mary Outerbridge who, according to legend, watched British officers playing the game in Bermuda in 1874, and brought it back to introduce it at the Staten Island Baseball Club. Another story has American tourists bringing back the equipment to play the game from England in the same year, with the first matches (it was frequently called 'Sphairistike' – the name given it by its 'inventor' a Major Walter Wingfield) played at Nahant, Massachusetts, and at the Newport Casino.

It did not take long for American players to equal and then surpass the British at the game. The United States has an awesome record against the United Kingdom in the Davis Cup, which was originally conceived by an American as a closely contested competition between the two countries. And from Bill Tilden in 1920 to Jimmy Connors, John McEnroe and Billie Jean King in

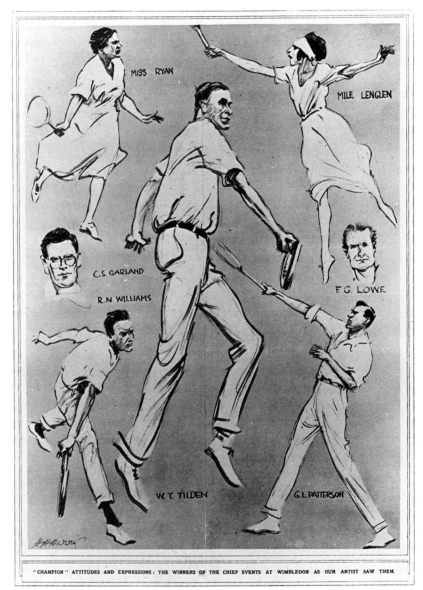

"CHAMPION" ATTITUDES AND EXPRESSIONS: THE WINNERS OF THE CHIEF EVENTS AT WIMBLEDON AS OUR ARTIST SAW THEM.

'"Champion" attitudes and expressions: the winners of the chief events at Wimbledon as our artist saw them.' *Illustrated London News*, July 1920.

recent years Americans have had their greatest triumphs at Wimbledon, whose very nature has been massively affected by two Americans – Jack Kramer, the pioneer of what began as 'the professional circus' and came to be called Open Tournaments; and Mark McCormack again, who currently represents many of the players, most of the sponsors, and even the All-England Club itself.

The first Anglo-American yacht race, 1851 – *America* winning.

In the glamorous history of Anglo-American yachting, one of the most famous names is that of John Stevens (1785–1857), Commodore of the New York Yacht Club, whose 170-ton yacht *America* was built specially to race in English waters. In a race round the Isle of Wight on 22 August 1851, *America* came first of 16 starters and won the cup presented by the Royal Yacht Squadron, which, ever since, has been known as the America's Cup. The subsequent history of the yacht *America* itself is exceptional. Largely rebuilt and renamed *Camilla* she was employed by the Confederates in the American Civil War, even having guns mounted on her when she was used as a blockade runner. Scuttled to avoid capture by the Federal Navy, she was later raised, commissioned into the rival Federal Navy, first as *Memphis*, later changed back to *America* and then employed in the blockade of Charleston. After service as a training ship for midshipmen, she was turned back into a yacht and, incredibly, on 8 August 1870, on the occasion of the first British challenge for the America's Cup, took part in the race, coming in fourth and beating the British challenger by some 13 minutes.

Many of the early figures in American yachting, all rich men, tended to employ British masters and crews – such as Charles Barr (1864–1911), the Scottish-born victor of several America's Cups.

In the equestrian field, from racing to polo and hunting, the owners, trainers, jockeys and the horses themselves all have the strongest Anglo-American connections. American jockeys have ridden in Britain from William L. Simms, the first American to win a major British race, in 1896 and Tod Sloan who pioneered the modern style of riding, to Steve Cauthen, the 1985 champion flat racing jockey; the races themselves are closely matched, with the Kentucky Derby modelled on the Epsom Derby; and the horses, too, such as the outstanding nineteenth-century Parole and Iroquois which was the only American racehorse to win both the Derby and the St Leger until Never Say Die in 1954. In the 1860s, by which time organized horse racing had developed a style of its own in the States, almost all the great sire lines were descended from stock imported from Britain. In contemporary times almost all the bloodlines are thoroughly mixed – British, American, Irish, French, Italian, Arab and so on, while the pedigrees of owners, trainers and the jockeys tend to match in transatlantic complexity.

The original Grand Stand at Churchill Downs, where the Kentucky Derby, modelled on the English Derby, was established.

In the world of boxing, prize fighting was common from the earliest days in the American colonies. It tended, frequently, to be the preserve of negroes, with two of the most famous names being Bill Richmond and the emancipated slave Tom Molineux (1784–1818), America's first black sporting hero. Richmond was the first black and, indeed, the first American to win boxing recognition in British prize fighting. Born on Staten Island (the

Tom Cribb fighting Tom Molineux,
28th September 1811.

home territory of so much American sporting prowess), he was
brought to Britain in the late eighteenth century by General
Percy, later Duke of Northumberland. He fought a number of
highly publicized matches between 1800 and 1818, including one
against Tom Cribb, the famous British champion. Later he
coached Molineux and became valet to Lord Camelford, the
boxing, horse racing and cock fighting devotee. Molineux himself, reputedly the son of a famous prize fighter, emerged as a
slave boxer in Virginia and, after gaining his freedom through
winning enough fights to buy it, he went north to New York
where he fought and won a number of financially rewarding
fights along the waterfront.

In 1809 he came to England with two white managers and,
assisted by Richmond, he, too, fought Tom Cribb in a gruelling
contest in bitter weather at Copthall Common near East Grin-
stead in December 1810. Cribb was a mean but powerful man
with huge shoulders and arms, but Molineux, the 'Great American Moor' as the British newspapers called him, was, though
shorter, much the more aggressive of the fighters. Despite the bad
weather, a huge crowd gathered round the roped ring that was
centred on a bowling green, to watch the two fighters, stripped to
the waist. While knocking the Englishman out in the twenty-
third round, Molineux stood accused of having weights hidden in
his fists. In the subsequent argument, Cribb had time to recover
and eventually won his fight in the thirty-ninth round. According
to contemporary reports, Cribb beat Molineux again the following year – 'an easier achievement since the latter had been much
exposed to alcohol and English women'. Molineux sadly died in

poverty in Ireland, though is reputation lived on, so much so that other boxers used his name and some years later a man called Jim Wharton made a considerable fortune posing as the reincarnation of the famous fighter.

Of all the great Anglo-American prize fights, and there were many, the most notorious was that between the English champion, Tom Sayers, and the American champion, John C. Heenan. It was held at Farnborough, Hampshire, on April 17th, 1860, creating an unprecedented amount of interest on both sides of the Atlantic. Despite the fact that the fight had to be held nominally in secret because it was illegal, the police made no attempt to prevent it and many leading public figures such as Prince Albert, Palmerston, Thackeray and Dickens were said to have been among the large crowd. After two hours and twenty minutes, with both fighters battered and exhausted, the crowd out of control, and the police about to stop the fight, the bout was halted by the referee who declared a draw. The British press saw the contest as a moral victory for the diminutive Sayers (he was forty pounds lighter than his opponent) but the Americans claimed that the intervention of the unruly crowd and the police had prevented Heenan from finishing the Englishman off.

The list of those excluded from this book on grounds of space is a long one, not least in this kaleidoscopic chapter. We could have followed Bonnie Prince Charlie's saviour Flora MacDonald on her journey of emigration to America after the Young Pretender had escaped to France. We could have looked at the life and times of Samuel Insull, the British-born Chicago capitalist and embezzler, the cabinet-maker Duncan Phyfe, or Benjamin Latrobe, the English architect who designed the Capitol after its destruction by the British. And should we pass by John McTammany (1845–1915) from Glasgow, whose achievements were not so humble? He, after all, invented the perforated music-roll, the player piano and, more importantly, a voting machine which used a perforated roll, and was the first to be used in an American election, if not in any election anywhere.

Alas, we must, but they are part of the Rich Tide none the less.

VISCOUNTESS DEERHURST
(VIRGINIA, DAUGHTER OF MR. CHARLES BONYNGE, U.S.A.).

THE COUNTESS OF ESSEX
(ADELA, DAUGHTER OF MR. BEACH GRANT, NEW YORK).

LADY ABINGER
(HELEN, DAUGHTER OF COMMODORE G. A. MAGRUDER, U.S.A.).

THE DOWAGER DUCHESS OF MANCHESTER
(CONSUELO, DAUGHTER OF ANTONIO YZNAGA DEL VALLE, LOUISIANA).

Photographs by Lafayette, Bond Street, W.

CHAPTER ELEVEN

Dynasties

It is a very curious fact that, with all our boasted 'free and equal' superiority over the communities of the Old World, our people have the most enormous appetite for Old World titles of distinction. OLIVER WENDELL HOLMES

The American woman? – why, she has beguiled, she has conquered, the globe; look at her fortune everywhere and fail to accept her if you can. HENRY JAMES

It is a truism to say that the intermarriage between members of the two great English-speaking peoples has cemented the bonds between them. From the days of the Revolution to the present day, such family connections have had a considerable, if not always apparent, effect on political, social and economic relationships. It would be wrong to try to draw any harder conclusions from transatlantic matrimony; none the less, it would be wrong to ignore it.

The Anglo-American marriage market reached its apogee in the late nineteenth and early twentieth centuries. In the three decades after 1870 well over a hundred such grand society marriages were concluded, a fact much written and commented about in contemporary newspaper reports. The sombre and cynical fact of the matter is that though love and romance sometimes played their part, as in the marriage of Jennie Jerome and Lord Randolph Churchill, most of these titled liaisons were primarily designed just to unite great British names and families with American money. One reason for this lay in declining land rents and property values in the late nineteenth century, making it increasingly difficult for many British noble families to maintain their estates. Fresh injections of income were needed. How better to get them than to marry an American heiress, since by United States custom great fortunes could be inherited as much by the female as by the male line. The evidence surprisingly suggests that it became almost entirely acceptable and indeed even fashionable to marry American wealth, though some snobbery did remain. In return, for a wealthy American family, marriage into a titled British family constituted the ultimate expression of social

Yosemite National Park, the great creation of the Scotsman John Muir.

PREVIOUS PAGES: 'America and the Peerage' from the *Sketch*, September 1903.

'The American Mother of Britain's Baby Lord High Admiral: the Marchioness of Donegall.'

achievement. As Richard Kenin has written, 'How perfect a meeting of circumstances. For the British aristocracy, whose titles were thought to carry far more distinctions than any of their European brethren, possessed just what the newly rich Americans wanted, a social pre-eminence based not simply on the speculative waves of finance but on the rock of primogeniture. If one's daughter were a duchess, one's grandson would without question be a duke. It was one of the most pleasant of certainties.'

Not all of these contract-seekers went to the legendary lengths of Lord Donegall, an eighty-year-old peer, who, at the turn of the century, actually advertised in the press for a wife who would exchange £25,000 in return for the rank of peeress.

Sir Bache and Lady Cunard walking in Hyde Park, 1915

By contrast, Sir Bache Cunard, the middle-aged grandson of the famous shipping family, who also found money when he married the American heiress, Emerald – born Maud Alice Burke (c.1872–1948) – demonstrated a clear case of money marrying

The 9th Duke and Duchess of Marlborough with their children. Oil painting by John Singer Sargent, which still hangs in the Red Drawing Room in Blenheim Palace.

ABOVE: The 8th Duchess of
Marlborough, Consuelo Yznaga del
Valle.

money. Emerald Cunard became one of London's greatest socialites, particularly during the inter-war period, and, as a close friend of Wallis Simpson, was a party to the latter's crisis-laden contribution to the Rich Tide. Since Emerald looked forward to succeeding Lady Airlie as Mistress of the Robes, a position of great honour and some influence, Edward VIII's abdication came as a great shock. She was mortified. 'How could he do this to me?' she is reported to have wept.

Some families did it again and again as with the eighth, ninth and tenth Dukes of Manchester – all of whom married Americans. As early as the 1860s the Prime Minister Lord Palmerston was to remark, 'Before the century is out, these clever and pretty women from New York will pull the strings in half the chancelleries of Europe'. Perhaps he had foreknowledge of Consuelo Yznaga from Louisiana who became the Duchess of Manchester, of Minnie Stevens who became Lady Paget, and of Mrs Arthur Post who became Lady Barrymore. These ladies were not only wealthy, they were also the society beauties of the age. As a wag said at the time, 'ready cash buys Norman blood', while *Society Magazine*, commenting on the trend, added acidly: 'The American republic was founded, it has been said, by housemaids out of place, and mechanics out of employment. It is being solidified by English aristocrats out of elbows.' All of this was socially cemented by the known liking that the then Prince of Wales, Edward VII, had for the cream of these young American

RIGHT: Left to right: Lord Longford, Emily Yznaga (sister of the Duchess of Manchester), HRH The Prince of Wales, Lady Arthur Paget (née Minnie Fiske Stevens), Lady Claude Hamilton, Mr Hall.

women, an attraction and intimacy doubtless developed by his early visit to the United States in 1860.

As we saw in earlier chapters, one of the greatest dynasties to play their remarkable part in Anglo-American relations over three generations had been the Adams family. Then there were the Barings, who married and remarried again and again into America. But two of the best-known aristocratic families with strong American links were the Astors and the Churchills.

'The Duke of Manchester and his bride, Miss Helen Zimmerman.' From the *Sketch* December 1900.

The Astors

A man who has a million dollars is as well off as if he were rich.

JOHN JACOB ASTOR

The founder of the Astor clan was the millionaire John Jacob Astor (1763–1848), who was born near Heidelberg and came to London where his brother had established a musical instrument shop. Remaining there for about three years, learning English, saving money and finding out about America – the country of his dreams – he had heard about the signing of the Treaty of Paris which finally ended the American war in the autumn of 1783, and decided to sail to America. On the voyage he became acquainted with a German who had successfully traded with the Indians, and by the time the ship had reached Chesapeake Bay he had decided to try his luck in the fur trade. He quickly built up a large fortune, eventually monopolizing the American fur trade, and when he died on 20 March 1848, he was worth a fortune of at least $20 million – which made him easily the richest man in the America of that time.

If John Jacob left London because he felt he would be unable to compete with the close-knit British business establishment, his grandson William Waldorf Astor left New York to settle in England because 'he longed for the respect and protection built into the English class system'. (Quoted by David Sinclair in *Dynasty: The Astors and their Times* (1983)). William Waldorf Astor was born in New York City. Like his father and grandfather he completed his education in Germany, but once back in New York he took a law degree at Columbia University before spending a brief period working at a law firm. Not enamoured by the prospect of a life in law, commerce or real estate, he became interested in politics and in 1877 he was elected to a safe seat in the New York Assembly as a Republican. Two years later he was elected to the State Senate. After a somewhat inauspicious year in the Upper House he was put up for election to Congress, but lost out to the Democratic candidate. In 1881 he won the Republican nomination for a safe District, but, despite an expensive and energetic campaign, he lost again. During and after the rather heated election he was humiliated by the press, who portrayed him, not altogether inaccurately, as a narrowly self-interested man, contemptuous of the common people.

For Astor, who saw himself as an American aristocrat, to be treated with so little respect was very hurtful, and it began to turn him against the United States. He might have come to Britain at this point or given up politics, but his career was rescued by President Chester Arthur, who appointed him American Minister to Italy, where he stayed for three years.

When his father died in February 1890 he became the head of the senior branch of the Astor family, with $8.5 million entirely at his disposal and an estimated yearly income of $6 million. Now he could do what he wanted. As an expression of his new position as America's leading aristocrat he planned to build the finest hotel in the United States on the site of his father's house, the Waldorf, completed in 1893, and a large mansion for himself on Fifth Avenue.

Astor's added wealth and power made him even more contemptuous of his native country, and in September 1890 he moved with his family to England. Many Americans interpreted his defection as a puerile reaction to his failure to be accepted by the upper (and lower) classes of his native land. Others maintained that he came to England to obtain, at any cost, a title which would provide a recognizable symbol of the innate superiority he felt he possessed.

As David Sinclair has written, ' "Knowing one's place" was the central principle of social harmony, and to a man as conservative and as steeped in the past as William Waldorf the idea of a title that automatically conferred unquestionable rank would have been appealing.' Astor himself said he finally decided to emigrate because of threats to kidnap his children, though there is no evidence whatsoever to support this claim. Not long after coming to Britain he was almost certainly behind the famous hoax about his own death by which he hoped to find out what people really thought of him. On 12 July 1892 most New York papers reported that he had died of pneumonia. The obituaries, which were generally complimentary, were read with glee by Astor from his London office: for once he had been given a good press.

In order to establish himself in British society and to act out his romantic fantasies, he spent millions equipping himself with residences fit for a nobleman. He rented Lansdowne House for $25,000 a year and, looking for a commercial headquarters, he bought a property at Temple Gardens near the Thames and converted it, at great expense, into an amazing mock Tudor-medieval office building, Astor House.

Later, Astor bought a mansion in Carlton House Terrace and, seeking a country seat, in 1893 he purchased Cliveden in Berkshire from the Duke of Westminster for $1.4 million, spending millions more refurbishing it and filling it with treasures and, at last, surrounding it with an enormous wall – which earned him

William Waldorf Astor
(1848–1919)

the title of Walled-off Astor (English upper-class pronunciation assisting the pun).

Also in 1893, in an attempt to make his mark in British public life he purchased the influential evening newspaper the *Pall Mall Gazette*. He quickly transformed it from a Liberal to a Conservative journal. When many of its staff left to found the rival *Westminster Gazette*, Astor recruited able replacements including Harry Cust as editor. Astor then founded a women's weekly, the *Pall Mall Budget*, and the *Pall Mall Magazine* (said to have been started by Astor after Cust, embarrassed by Astor's insistence that his own writings were to be published in the *Gazette*, suggested that his work was better suited to a literary magazine).

It was the beginning of a new age when newspaper proprietors spent limitless amounts of money in paving Fleet Street with gold. Later, Astor bought the *Observer*, ostensibly to gain the services of its influential editor, J. L. Garvin. Through his newspaper empire Astor had found an occupation which befitted a gentleman and one which enabled him to exert an influence on the political and social life of Britain. But he was not satisfied – it was doubtful if he ever would be – he had not won the honour and respect he longed for. His quixotic thirst for recognition could only be quenched by a peerage. In 1899, after completing the necessary five-year period of residence, he became a British citizen, for which act he was branded a traitor by the American press and public. At the same time he published a complicated genealogical tree in the *Pall Mall Magazine* which dubiously appeared to demonstrate that he possessed noble blood, but he received only ridicule when experts refuted his claims. He gave hundreds of thousands of dollars towards the war effort in South Africa, to universities, to hospitals and to charities but, while this munificence may have helped his cause, a peerage was still not immediately forthcoming.

If Astor was not a baron, at least he could live as if he were one. In 1903 he bought the thirteenth-century Hever Castle in Kent, and again spent millions reconstructing it according to his idea of what a nobleman's fortress should look like, even diverting the River Eden to create a boating lake. He built a mock-Tudor village around the castle for his guests, and to finish it all bought fantastic paintings and treasures including portraits of Henry VIII and Anne Boleyn by Holbein, Cardinal Richelieu's sedan chair and Martin Luther's bible.

The Great War finally gave Astor the opportunity to get what he wanted, his gifts to war charities in 1914 and 1915 winning him a place on the New Year's Honours List of 1916. The following year he was promoted to the rank of Viscount Astor.

The Astor stately homes.
ABOVE: Cliveden Place.

LEFT: Hever Castle.

Nancy Astor (1879–1964)

The liberal press, denouncing his elevation to the nobility, claimed that he bought a peerage from the party in power. Astor in fact only attended the House of Lords on two occasions – when he was introduced in 1916 and then in 1917 when he became a Viscount. On the surface this was quite surprising given his huge efforts to obtain a peerage. However, by that time he had become almost a recluse and, moreover, he was still not interested in active politics nor, despite his medieval romanticism, was he ever practically imbued with a sense of *noblesse oblige*. He spent his last years in Brighton where he died in 1919. His sons, Waldorf and J. J. Astor, inherited his considerable Anglo-American fortune.

William Waldorf Astor got his title, but ultimately failed to become a part of the Old World aristocracy. He was never really accepted by the English social élite. This is perhaps because the only effective way of assimilating into the British upper classes was considered to be by marriage, like Jennie Jerome, or by receiving the upbringing of an English gentleman, which Astor's sons Waldorf and John Jacob had.

Waldorf, the second Viscount, was born in New York City in May 1879, but left America as a child when his father went to Italy. At nine he was sent to an English prep school and then on to Eton where he excelled at both work and sport. At Eton he was trained to adopt the social responsibility and graces by which the British upper classes were defined. He came down from New College, Oxford, in 1902 with no very clear idea of what he might do with his life, just a vague feeling that he wanted to undertake something useful and worthwhile, and for some time he devoted his attention to the development of a stable of thoroughbred horses which was to make him a leading figure in flat racing circles. Apart from that, he enjoyed the leisured existence of the English gentleman of his day, but in 1905 even his hunting, shooting and Swiss winter sports had to end when angina and traces of tuberculosis were diagnosed.

Given this ill health, Waldorf might have been expected to withdraw from public life, but then he met Nancy Langhorne Shaw, the daughter of a Civil War veteran and Southern gentleman, whom Henry James would describe as 'full of possibilities and fine material, though but a reclaimed barbarian . . .' Nancy, a divorcee, was wooed in Virginia by the Ulsterman Angus McDonnell, the second son of the Earl of Antrim, who, like several other second sons of the peerage, went abroad to seek his fortune. He was besotted by Nancy but the romance did not develop, and in 1904 she came to England for the winter season. She fell in love with Lord Revelstoke, the head of the Baring banking house, but the romance broke down because of an alleged affair of Revel-

stoke's. Nancy was heartbroken and after the break-up returned to America, but by this time she was set on acquiring a British husband. According to the story, she wrote to Herbert Asquith for his advice as to which of the men she became acquainted with in England she should consider marrying. As Asquith could not help, she returned to England in December 1905, met Waldorf, who was captivated by her charm, and in the spring of the following year their engagement was announced. William Waldorf would of course have preferred his son to marry a British noblewoman but he did not actively oppose the match, and as a generous mark of this he gave them Cliveden as a wedding present.

In 1910 Waldorf decided to pursue a political career. After one defeat he entered Parliament in December as the Unionist member for Plymouth. The following year his father put him in charge of his newly acquired newspaper, the *Observer*, where, working closely with the editor, J. L. Garvin, Waldorf enhanced his

influence in the Tory party. During the Great War Waldorf's
political career began to blossom. He served as the Parliamentary
private secretary to the Prime Minister, Lloyd George, the Parliamentary secretary to the Minister of Food (1918) and later to
the Minister of Health (1919–20). On his father's death Waldorf
was forced to resign his seat. He wanted to decline the title and
remain in the House of Commons but this was not then consti-
tutionally possible and he thus became the 2nd Viscount Astor.
His wife Nancy, Lady Astor (1879–1964), campaigned in his place
and won the seat for the Conservatives which she was to hold
right up until 1945.

In her electioneering Nancy Astor made much of the Ameri-
can-Mayflower connection, stating in her acceptance speech that
'I am a Virginian, so naturally I am a politician'. To mark the
historic occasion, she was introduced to the House by Balfour and
Lloyd George – both former Prime Ministers. As Lord Lothian, the
British Ambassador, said later to the Virginia Legislature: 'I shall
not soon forget the sight of Lady Astor's trim little figure dressed
in appropriate black, advancing from the bar in the House of
Commons flanked by Mr Balfour and Mr Lloyd George . . . That
was your second conquest of Britain.'

Nancy's political career was active and varied, with temperance and women's rights as her particular concerns. It was she
who said: 'I married beneath me – all women do' – though such
precociousness and her blinkered support for the appeasement of
Hitler won her and the 'Cliveden Set' many enemies, including
the life-long antagonism of Winston Churchill:

'Winston, if I were married to you, I'd put poison in your
coffee.'
'Nancy, if you were my wife, I'd drink it.'

Of her arrival in the House she said, 'I am a novel principle and
have to be endured'. Of her time there she would say, 'I don't
know whether I have become a force in the House of Commons as
much as a nuisance,' and of her last sad day in the House on 15
June 1945 she remarked, 'I leave the House of Commons with the
deepest regret . . . I don't think any other assembly in the world
could have been more tolerant of a foreign-born woman, as I was,
who fought against so many things they believed in . . . I am
heart-broken . . . I shall miss the House, but the House won't miss
me. It never misses anybody.'

Nancy Astor quite simply broke new ground. An American,
married to an MP, who was the son of another American, with
her Virginian power and vivacity, not to say her ambition, played
a crucial role in forwarding the rights of women in that never-

J. J. Astor and his son, October 1932.

before-breached bastion, the British House of Commons. Never forgetting her American roots, she brought to British politics a spirit that 'either charmed or repelled', the most lively, if flawed, woman politician of her generation.

Waldorf eventually gave up active politics but, as the proprietor of the *Observer*, he continued to exert an indirect influence on public opinion. Outside the world of politics and journalism Waldorf's main interest was horse racing. He built up a successful stable and, although he never had a Derby winner, he won 11 Classics and possessed one of the country's top studs. In his turn, Waldorf's son, William, the 3rd Viscount, followed in his father's footsteps – at school, university and as a Tory MP – though he is most often remembered for his heavy involvement in the Profumo Affair in the early 1960s.

John Jacob Astor (1886–1971), William Waldorf's second son, was born in the United States and like his older brother he was educated at Eton and New College, Oxford. He then joined the Life Guards, spending three years in India as an aide-de-camp to the Viceroy, and winning a reputation as a brave tiger hunter. Early in the First World War he was sent to Belgium and was seriously wounded at Ypres. Invalided home he became attached to Lady Mercer-Nairne, the young widow of a fellow officer killed at Ypres, and in 1916 they were married. The match pleased William Waldorf as Violet was the daughter of Lord Minto. After the wedding J. J. Astor returned to the Front but he was badly wounded at Cambrai during the last German offensive and lost a leg.

Leaving the Life Guards as a major he inherited Hever and the Carlton House Terrace home on his father's death, as well as a large stake in the Astor fortune. In 1920 he stood as the Conservative Coalition candidate for the safe seat of Dover but lost to a Tory right-winger who opposed Lloyd George's coalition, which J. J., like Nancy and Waldorf, and many Conservatives, then supported. On 23 October 1922 he bought *The Times*. Within a month he was elected for Dover. In contrast to Nancy he was a reticent and rather shy individual and was not cut out to be a politician. However, as proprietor of *The Times* he, too, exerted influence on the political life of Britain.

In 1956 J. J. was rewarded with a baronetcy for his philanthropic efforts and his service to the country. He was now called Baron Astor of Hever, the same title held by his father before he became Viscount. He died in 1971. Born an American, through education and upbringing he, like so many of his family, had become the quintessential English gentleman.

The Churchills

On 12 August 1873 the celebrated American beauty, Jennie Jerome, was invited to a ball given by the Prince and Princess of Wales in HMS *Ariadne* at Cowes for the Tsarevich and Tsarina of Russia. There she met and fell instantly in love with Lord Randolph, the younger son of the seventh Duke of Marlborough and a leading member of the Prince of Wales's social set. They met again on the following day and by the third they had decided to marry. Randolph's family did not approve of the match as a Marlborough was expected to marry into the high peerage. Randolph responded by sending his father Jennie's photograph adding that 'she is as nice, as lovable, and amiable and charming in every way as she is beautiful, and by her education and bringing-up she is in every way qualified to fill any position'.

The Duke was not convinced. 'Under any circumstances an American connection is not one we would like,' he said. 'You must allow it is a slight coming down in pride for us to contemplate the connection. From what you tell me and what I have heard, this Mr Jerome seems to be a sporting, and I should think, vulgar sort of man. I hear he owns about six or eight houses in New York. (One may take this as an indication of what the man is.)' For good measure the Duke went on: 'It is evident he is of the class of speculators.'

Leonard Jerome, dubbed the King of Wall Street and Father of the American Turf, was indeed a dashing entrepreneur who was, incidentally, related by marriage to George Washington, while his cousin was James Roosevelt, the father of Franklin Delano Roosevelt, making Winston and Franklin eighth cousins once removed. Jerome was the founder of the New York Jockey Club and the builder of the Jerome Park Racehouse. He had also built himself a large mansion on the corner of Madison Square. Jennie's mother, Clara, was a good-looking fashionable lady, but in 1858, bored by her husband's womanizing (Jennie had been named after the famous singer Jenny Lind, one of Leonard Jerome's favourites) and perhaps also by New York social life, she moved to Paris with her three daughters – Jennie, Clara and Leonie. Enjoying the Paris social scene where they were well received at the Court of Napoleon, they remained in France until the defeat of the French army and the imminent arrival of the Prussians in the capital forced them to depart for England.

Jennie's mother, though something of a snob, was not particularly pleased with her daughter's engagement to Randolph, for she hoped that Jennie would marry an actual duke, or some foreign aristocrat. However, Leonard Jerome approved of the match, until, that is, he heard about the Duke of Marlborough's low opinion of him. The Duke insisted that the couple should spend a while away from each other, hoping that Randolph would change his mind. However, as they remained very much in love, the Duke reluctantly gave his assent to the marriage. At least if Jennie could supply a handsome dowry and thus inject some much needed new wealth into the family the match would not be too much of a disaster. Unfortunately, though, Leonard Jerome was not as rich as everyone thought, and had suffered badly during the Wall Street Crash of 1873. As a result, the marriage negotiations between the two families were far from easy, but after much deliberation, a mutually satisfactory settlement was reached, and on 15 April 1874 the couple were married at the

Lord Randolph Churchill (1849–95) *c.* 1880.

Jenny Jerome, Lady Randolph Churchill (1854–1921), 1888.

The 'Anglo-American' magazine, with Lady Randolph Churchill on the cover of the first issue, November 1898.

British Embassy in Paris. The Duke and Duchess did not attend.

Two weeks before the wedding Randolph had been elected to Parliament as the Member for Woodstock – and thus began his spectacular political career. But his first year married to Jennie was largely spent enjoying the social round, the only brief interruption being caused by the premature birth of a son – Winston – on 30 November 1874, one who in later life was to become the first foreigner since Lafayette to be given American citizenship by Congress, and, on whose death, the President of the United States was to order that American flags were to be flown at half mast.

The parents' fabulous social life was ended by the famous row between Randolph and the Prince of Wales over the affair which Randolph's brother, the Marquis of Blandford, was having with Lady Aylesford. When the Prince heard about the affair while visiting India with Lady Aylesford's husband, he insisted that both the Blandfords and the Aylesfords divorce each other and that Blandford must marry his mistress (who as it turned out was pregnant). To Randolph the Prince's demand was totally unreasonable. Knowing that the Prince himself had earlier had an affair or flirtation with Lady Aylesford, and happening to own some revealing letters to prove it, he threatened to publish them unless the Prince retracted his demands. The Prince reacted badly to what amounted to an act of blackmail. He swore never to attend a gathering at which the Churchills were present, and Jennie and Randolph were consequently ostracized by the social élite.

Blandford did not marry Lady Aylesford, though he did divorce his wife and later in 1888 became the second Churchill to marry an American, being betrothed to a rich widow, Mrs Lillian Hammersley, who was to become disparagingly known as 'Duchess Lily'; 'A common-looking and badly dressed woman with a moustache and a fortune amounting to some $5 million', according to a contemporary magazine report, and by other accounts 'jolly but vulgar'.

After the Blandford scandal Randolph's father wisely accepted Disraeli's offer of the Vice-Regency of Ireland and Randoph accompanied him to Dublin as his private secretary. Following four profitable years in Ireland, Randolph came back into the mainstream of English political and social life, becoming famous as the leader of a small group of Tory backbenchers (with A. J. Balfour, Sir Henry Wolff and John Gorst) who became known as the Fourth Party because of their vigorous opposition to Gladstone's administration. Randolph, a brilliant debater, brought life to the Commons (and brought the best out of the Grand Old Man – Gladstone – who relished Randolph's challenges on the floor of the House).

In 1885 Randolph was rewarded with a plum post at the India Office, and over the next few years rose to become the Leader of the House of Commons and the Chancellor of the Exchequer. However, he was often his own worst enemy, and after falling out once too often with Lord Salisbury, then Prime Minister, over a question of policy, he offered to resign. Perhaps to his surprise – for, although he had several enemies in the Cabinet, he had thought himself to be indispensable – Salisbury accepted, and Randolph went into the political wilderness and never really returned.

During his mercurial rise and fall Jennie, despite the rapid decline of their marriage, played an active role in her husband's political career – organizing public meetings, canvassing votes and speaking at the hustings. She helped to found, with her husband and others, the Primrose League, a Tory political–social organization which still exists today. During the Boer War, as Chairman of a Committee of American Women in Britain, she directed the raising of money to equip a hospital ship, *Maine*, which under a British chief surgeon was staffed by American doctors, nurses and crew.

Afflicted with syphilis, Randolph's physical and mental faculties gradually but irrevocably deteriorated and, not surprisingly, his relationship with Jennie worsened. Once so sharp in Parliament, his speeches were increasingly punctuated by embarrassing lapses of thought and outbursts. Finally in January 1895, after a world cruise taken with Jennie had failed to revive his health, he died, aged only 45.

Throughout their married life Jennie had attracted numerous admirers. She fell deeply in love with an elegant Austrian nobleman, Count Kinsky, whom she probably would have married had the Count not been forced into a dynastic match by his parents shortly before Randolph's death. Later in 1900, she scandalized London Society by marrying a handsome young officer, George Cornwallis-West, who was only 16 days older than her son, Winston. For a while, though short of money, they were happy, but Cornwallis-West eventually left her to marry the famous actress, Mrs Patrick Campbell, who ironically was the star of a play written by Jennie when she was 64, *Borrowed Plumes*.

In 1918 Jennie married for the third time, to Montagu Porch, who at 45 was younger than Winston. Three years later she died after a domestic accident. Jennie had a considerable effect on her husband, on her more famous son, and on the politics and social scene of a generation. Witty, charming and astute, she was the epitome of those glamorous marriages that did so much to give the roots and branches to the greater Anglo-American family tree.

In contrast to Randolph, the ninth Duke of Marlborough like the eighth (Lillian Hammersley's bridegroom) married an American purely for money. Consuelo Vanderbilt was an extremely rich heiress of only 18 when she was forced, in 1895, by her domineering social-climbing mother to marry the Duke. This arranged marriage was assisted to its conclusion by those two American-born ladies, the Duchess of Manchester and Lady Paget. Consuelo later said that when he proposed to her 'there was no need for sentiment', for, as she added, 'in a small room in the church itself,

Lady Randolph Churchill at her residence in Brook Street, August 1914.

THE GRAPHIC

AN ILLUSTRATED WEEKLY NEWSPAPER

No. 878.—Vol. XXXIV.
Registered as a Newspaper

SATURDAY, SEPTEMBER 25, 1886

WITH EXTRA SUPPLEMENT

PRICE SIXPENCE
By Post Sixpence Halfpenny

"VICE VERSA"—THE OLD CHANCELLOR OF THE EXCHEQUER AND THE NEW

the bridegroom and the bride's father signed an agreement giving Marlborough a dowry of $1.6 million in cash and the income from $2 million in gilt-edged stocks'; other subventions later given to the Duke and Duchess and their sons brought the total close to $20 million.

The marriage was an unhappy failure, ending in a separation in 1906, though, as a result of the business-like matrimonial contract, after the divorce was officially concluded 14 years later, the Duke continued to receive a $100,000 pension from the Vanderbilt fortune, allowing him, incidentally, to rebuild

The Duke of Marlborough and his bride, Miss Consuelo Vanderbilt, married in New York, November 6th, 1895.

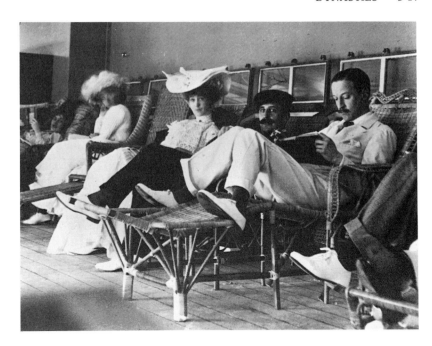

Miss Jacobs, Miss Dempsey, the
Duchess of Marlborough, Mr Bruce,
the Duke of Marlborough, from the
Durbar, Delhi Album, 1902.

The Duchess of
Marlborough at a Women's
Municipal Party in Battersea.

Blenheim Palace on the proceeds, to the benefit of countless contemporary British and American tourists. He later married another American while Consuelo found similar solace with a Frenchman, Jacques Balsan. While Consuelo always found it difficult to adjust to the stuffy and highly formal social life of the Marlborough family, after separating from the Duke she became actively involved in the women's rights movement. She founded women's hostels, wrote and lectured, promoted women's education and won election to the London County Council as a Liberal member. Like a number of other twentieth-century American expatriate women, she found no barrier or disincentive to assisting sections of British society in their political aspirations, and did so with vigour.

Jumping a generation, and reversing the family pattern, Winston Churchill's son Randolph married in 1937 Pamela Digby, daughter of Lord Digby, who later, long after her divorce and Randolph's death, married the outstanding American Democrat and diplomat, Governor Averell Harriman, became an American citizen and is still one of Washington's most celebrated political hostesses. She spent the war years living in Downing Street and thus is a woman who, more than any other, has had a unique viewpoint of Anglo-American relationships over the last 45 years. She was brought up at Minterne, the Dorset estate which had belonged to the first Sir Winston Churchill.

Randolph Churchill married Pamela Digby at St John's Church, Westminster, October 1939.

Sir Henry Channon and Lady Honor Guinness leaving St Margaret's, Westminster, after their marriage in July 1933.

There are many other Anglo-American family links that loom large in the present century, from Prime Minister Harold Macmillan (later the Earl of Stockton) whose mother Helen (Nellie) Tarleton Belles was a sculptor and singer from Indiana, to the redoubtable American-born Sir Henry 'Chips' Channon (1897–1958), the Oxford-educated beau who married Lady Honor Guinness, the eldest daughter of the Earl of Iveagh. A leading socialite in the 1930s, a close friend of Emerald Cunard and another supporter of Wallis Simpson, he became the Conservative MP for Southend, a seat now held by his son Paul, a senior minister in the Thatcher government. Today many British politicians from all the major parties – including Anthony Wedgwood Benn and David Owen – have American wives.

It is easy to consider the Anglo-American dynasties as a mere curiosity. That is far from being the case given the range and degree of political and social importance of the participants. Some were phenomena, creatures of their period and prisoners of its values; others, like the Adamses and the Churchills, as we have seen, have had an essential and lasting effect, as central to the Rich Tide as any other subjects in this book.

Back in the dark days of 1940, Winston Churchill himself seemed to be thinking in tidal terms when he spoke of the way in which the British Empire and the United States were going to be 'mixed up together in some of their affairs for mutual and general advantage'. Churchill said majestically and yet simply, 'For my own part, looking out upon the future, I do not view the process with any misgivings. I could not stop it if I wished; no one can stop it. Like the Mississippi, it just keeps on rolling along. Let it roll. Let it roll on full flood, inexorable, irresistible, benignant, to broader lands and better days.' Arguably both in war and peace, the Rich Tide has contrived to fulfil many of Churchill's dreams over the past four and a half decades – in essence if not always in grandeur. The future, however, may be a little cloudier . . .

Winston Churchill beginning his speech called 'The Sinews of Peace' in Fulton, Missouri, March 1946.

CHAPTER TWELVE

The Tide of the Future

As we mentioned in our Acknowledgements, after we completed our study of The Rich Tide in the past, we conducted a varied series of interviews with both Britons and Americans about the way they perceive the Rich Tide in the present and future. These conversations produced a potent cocktail of mixed emotions – reassurance from many Americans, self-doubt from many on the other side of the Atlantic. Optimism was often tempered by doubt and pessimism was almost always tempered by regret.

There is no doubt about where the Reagan and Thatcher administrations stand on the Rich Tide. President Reagan, Vice-President Bush, Caspar Weinberger and Margaret Thatcher were all unequivocal in their enthusiasm about its present status and their confidence about its future prospects. 'Britain,' the President observed, 'is without doubt the single foreign country which is best known in the United States.' And is there a special bond that exists between the United States and Britain that does not exist between the United States and any other country? 'The simple answer is yes. While we share a common language with a number of countries, and a common culture and legal system to varying degrees with a somewhat smaller number, the UK has been the common source from which the shared elements are derived.' And do our shared historical ties still mean anything in America today, or are they now largely irrelevant? 'While the sources of cultural and intellectual inspiration of the United States are more diverse than they were when the country was younger, English language, law and culture continue to be of very real relevance to us. In addition, what the United States can contribute to the UK in this area is substantially greater than it was as recently as a generation or two ago. Paradoxically, the increased diversity in the world around us has contributed to strengthening the bonds between our two countries.'

Many people have predicted that the bonds between our two countries will have weakened considerably by the turn of the century. What did the President think? 'Given past history and the

President Reagan and Mrs Thatcher
walking through the woods at
Camp David 22nd December 1984,
during her stopover after visiting
China.

likely need for an even closer relationship in the future, the bonds
will probably be even stronger than they are now. We live in an
insecure world and it is only through such a mutually supportive
relationship that the two oldest English-speaking democracies
can advance the vision and the ideals which they share.' And the
President added a postscript, 'The present relationship between
our two governments is perhaps the closest that it has been for
some years.'

Vice-President Bush was equally confident about the future bonds between the two countries, though he added a rider. 'It would, I think, be a disservice to the relationship between our countries to deal with them in a particularly personal or sentimental fashion. Let's face it, Britain is wrestling with some daunting economic and sociological problems – unemployment, inefficient industry, militant trade unions and remnants of the class system. All these issues confront Britain's leaders and they comprise a formidable agenda. How these issues are dealt with will, in the long run, determine how relations between our two countries will evolve. However, I have great faith in the quality of British character and the strength of Britain's leaders and hope and believe that at the end of the century our bonds will have been strengthened as Britain emerges into a new century free of some of these problems which consume so much time and effort today.'

The Vice-President's final comments were essentially positive. 'Despite all I have said about the issues being dealt with by the British government today, the sense of something special will always endure. Our countries have shared so much down through the years that there is still a sense of family that comes to the fore when world issues are discussed.'

Caspar Weinberger felt equally strongly about the sense of family. 'I think when Americans get to go to England – even Americans who don't have English ancestry or English roots – they feel a sense of kinship, and I think that that is not just rooted in history, but it's rooted in shared ideals and an acceptance of shared values. I think that, yes, there is a special bond that I don't sense with other countries.

'I know that there's a certain fashionable school of people – and I've heard some of them at recent conferences that the Woodrow Wilson and Smithsonian Institute sponsored, along with Ditchley – that says the relationship and the ''Special Relationship'' and all is exhausted and completed now. But I don't think that. I think it's been woven into the fabric and background now of a great many individuals, so the reason that those ties just aren't thought of so much or perhaps spoken of so much is not because they're weakening. It's because they're becoming so much a part of the background and the shared assumptions that people don't even single them out – they've just become ingrained, an indivisible part now of so many individuals.'

And when America supports Britain over the Falklands, or Britain supports America over Libya, is that long-standing loyalty and friendship or is it purely strategic? 'Oh no, I think it's a good mixture of both. You could make a lot of arguments as to why

Vice-President George Bush.

there was a strategic or military reason for neither to have helped the other in the two instances you've mentioned. Indeed many people, of course, made those arguments. But certainly our administration never had the slightest hesitancy in supporting to the fullest extent we possibly could the enormously difficult and skilful effort that Britain made in the Falklands and – as was quite apparent – Britain was the only country to support publicly in the way that they did the action we felt we had to take in Libya. And that was a very courageous act by Mrs Thatcher, to do that in the face of what she knew would be very strong opposition.'

And, governments apart, did contemporary Britain still matter to America? Was Britain still making a contribution to America and Americans in terms of people and ideas? 'Very much so. There's enormous expertise on the scientific side and on the managerial side and there's a great deal of capital being invested from England in the United States, and a continuing interchange in military and defence matters. There's the more intangible interchanges, too – ideas, the fruits of scholarship, the Americans who study in the English universities are both bringing and carrying back a great deal. I think the Rhodes idea is still very much alive.'

Margaret Thatcher felt the same way. 'Certainly there is a tide still flowing from Britain to America, both of people and ideas. Cheap air travel brings the United States in reach for an unprecedented number of our people. We are the largest foreign investor in the United States. When you think of the flow of ideas over the last fifty years, you call to mind the economic theories of John Maynard Keynes; the British contribution to the development of radar, the jet engine and the atomic bomb; more recently the discovery of the structure of DNA; the development of optical fibres; the influence of British drama. That is an impressive list, not just in quantity but in quality.'

Caspar Weinberger, Secretary of Defence.

And the most important contributions we are currently making to each other? 'From the American side the contribution which I would stress most is that of the enterprise culture, which rewards initiative, encourages people to set up their own business and to be self-reliant, to provide for their own families rather than look to the State to do so. I would also single out respect for hard work and success rather than for rank or birth as a major and beneficial influence from the United States.

'In the other direction I would single out, in the field of ideas, the quality of our scientists and engineers. It was no surprise to me that the United States were keen to have access to the best British brains in support of their Strategic Defense Initiative and in other fields like the space programme and medical science. I also believe that they still value our advice on international issues because of our unrivalled experience in certain parts of the world.

'When it comes to people, the list is almost endless. Men like Neville Marriner, Georg Solti, or Raymond Leppard in the world of music, and Alistair Cooke in the press. Hollywood still draws on British talent, and American shopping malls have branches of Laura Ashley, Conran's, Burberry's, Jaeger and many others.'

Mrs Thatcher felt that people tend to play down the Special Relationship far too much, to be almost shy about mentioning it. 'I am proud of the Special Relationship. It stems from the time we stood alone together against dictatorship in the Second World War and later in Korea. We are both countries who have fought for freedom and that creates a special bond. Of course there has been a change. But we still share basic fundamental values: democracy and liberty under the law, free enterprise societies. Britain and the United States forged together the main institutions of the post-war world such as the United Nations and the North Atlantic Alliance. These shared experiences have created a habit of working very closely together right across the board in defence, foreign affairs, high finance, not just as a reflex action but because both sides positively value it and find it useful. We have a unique relationship in the nuclear and intelligence fields. We communicate with each other much more easily than other nations.

'None of that will change. It is sometimes suggested that the growth of the European Community will weaken our relationship with the United States. But I absolutely do not accept that it should do so. I have never seen closer cooperation in Europe as an alternative to a close relationship with the United States, but something to be pursued in parallel. We have enormous reason to be grateful to America in this country: for its contribution to our defence and the way in which it defends freedom worldwide. As long as we remember that, the Atlantic will continue to unite us and not divide us.'

Lord Franks has a unique perspective on the relationship between Britain and the United States since the war. He went to Washington as British Ambassador in 1948. 'When I first went to the United States, Britain and America were still partners — unequal partners, admittedly, but we were still partners. We took care of things in Asia and Africa while they were taking care of things elsewhere. If I had gone to America ten years earlier, before the war, I would have found Britain and America to still be equal partners. Before the war the United States was still the sleeping giant, not looking at the whole world, while we still had a world empire. Their economic power was already greater than ours before the war but our global responsibilities were still greater. That had all changed by the fourth year of the war. Only America managed to pursue its war effort without throttling back civilian production. And when Japan gave up, Americans overseas numbered about ten million. Immediately after the war fifty per cent of the world's production resources were in the United States. And then, after two years of hesitation, with the Marshall Plan the United States took up their world role. That was a key moment. Marshall's speech at Harvard, June 5th 1947.

'To come back to 1948 when we were unequal partners: we

Lord Franks, then Sir Oliver Franks, on his way to take up his post as British Ambassador to the United States.

were still the first to be consulted. There was an intimacy that was not shared by anybody else. I remember June 1950 during the Korean War; the Americans were very concerned; things were not looking good. And Lord Tedder and I were summoned to meet with Omar Bradley. No other country was there. It was quite natural – it was just the British.'

When did we cease to be even unequal partners? 'That collapsed at Suez in 1956. That was the end of any real form of partnership. It was renewed a little under Macmillan and Kennedy, then weak again under L.B.J., who just wished that the whole world would go away . . .'

Peter Jay, himself the British Ambassador to Washington from 1977 to 1979, reflected on the same period: 'There is no doubt, in my opinion, that there was an historically freakish and extraordinarily wonderful period between about 1941 when the Atlantic Charter was written and about 1951 when the two

President Kennedy and Prime Minister Harold Macmillan during talks in Bermuda 21st December 1961. The five-hour talks covered Berlin, the Congo and nuclear tests.

governments together (with only minimal consultation with our loyal allies, the French) re-drew the economic, financial, functional map of the world in a way which I think was amazingly imaginative, extraordinarily bold and basically right. And almost all the genuinely global and also the Western institutions which structure international relationships were created during that period. That was an exceptional period, but there never was a period when Britain had a veto, there never was a period when "Will Britain go along with it?" was a dominant factor. There was a period when the United States in the forties found it convenient and necessary to co-operate to quite a high extent. And it was possible for people like Oliver Franks to do some very fruitful work. That was partly because the principal subjects which they actually talked about were in themselves world-shaping subjects, and you don't talk about world-shaping subjects now because everybody knows we haven't a chance of shaping the world. We can only talk about rather marginal and rather cosmetic issues.'

Former Prime Minister James Callaghan mused about the current balance of power between Britain and America, and indeed about the Special Relationship itself. 'I think the first time the phrase was used was in a speech by Churchill that I listened to in the House in November or December 1945. I'm pretty sure that's almost the first time we ever heard it. And it arose because of the intimacy of the war, obviously. It arose because we made special arrangements in which we were jointly operational with the Americans: for example, Bretton Woods, the setting of the

James Callaghan.

post-war monetary scene; for example, the nuclear arrangements in which they rather diddled us as a result of the MacMahon Act; for example, the communications network, the intelligence network, with GCHQ here and the National Security Authority at Fort Meade in Maryland. Those are the kind of things that formed the Special Relationship, plus of course the natural diplomatic exchange that grew up. But those things were merely the tangible evidence of this Special Relationship which was then derived from what we conceived to be our joint interests. Now they are almost a reason for the existence of the Special Relationship. That's the difference.

'*Then* it was a Special Relationship because our interests were the same, our objectives were the same – to rebuild an independent Europe; to prevent it falling under Soviet domination; to contain Soviet expansion; to have an international trading system that would support both the dollar and sterling. We were a world power, but with the dissolution of Empire – the Commonwealth has not taken its place in the same sense – our interests and our objectives are now not – and I say this with regret because I have loved that partnership – are now not necessarily the same as those of the United States.'

In what way do they differ? 'First of all there was the European Community, which is now a third area, and you look at the areas of tension. You have an area of tension between the United States and Europe of which we are now a part on agriculture, on trade relations, on attitudes to the Middle East or to Latin America. All these, I think, are areas where the European outlook, the European interests are not the same as those of the United States.

'Nations live by their long-term interests. And it is not in our long-term interest to follow some of the things the United States is doing. I don't say this as a matter of rejoicing. But I see every year the European bond becoming stronger, even though there's no particular affection there, and the American one becoming weaker. And as long as we have American nuclear bases here – and they supply us with Trident or Polaris or whatever it is – that will, I fear, become the real substance of the Special Relationship instead of merely being the expression of it.'

But, emotionally, to whom are we closer today? 'I should say that the average British citizen still feels closer to America than he does to France or to Germany.' And what about America's loyal support of us in the Falklands – was that a tribute to the bond? Was it a sort of last gesture to the Special Relationship? 'I hope it wasn't the *last* gesture, but I think it was a gesture to the Special Relationship in which all the old nostalgia came to the surface

OPPOSITE: Cover of *Time* Magazine on the theme of Swinging Britain, 15th April 1966.

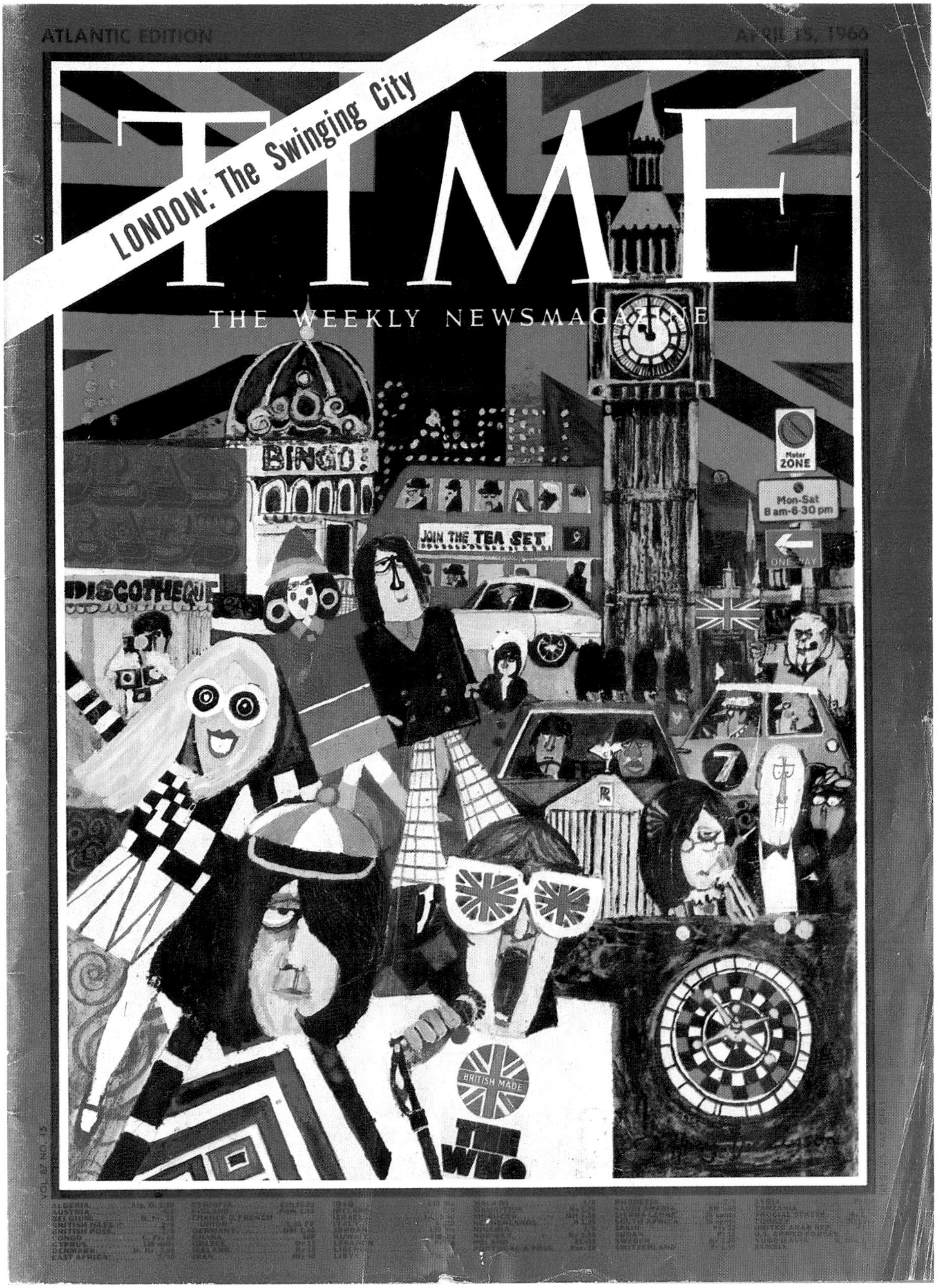

ATLANTIC EDITION
APRIL 15, 1966
LONDON: The Swinging City
TIME
THE WEEKLY NEWSMAGAZINE
BINGO!
JOIN THE TEA SET
DISCOTHEQUE
Meter ZONE
Mon-Sat 8 am-6.30 pm
ONE WAY
BRITISH MADE
THE WHO
VOL. 87 NO. 15

about Britain fighting again and I have no doubt in my mind, talking to people like Haig and others, that this was a dominant sentiment among a great many of them. Not among Jeane Kirkpatrick; she didn't feel that way at all. But, then, there will be more and more Jeane Kirkpatricks as the days go by: fewer and fewer Al Haigs – after all, he's been Commander-in-Chief of NATO, hasn't he? So we were lucky in that sense, I think. There will always be, I think, this core of sentiment about us, but sentiment is not the stuff on which you build a special relationship. We can't continue to live in the role of that of an impoverished but rather admired poor relation.'

And governments apart, and special relationships apart, did Mr Callaghan think that British brains still have a larger than proportionate influence? 'I would have thought that British brains are very much valued in the United States. Very much. And individually they think we're pretty good. Collectively, they don't think much of us.' A point that was to be echoed by Harold Evans when he said, 'The big difference between England and America is that the Americans have wonderful systems. We have wonderful individuals – and lousy systems.'

Harold Evans also took up the subject of the Falklands and America's decision to support Britain. 'That I thought was a decision taken by President Reagan which could have been taken by President Carter. It was one based on human rights in recognition that it was democracy against a dictatorship and that we were important for that reason, which is a philosophical approach. We were also important pragmatically because we were the strong European ally.'

David Owen felt much the same way. 'I think they supported us for both emotional and historical reasons. And I think the pragmatic reasons would have kept them in their position which they started off with – trying to play the honest broker. And I think the reasons, who knows, are perhaps the links between the services, which are very, very strong and I suspect that was probably more important than the political reasons. In many ways it was a remarkable act of friendship that they paid such a heavy price economically in their relationships with Latin America. I think it was also a slight sense of what was right and wrong and I think it was so clear to them that the Argentinians were the aggressors. I think that a sense of right and wrong in the United States is pretty strong.'

'That tells you something,' added Clay Felker, the creator of *New York* magazine, 'that in a real crunch the United States will always stand by and back England. So to that degree it is a permanent relationship.' 'I think first of all', said Alistair Cooke,

OPPOSITE: Cover of *Punch: Our American Heritage: The Transatlantic influence in Britain.* Cartoon by Ronald Searle

there was a sentimental desire to be on Britain's side, but I think that the main thing was that they felt that this was British territory and Americans didn't know much or care about the Malvinas and how long this has been going on, and the Argentine's very strong claim to own this. I mean, nobody brought up the thought that, for instance, if Long Island were British, it would therefore still be British because the historical background was about as far off!'

James Reston is an optimist about the future of the Rich Tide. 'First of all you have to remember, I think, that in the critical periods in the relationship between the United States and the United Kingdom, in the first decade of this century, and before the Second World War, the great power of business was essentially isolationist. The business people were the people who thought ''Well, America is not a country; America is an empire. It doesn't need overseas trade or anything else.'' Now you have a dramatic

VJ Day, celebrations 1945: girls draped in the Stars and Stripes dance in Trafalgar Square.

Anglo-American co-operation: British taking over a zone from the Americans, June 1945.

change. The multinationals are taking the best of the brains out of the universities; they are deeply involved in the world. They are a new force in the politics of co-operation, in my view.'

Despite the change in the relative power of the two countries, Britain, he felt, still had an important role to play. 'We are, I believe, getting what I would call some reverse lend-lease in diplomacy. That is to say, here is Reagan who thinks he has a doctrine – and whenever anybody has a doctrine, you want to keep your fingers crossed – but here he is, he thinks now he is going to intervene all over the place or he is going to use sanctions here and there in the other places; and Britain and the other partners in NATO who have far more experience in the world than we do are saying, "Now, come on . . . take it easy there." And therefore there is a very influential calming voice, an experienced voice, coming from the United Kingdom, I think, and the rest of the world, to America which is desperately needed here.

'There is a fundamental difference between the New World and the Old World. Remember the old signs that used to be in the country store here: "The improbable we do today and the impossible – give us until Monday." That is still the attitude here that we can *stop* communism or we can *go* to the moon, or we can build a shield against offensive nuclear weapons. Well, the experience

James Reston.

of the Old World – if I hear it right – is saying to us: Look, in a way Hitler thought that – that if everything in his massive plan worked to perfection and there were no accidents and it didn't snow in Stalingrad and so on, why then he would indeed see a German Empire of a thousand years. But I think Europe is saying: You know, you may be smart over there in Washington, but you can't repeal human nature. Everything is not down to the point of perfection. Nirvana is not inevitable.'

Harold Evans took up the same theme: 'The Americans bring a very emotional approach to foreign affairs in the sense of the Soviet Union being all evil and we are all good. The English bring a

Harold Evans, then editor of the *Sunday Times*.

common sense pragmatism to it. Look, those men may have ill designs, but they're not all evil, and we're not all good, and it's possible to make arrangements with them. And I think that's a very important influence. Because the most dangerous influence in American foreign policy is the messianic tradition – that we've got to go out like the Crusaders and conquer. They see themselves engaged in the struggle between good and evil. We, rightly or wrongly, see ourselves engaged in the struggle between not so good and not so bad.'

Back to James Reston: 'I think there is an affectionate eye here at this side of the Atlantic in regard to Britain and I do not think there is the same the other way around. I think I see even in the headlines these days in Fleet Street a kind of mockery, and there is a fear, quite naturally I think, of cultural aggression. But there is a holding back again what I think is a good thing which is that we should get all mixed up together. As soon as somebody suggests that Sikorsky should buy the helicopters or that maybe the British Leyland company should make a deal with a US company, there is – and I understand this – a quite natural outcry that you don't want to be taken over: it is one thing to lose the Colonies but it's another thing to be colonized.'

Alistair Cooke also felt that the flow of transatlantic opinion was not always fair to the United States. 'I have always made a point of saying that the British are lucky that the American pre-conceptions of the British are very flattering. Everybody reads *The Times* and they have Chippendale furniture and so on.

David and Debbie Owen.

And the British pre-conceptions about America are still that it's materialistic, that it's vulgar, and got a kind of boisterous vitality that's not anything you'd want. And Americans are able to shut out from their minds the fact of appalling brutality and hooliganism in English soccer, for instance.'

James Reston had one further point to make about British attitudes today. 'There is one thing I must say that rather sticks in our throats over here – and I put it to you in my plain Scottish way – you know we get a sense here – and now I'm talking about governments and attitudes of governments and maybe attitudes of the Press – that if only the British were in charge instead of this cowboy from Hollywood, all would be well, because you know so much more. Well, our answer to that is – when you were in charge you had two world wars in twenty years. We've now gone through the two generations since these clumsy giants took over, and our record is not so bad.'

As an American living in Britain, Debbie Owen said that she almost wished for the Special Relationship to become less and less. 'I think that the Brit is a European. The rhythm, the values are much more European than American and it seems to me that if there is going to be a strength and a new realignment, it should be a European one.' David Owen felt the same way. 'I think that politically Britain ought not to go on trying to boost a sort of relationship in a rather artificial way and I think that in recent years there's been a slight tendency to try and revive something which isn't there. I think that Britain's destiny is European predominantly. Though I think because of this language, because of this empathy, because of this sort of history, there *will* be times when Britain has a peculiarly close linkage acting as a link between Europe and America as long as we don't make too much of it.

'I would think that the Americans give a higher priority to the Federal Republic of Germany of all the European powers and to Japan as the centre of gravity in American politics increasingly moves away from the east coast, and more and more Presidents, Vice-Presidents and key senators are from the South or from the West. I think there is more and more of an orientation towards the Pacific. I think the Atlantic is nowhere near as dominant in their outlook. And for these reasons I believe it's high time Europe took more responsibility for its defence and realized that economically it has to build up its industrial strength and it must not expect America to think the Atlantic is more important than the Pacific. If we understand that and build up a European relationship then I think we will have a better one with America.

'So often I think we simply do not understand. It is typical how

Britain does not understand President Reagan, for example. You get almost all the British intellectuals and the left of centre who are scathing and have never understood the extent of Reagan's appeal. I mean, here is a man, a two-term President, massively popular, great empathy, and we say dismissively – What was he? – just the two-term Governor of California. California – which in terms of gross national product is the sixth largest country in the world. We underestimate that man and have consistently under-estimated him because we aren't prepared to understand that whole western Californian culture.'

On the political issue, Alistair Cooke was in no doubt. 'I don't think there is a Special Relationship. I think since Kennedy there hasn't been a Special Relationship. I remember 1961, down at Palm Beach. I was the only correspondent with the White House Press Corps. Which in those days was twenty-two guys – very manageable. Kennedy was going to Europe. He was going to Berlin. He was going to see De Gaulle. So I said to him when it was all over, "Have you any plans to go to London?" And he said, "No." Later on he said to Larry O'Brien, "Why go to London? England doesn't matter a damn any more."''

An obituary which would probably come as good news to Peter Jay. His view: 'This Special Relationship is a bit of a pain in the neck. It's something that has to be formally celebrated every time the British Prime Minister goes to dine at the White House and the President gets up and mentions it and all the British officials heave a gigantic sigh of relief because seven months of diplomacy have paid off and he has included the phrase in his speech. All of that seems to be ghastly. If that's what it was about, getting this empty phrase mentioned in a quick speech written by a junior speech-writer in the White House so that the President could deliver it over dinner when he entertains the British Prime Minister today and he entertained the Israeli Prime Minister yesterday and the Egyptian Prime Minister tomorrow, it would merely illustrate how absolutely empty the whole thing is.

'All of those things in my opinion, the official symbols of the relationship and certainly any attempts on the part of British ministers and officials to think there is some real substance in it, is dangerous and distracting from what is the reality, which is that the relationship between Britain and the United States (as to 95% of what's important about it) is not a relationship between two governments. It's not the property of two governments, it is the relationship between two peoples. It is not a relationship between each and every one of them on either side, but none the less it is a relationship whose values, whose successes, whose failures, whose strength, whose fruitfulness comes from what happens when private citizens whether employed in a professional or artistic capacity or in a purely personal capacity meet one another and travel backwards and forwards and that is what 95% of it is all about. The relationship between the governments is – and is almost bound to be – conspicuously weaker than the relationships between the people. It is all enormously complicated – and it has been for twenty-five years – by the whole problem of Britain's relationship with Europe with a capital E not least and indeed predominantly because Britain's identification with Europe with a capital E, has been an object of American policy. Madly and mistakenly and self-destructively for both Britain and the United States, in my opinion, but none the less it's been a major object of policy and all the things which in fact make the United States' relationship so crucially important to the British people – and sometimes the British government – are seen by continental Europeans as objects of suspicion, as well they might be, for very good reasons.

'In any case it's important to understand the United States' attitude to Britain in governmental terms. You have to understand that Washington, like any gigantic world power centre, is a great parallelogram of forces. The element in those forces which is represented by external events, if you exclude for the moment the military capability of the Soviet Union, is absolutely tiny as compared with the influence of the Steel Lobby or American Labor, which is at a very low ebb at the moment, or any other industrial, political or domestic Lobby. The whole external world is one per cent.

'So I don't think that the whole external view is very important, let alone Britain in particular. I mean, far more important is Israel, to some extent Egypt, Japan – and in a media-dominated world it's the squeaky hinge that gets the oil. It's the places that are going wrong that get the attention, not the places that are going right, and it's largely a British fantasy to think there is some kind of special inside track, reserved for the British. It is just not true.'

So if the Rich Tide is not the Special Relationship, what is it? According to Alistair Cooke, it's 'the subterranean flow'. 'I think there's a stronger subterranean flow than there's ever been – between experts. I find that, for instance, absolutely top, first-rate doctors here have their pals in England. And I think this is true of jurists. Warren Berger, for instance, you might say is an anglophile. He knows a great deal about British law and thinks it is the sheet anchor of American law. It's true of scientists too. They all know their opposite numbers and they completely bypass, it seems to me, and obliterate all the standard preconceptions and misconceptions which go on and on among ordinary people.'

Not that the picture is a simple one. 'My best friend here in New York is a retired investment banker who was born in Hungary and brought here at the age of two. He loves statistics and so we exchange them. And so when I got the latest Bureau of Labor statistics I called him up and asked him about the WASPs in New York. I said, "What would you say, Paul, is the percentage of WASPs in New York?" He said, "I don't know, it's very low. I would say it's about 30%." I said, "6.5%," and he said, "What? It's an absolute scandal. You ought to get food stamps."'

Harold Evans took up the theme of law. 'I agree that the long line of Englishmen who gave us habeas corpus, Magna Carta, the Bill of Rights, had a tremendous influence on the United States and that the common law system was embedded here by Englishmen. However, it is viewed with a different philosophy in the sense that the United States believes in free expression and equality and basically England doesn't. England is still in the words of Thomas Jefferson "a Tory country" which believes that rights are natural to the Crown which gives some of them to the people. Jefferson said that was the Tory concept which came from the Normans landing in England and all those French lawyers. And I think that's still true today. In the United States, by and large, all the information belongs to the people; in England, you give out to the people bits of information because all the rights belong to you, particularly under Mrs Thatcher, who's a true Norman. She's a Frenchwoman really, you know, she's not English – there's this fiction of her being born in Grantham which is just a kind of French propaganda trick. You see all this very dramatically in attitudes to things like people who are injured in aircraft accidents or by drugs; no free speech can be prevented in the United States in defending the rights of these people who've been injured by other people exercising their property rights. In England no such free speech is allowed, because property rights are protected. These are all Norman concepts – property.'

Evans thinks that 'the United Kingdom is still giving a certain amount here. We're obviously not giving any economic stimulus but I think we're giving a stimulus of ideas. The United States seems to me obsessed by money and numbers. Conversations in New York are usually about numbers. Conversations in England are not necessarily about numbers – they are more apt to be about ideas. We provide for eccentricity, we have irony and humour; I think common sense and pragmatism allied to extraordinary flights of fancy intellectually and in cultural and literary terms are the English strengths which are still capable of being exported to the United States and in fact are being exported with many of our people. And at the same time we know what the English weaknesses are. My wife, Tina, has a theory that the ideal is called Transatlantica. It's an island in the middle of the Atlantic which has the tolerance, the humour, the pragmatism, the literary skills, the irony of England allied to the numeracy, the openness, the egalitarianism of the United States.

'I find the paradoxes in the United States fascinating. I still can't explain them. The United States has a freer flow of information than any country in the world, but less debate. You can be arrested here for saying anything good about a Soviet disarmament proposal even though we might be able to manage it to our own interest, whereas in England it would be taken and analysed thoroughly. America is such a large, diverse country which needs unity that it can't risk satire and irony. It doesn't understand them; it doesn't want them; it puts a premium on unity. Since in England, by and large, you have a unified nation, you have to put a premium on diversity – and you get diversity. In this country the star system is essential. The star system in my judgement should be part of the American Constitution, because I don't think the country could be unified without it, without the ability to recognize the same people. The country is desperately thirsty for symbols. What England tends to do is to be rather cynical and undermining of celebrity. Celebrity here goes crazy.

'I don't think I've ever heard the word "eccentric" used in the United States except by an Englishman, because the Americans have a word for it – it's an interesting word – they'd say "crazy". Which is very different. We don't say anybody who's eccentric is crazy. He's just eccentric. In other words he's a civilized human being who doesn't wear any socks, or whatever. But with the Americans he's "crazy" and why – because he has bucked the system and America wants everybody to stay in their place and operate as part of the system – unless they are a celebrity when they get special status and recognition.'

So how is the Rich Tide operating today? Peter Jay felt that there was something of an analogy between the intellectual balance of trade and the actual economic and financial balance not so much of trade but of investment. 'In other words, quite a bit of the raw material – in terms of money and of inventions and of people – that would be very small in relation to the total size of the American GNP but none the less significantly worth something flows from the UK to the United States. At the same time a dominantly processed culture with all its wonderful achievements in medical science, other forms of natural science, government and many other things like the arts, flows back the other way. A simple balance sheet is difficult to draw up. If you were to ask a young, intelligent bright person growing up in Britain where the pole of the civilization that he lives in is, then he or she would probably say that it is manifestly in the United States. And indeed I have always taken the view for my own children and in general that having the United States as one's backyard is one of the most gigantic and most precious and valuable assets of being an Englishman, and an asset which is not wholly shared by Frenchmen, Germans, Italians or others. And therefore, if that's where the action is, as it were, the place to which the inputs come and from which the outputs flow, then it seems to me – unless one takes a narrow and parochial view – an enormous source of opportunity and of strength to be part of that very big culture. In other words, to use a historical analogy it's rather like having a farm which in various respects is quite good and prosperous, which operates in the orbit of a market town which is 25 miles away. Now, if you ask the question "Do you get more from the market town than you send to it?" ultimately that's a dotty question because each farm is in a state of equilibrium in its exchanges with the market town. Otherwise it would not be viable. And equally obviously if you ask from where it gets what it has, it gets it from the market town; and if you ask where it takes what it has to offer, it takes it to the market town. So you live, if you like, as a planet going round that sun – to change the metaphor! – and that seems to me not to be a sort of negative or depressing or humiliating or protestable fact but on the contrary to be a wonderful fact, and thank God that the sun, in whose orbit we circulate, is as free, as open, as liberal, as enlightened, as creative, as rewarding, as attractive – and as English-speaking – as it is.

'What it comes to, I think, is that in terms of raw inputs of people, ideas, inventions and creations, England, relative to its size, is still making an important, significant contribution and one which incidentally the Americans greatly welcome. It varies enormously from field to field. There are areas in which it is really quite disproportionately large and areas in which it is negligible. But none the less it is being made. At the same time if you ask where the English consumer is getting his culture, and I don't mean that in the sense of fine arts but in the sense of lifestyle and wealth, he is getting it predominantly from the United States. And the crucible, as it were, where the inputs are processed and turned into the outputs, is mainly in the United States and nothing in my opinion could be more fatuous than to try and impose some kind of cultural emotionalism which says that this is a bad thing and that we must institute our own mini officially sanctioned licensed crucible which will take over this role. The perennial error of English people is to bemoan the fact that somehow Britain is not successful in what they imagine should be its role – being like the United States – and to lose sight totally of the disparity of scale. So it seems to me that's how it works. That's the market place, that's the crucible, that's where the action is, not wholly but predominantly. Thank God it's available to our creators, inventors and thinkers, and thank God it's accessible to our consumers. But that's where the transmutation takes place.'

Perhaps the most successful British company operating in America is Hanson Trust, led by Lord Hanson in Britain and by Sir Gordon White in the United States. 'In Britain, we've always had very good ideas,' says Lord Hanson. 'What we have lacked has been the energy to put those ideas into practical use particularly on a large scale. The Americans have got tremendous energy and they've got the ability to convert the energy into a practical effect, because over there they never say a blanket no to anything. If a travelling salesman calls, they will always say "Well, what is your product?" because there may be a germ of an idea there that might help them to do something a little bit better. Over here we tend to be rather negative.'

James Hanson feels that the atmosphere for British business in America has improved. 'In particular, I think, since the present government has been in power for the last seven years or so.' Gordon White agrees: 'When I first came out here twelve years ago, not only were they not really that interested in even looking at a British balance sheet, and one was scarcely able to cash English money in a bank, but the general feeling about the British was that we had gone down the tube. During the intervening period of time, and particularly with the advent of Margaret Thatcher, and an obvious turn-round in the power of the Union Barons, the atmosphere is changing, and it's changing very rapidly.' In this climate both men feel that British impact within American business can grow – just so long as the British realize that they must play according to American rules. Says White, 'I am not prepared to say "We in the UK do it this way". In fact I did have a man out here for a while who used to say to Americans, "Well, we in the UK do this . . ." I finally said to him "If you go rabbiting on about 'we in the UK', I'll throw you out of the window."'

There are many such lessons to be learned. Says Hanson, 'In England, if you make a take-over, the first person you call – or the first person we'd call – is our banker, our merchant banker; in America the first person you call is your lawyer. Within very short order, you are in the hands of the lawyers whatever you're doing;

Lord Hanson and Sir Gordon White.

you're going to get sued whether you're doing something very correct or if you are doing something that is in fact sueable.' Adds White: 'The lawyers also have a tremendously powerful lobby and the system is very simple: they can take legal cases on a contingency basis, which we're not allowed to do in England. You've got to pay your legal bills in England. Your lawyer can't work for you for nothing and take a piece of the fee. I'm a Yorkshireman, I have always done business on the basis of a handshake. That won't work here. They don't believe you. Once you've agreed to do something, they'll bring in lawyers by the dozen and then the legal papers begin to mount up. They don't believe in the fact that you can keep your word or would keep your word. Maybe it's because it's such a big country, and they're used to having to deal with strangers . . .' Both men feel that the British influence on business in America can grow, provided that the Britons learn the lessons. 'Forget the two-hour lunch.' 'You cannot survive here if you are inefficient.' And so on. Perhaps some of the ground lost after the war can be recaptured. 'If we could come out here as we did twelve years ago without any money and still make it, then after the war ICI should have owned Du Pont,' says White. 'If you take Cunard and White Star – after the war they had so much money, they could have come over here and bought any number of companies. I consider that we owned 25% of this country before the war and I'd like to buy it back again.'

And what of American business impact on Britain? Lord Hanson concentrated immediately on the impact that the Americans were going to have on the financial market in Britain, particularly following the 'big bang'. 'London's position as a financial centre has strengthened again lately, and brokerage houses are eager to move in,' he said. 'They're going to chop the City of London to ribbons,' added Gordon White, 'at least on underwriting.' Lord Hanson particularly admires the professionalism of the American motor car companies and oil companies. 'They're all aggressive, very, very tough, very successful. You can't really tell that Ford is not a British company, but they keep giving it new blood from America in an industry which is essentially American. And when they choose to expand in the UK they are building from such a massive base.'

In the field of fashion Zandra Rhodes considers that we are 'amazing ideas people. In a country of individuals we are prepared to go out on a limb as we did at the time of Carnaby Street or the Sixties. We have been responsible for most of the recent fashion trends – like the mini skirt, the punk look, coloured hair or the Boy George look – but we never seem to reap the monetary rewards or get the credit for it either. It's the Americans who are the brilliant marketeers. I have learned all my marketing from Americans. If we are to have a full impact on America we have to learn not to put ourselves down. But there's no doubt that where Paris used to be the arbiter of fashion there are now four centres: Milan, London, Paris and New York.'

Clive Barnes was a critic in London before he moved to New York to become a critic for two New York newspapers, first the *New York Times* and now the *New York Post*. Which way does he feel the tide is flowing in terms of ideas at the moment between Britain and America? 'Probably more is coming from England to America, but conceivably more is originating in America that England doesn't see. If you take the *New York Times* and have a look down the theatre listing, you would be amazed at how much has come from London; that is, in terms of plays, only to a much lesser extent in terms of actors. In fact, whereas almost every American actor can handle a very fair English accent, the English actors who can handle an American accent are very rare. At one time you could count them on the fingers of one foot. It was very rare indeed. There was Peter Finch and almost no one else. I mean, it always amazes me that Olivier can't do it. If you watch him in *Long Day's Journey Into Night*, which is of course a television classic, a movie classic, or whatever, you see in the first act that he tries an American accent – and he did it exactly the same on stage – and then, almost at the same point when he goes off stage for the

Zandra Rhodes.

first act, you can almost hear him off stage saying, "Screw it, the guy was Irish anyway." Then he comes on and tries to do an Irish accent, quite forgetting that he can no more do an Irish accent than he can do an American accent, because English actors can't do Irish accents either. Then at the end, at almost the last moment, he moves into his own voice and he's absolutely magnificent. Of course, the other film version of *Long Day's Journey Into Night* is Ralph Richardson. And Ralph doesn't make any attempt to do any American accent at all.'

Why is it, then, that British actors fail to master American accents? Is it because they don't have to, because there seem to be so few American plays in Britain? 'I don't think it's that. I think that the English accent is associated with acting and with the arts in American schools. The English accent has a certain position in American society. It is regarded as rather classy or something. I remember getting into a cab in New York and telling the cab driver where I wanted to go and he immediately said, "Hey, that accent – what is it? English, gay or just affected?"'

Clive Barnes.

And what about the trend in musicals? 'Well, the trend in musicals tends to be that America sends Broadway musicals to the West End and the West End sends Andrew Lloyd-Webber to Broadway,' he said. Andrew Lloyd-Webber himself disclaims that sole billing, but with the work of Tim Rice and the recent production of *Les Misérables* in mind, as well as his own work, agrees that right at the moment most of the ideas in musical

Andrew Lloyd Webber and Tim Rice.

theatre are coming from London to New York. 'It's partly economic in that the costs here are very much less so the possibility of being able to try productions with younger people and new ideas and indeed put on work that is likely to break new ground is much greater. It's much easier here than on Broadway where it could cost you four million pounds before you even cough. I think that the talent is pretty firmly based here at the moment, and we are also encouraging a hell of a lot of Americans to come here and work on British productions, but the fact is that you cannot afford to take chances on Broadway, and therefore Broadway tends to rely on tried and tested material. And what better testing market is there than the West End, or the RSC and the National Theatre?'

In opera and ballet Clive Barnes saw the picture as very different. 'In opera the trend is very much in favour of the Americans. America produces many, many more opera singers than Britain does. Chiefly because in almost any field of human endeavour the number of champions which you produce – and it's particularly true of what you might call physical endeavour, whether they're opera singers, sprinters, swimmers, dancers or skiers – the number of champions that you produce is fairly dependent on the number that you train. America trains many, many more opera singers than does Britain and consequently it produces many more champion singers. Although there is a surprising flow considering that England has only taken her native opera seriously really since World War II. There's a surprising flow of singers, conductors and musicians considering that until World War II Britain was regarded, as the Germans used to say, as a land without music.

'As far as dancers are concerned, British ballet has passed through a certain decline in the last ten years, since the retirement of Ashton and Fonteyn and the non-utilization of Nureyev. Those great days seem to have dissipated somewhat, so where the Royal Ballet at one time could arguably be thought of as the world's finest company, I do not think anyone would make that claim for it now. So British ballet is not nearly so important in America as it was, probably not so highly regarded in America as American ballet is in Britain.'

Paul McCartney feels pretty bullish about the current state of British popular music, and its impact on America. 'We're having a run at the moment . . . This is our biggest major run since the Sixties. We're really doing it. We had a good run in the Sixties; before then it had been all-American really, with Elvis and with Chuck Berry and the guys; then musically it became Britain and then it sort of swung back to America. Like a pendulum really. It's our swing at the moment with a lot of the American guys like

Springsteen coming into the thing, but we are having a good run at the moment – the British. The British always go down quite well in America, and we just happen to have a few talented people now. I think the Americans were not really interested in the punk revolution – that barely touched them. It was a little too down-market, I think. But now you're starting to have a real resurgence.'

So, considering the size of the population, would he say Britain is doing pretty well? 'I'll tell you . . . I have a map of the world, a music publishing map, which gets hidden away in Linda's cupboard at home. I happened to be in there putting a record on and I was looking at this thing. And it's more obvious on this publishing map, because we're dealing in territories, so there's a sort of red-striped territory for Russia or whatever, and you look and you see little old Britain and you see to our right this huge Russia and Europe. Then you see to our left this huge mammoth America; down at the bottom you see South America, again a huge entity. And I was just looking at the thing and thinking Bloody hell, there's little old us operating out of little old London and we're selling our music in all these places. You know, it's like a British Empire resurgence – in music. This little island, you know, still having its influence. Pretty cosmic eh, Dave?'

Paul McCartney.

What, then, did Paul think was the secret of our success; why did he think we make such a musical impact on America? 'Ancient civilization; the European stuff; I think we're part of all of that. And there's a sort of arrogance like from Liverpool, who don't realize we're not top of the world any more. You know, this Cup Final was exactly the position the Liverpool people think they ought to be in. You know, we don't feel surprised, like Peterborough. It's our rightful place. And I think the British are a bit like that. An ingrained thing. I mean, when I drive people around near where I live, I drive the Americans past the local hotel and it says "Rebuilt in 1492". There's your reason. They haven't got anything older than two hundred years.

'One of the reasons I always cite for the Beatles' success in America is this sort of innocent arrogance. It wasn't a sort of arrogant arrogance, not a sort of off-putting thing. It was just "Hey, you know, we like ourselves. Why shouldn't you?" We said to Brian Epstein, "We're not going to tour America, Brian, until we've got a Number One there." Nobody had ever dared to say that. But we had seen Cliff Richard go over, be third on the bill to Frankie Avalon, the little fish in this huge big pool, and then come back to England and be a star again. And Adam Faith did the same thing. They were huge here but nothing over there. So we noticed this; and we were just the next generation. So we said,

"Not until we have a Number One", which was the height of this kind of innocent arrogance. But we were in Paris one night when they were on the phone and they said, "Hey! 'I Wanna Hold Your Hand' is Number One." So that when we went to America these guys said, you know, "Well, how do you find America?" We said, "Turn left at Greenland." And anything they could say to us, we would say, "But we're Number One in your country." You know, we had the ultimate answer for anything.

'And today you've got Live Aid and Geldof! Talk about innocent arrogance. Who's done that, man? There's no government got that together. He was probably the only man who could have done it. But the innocent arrogance certainly helped.'

David Hockney thinks that English artists will continue to be attracted to the United States for the same reasons that he was: space and climate and privacy. 'You know, you can live very privately here. You can live privately in London too, but here in a sense one thinks maybe they're less interested in what an artist like me is up to up on the hill. So I just proceed at my own pace, and I like that. That's the reason I am here.'

Hockney feels that one of the main reasons for the cultural vitality of America is their more universal approach to the arts. 'The line between what one would call the popular arts and high art; in England they seem to make that very clear, in America they don't. There was a headline in the *Guardian* last year that said "The art world doesn't know the difference between Jacob Duck and Donald". The article then goes on to tell you that Jacob Duck was a seventeenth-century Dutch painter of lively interiors. But the insinuation in the headline was that Jacob Duck was Art with a capital A and Donald Duck was not. Well, I wouldn't go along with that. I know perfectly well that Donald Duck is one of the greatest artistic creations of the twentieth century. A wonderful invention, and he's alive. Now, in America you wouldn't have got that distinction. You wouldn't get that headline, which somehow seems to belong to a rather snobbish attitude to art that I wouldn't share.

'I mean, I am still amazed. Again, I was rung up the other day and they said, "Could you make art in Los Angeles?" And I thought, this is amazing. It's as though no works of art were made here. I pointed out that they were: great movies – *Modern Times*, *Citizen Kane*, *Singing in the Rain*. They're great works of art. They will survive. Not seeing them as art is not seeing what art is, it seems to me. I know it's not painting, but it's art. I think there's a lot of confusion at the moment about what art is, but certainly art must move you, I think. The difference between art and design is that design doesn't have to move you. Art does.

David Hockney in Paris.

'Of course some art is exportable, and some is not. But I do think that if Britain could break down some of the false distinctions about art as they have done here, then there would be more vitality and British art would have more of an impact on America.'

Alan Coren thinks that this is a static time in terms of humour as far as influence is concerned. 'If you want to go back a bit, the image the Americans have always liked of Britain is of a British Tourist Authority world with dotty eccentrics in it, P. G. Wodehouse was enormously popular, so were the Ealing comedies, A. E. Matthews, David Tomlinson; whenever Disney wanted to make his films about Britain, he chose characters out of P. G. Wodehouse or P. L. Travers. He went deliberately for the things that we had not addressed seriously – the daft English enforcement of an international idea of rather dotty, middle-class eccentrics with good accents; lots of public-school stuff; pre-Edwardian Three-Men-in-a-Boat stuff. America continued to take this from us right up to probably the mid-1950s. Films from Britain begin to be important in the late 1950s as Americans begin to become aware of Woodfall Productions. They begin to learn about English satire. And the English writers begin to sell there in large numbers. In addition to satire on television, our satirical films like *Darling* were enormously successful. (*Ramparts*, *Monocle*, *Good Looks*, *Harvard Lampoon* were all to be influenced by English satire.) There had also been something very spontaneous in the rise of Mort Sahl and Lenny Bruce in the States. Sahl and Bruce then come over here, their records are bought. Shelley Berman's records sell . . . Bob Newhart . . . we begin to get very interested in the new modern American, smart, wise-cracking stuff with a political edge. There begins to be an interplay – a brief one. Then it all goes a bit flat. When Kennedy went, the idea of an intellectual America that can snipe at itself and is tough enough to take satire, that went too.

'American humour today is not nearly as edged as it used to be. That's why *Lake Wobegon Days* is such a significant best-seller. It's sold about three million copies in the States in hardback. It's an absolute return to the values of Huck Finn, away from Woody Allen and the smart New York intellectual Jewish thing, because that's more and more a minority, and back straight into the heartland of crusty old humour, barbershop quartets and the charm and comedy of the-greatest-character-I-ever-met; a *Reader's Digest* thing; it's read an enormous amount in America. Their situation comedy is very family situation comedy; even when it's black. Even ''Cheers'' which is probably the best thing they've got going for them at the moment is still about a family

Alan Coren.

pub with very recognizable characters that have very warm, very human, very loving relationships. You don't see much tart television. The same is true of the *New Yorker*. The *New Yorker* is now much, much blander; its cartoons were much more satirical in the Sixties under Kennedy. If you look at it now, most of the cartoons are corporate cartoons, jokes about corporate jargon, about Yuppies, about the Hamptons . . . all that sort of thing. It's blokes coming home to a house with a pool and a Mercedes in the garage and it's about middle-class values and about families. And I think that a hell of lot of that is to do with Reagan. Presidents are enormous inputters of cultural atmosphere, and an idea emanates from them and it is very strong.

'At *Punch* we use a lot of American cartoonists – about thirty per cent of our cartoons – but we're using the cartoons they can't sell over there because they're sharper or dirtier or smuttier. Smut's almost gone out in America. Comic smut used to be marvellous, and they were very good at it. But the last time I was there, so many of their areas for comedy have become unacceptable because they're taken seriously. If you make a joke at a New York cocktail party, they look at you and they say, ''Well, I don't think you're taking that very seriously, Alan. Many people have small dicks . . .'' and it's, you know, the Small Dicks Society of America and the Anti-Small Dick Defamation League . . . It's all like that. And I think we're moving apart. It's un-American to take the piss out of America. You'd have a hell of a job writing *Catch-22* now, about America. There hasn't been a satirical novel about the Vietnam War. That seems to me extraordinary in a culture like that. Vietnam demonstrated itself to be a failure, which America can't stand; and it never approached it satirically. There should be a television series like ''M.A.S.H.'' about Vietnam but there isn't.

'I think we're clearly growing apart at the moment. I don't think we can offer an image of Britain that America wants to laugh at right now because quite clearly the ones we talked about – the P. G. Wodehouse, silly-ass, green-shire England is gone. They are very much aware of our problems. They are very much aware of Thatcher. In some ways they respect us too much because of Thatcher. I would say that it is a great shame that we don't share as much comedy as we used to. Because I think when you share comedy you reach cultural understanding in a much better way.'

On a wider level, Clay Felker was more optimistic. 'The obvious traffic from England to America is cultural, and I think that it is as strong as it has ever been, and in fact right now it is at one of its historic spikes upwards. Because we are in a very bleak period in America culturally – playwrights seem to be almost non-existent and English playwrights are turning out one marvellous thing after the next. I think that it's because in America now we do not have a central belief system which gives us a unified audience. A unified audience stems from a unified set of national values. And our values are so diffused now that it is very hard for our culture to come upwards from an audience, whereas English values are essentially unified. Churchill said, "This pudding has no theme." We have no theme. This is a marvellous diffused country, but it's being held together now by one man's personality.

'American journalism too is in a very slack period in terms of innovation, and the British have more vigour, some of which I don't approve of but a lot of which I do. You care about language more than we do. And out of that inspired use of language comes the ability to persuade, the ability to inspire. We just don't use our basic cultural resources as well as you do. I don't know the answer to it. Sometimes I think it has to do with the fact that the use of the language is such a signifier of class that it takes on greater use in the UK than we make of it in the United States. Also it may be that an island nation without as many people has had to survive because of the language. Whereas we can survive with just sheer economic weight and force of numbers. We don't have to be very subtle. I have many times observed that Americans don't understand when they're being insulted by the English. It goes right over their heads. We tend to take out our violence, our aggressions in other ways.

'The greatest thing that England can do is to build up its cultural attractions which are its theatre, its music, its dance – all the things that it does so brilliantly. Every time I see a slash in the Royal Shakespeare Company or the National Theatre budgets, I say to myself, "Don't they realize that this is one of the great money-earners that they have?" Why make cuts in the BBC World Service? England's power will only come from its culture and its ideas. And things like the *Economist* are a good example of the way Britain could be influential. A weekly magazine, it sells twice as many copies in America as it does in England. I read an English magazine that informs me about Asia, *The Far Eastern Economic Review*. Even its name is an English idea. It's put out in Asia but it's not called the "Asian Economic Review". It's called from London *The Far Eastern Economic Review*. You've lost your imperial mission, but your imperial mission is still there in terms of culture and ideas.'

There was one subject on which almost everybody had something to say. President Reagan spoke about 'our shared language',

Peter Jay.

and Andrew Lloyd-Webber talked about our 'one tremendous piece of luck, which is that we speak English and so do the Americans. I think the only European group who have really broken through internationally in the last ten or fifteen years has been ABBA – and that was with very carefully put together English lyrics.' And Peter Jay summarized it thus: 'The one overwhelmingly important fact about the relationship which in my opinion is many thousandfold more important than almost all other facts put together is the language. It is so obvious and so palpable that people turn aside from mentioning it, but if one is trying to explain things it seems to me that one has got to recognize that fact. It is absolutely transforming.'

Alistair Cooke had some words of warning. 'There is this very dangerous thing happening now which is lots of people not learning English at all, and state laws which allow voting in two languages and so on. Not only splitting up into the ethnic ingredients of the melting pot, but unmelting the melting pot itself. This was something that Teddy Roosevelt was concerned about when he said, "We cannot go on having hyphenated Americans. There's only one language." And the Hearst newspapers did a great deal. When I first arrived here, the very first thing I ever covered was going up to P.S. 45 in the Bronx and I found it very moving to find the parents of first-generation children, Italians, going and learning English at night. The parents learning English at night! Now the children are not necessarily learning English by day. This is especially true in Florida and California. I think there's a great danger of not only German republics but Quebecs in our future if people take pride in being Puerto Rican and so on and screw you for being an Anglo!'

Harold Evans took up the same theme: 'I feel very emotional about the English connection, the language. I think in twenty years' time the United States will be even less related to England. We know that the largest immigration here is Mexican, Latin American-speaking. By a folly of President Carter in 1976, English is no longer the enforceable language in the schools. English was the great integrating force of the United States when the Armenians, the Poles, the Germans, the Italians came over, they all had to learn English. The second generation, they all speak English today. Now in the schools they are required to teach languages to any minority. They say the schools in Chicago are teaching twenty-three languages. And certainly many parts of the country where Spanish is dominant, the Anglo-Saxon connection is being lost. The biggest immigration into the United States now is from Asia and from Central and Latin America. It's going to be a hard job to hold on to English as the major tongue here in twenty or twenty-five years' time, the way it's going.

'It's actually wrong in two respects: it's wrong as part of the cohesion of the country and its sense of identity and it's wrong also because when they go in the market place at the moment, they still have to learn English and speak English and they can't do it very well. So the Bilingual Education Act is costing billions of dollars and it's weakening the unity of the country. If you look a hundred years ahead the biggest threat to the United States is what the Indians used to call fissiparous tendencies.'

James Reston echoed the same concern: 'The old immigrants – and we're all immigrants in a way – have been a little frightened by this Hispanic invasion; not because of the people but because of their attempt to insist on dual language; and the country is saying to the new immigrants, "Don't do that – in the first place it's bad for the country and it's very bad for your children. They won't have the opportunity in a world of English-speaking people if all they can do is master their own tongue."' Reston, however, was more confident than Harold Evans about the resilience of the English language. 'Churchill was right in saying that the greatest thing that had happened in his time was that the English language had become the language of the world. That's even more important now because it clearly has become the language of the business world, and that's terribly important because for the first time in history we really have a world economy. And that business is done in the English language. In any case, English is the established language – that's the status quo – and one of the great failings in this country is in its education in languages.'

Clay Felker adds to that: 'The more powerful America gets, the less likely it is to want to learn foreign tongues. Asians are rapidly ascending the heights in the United States, but Americans don't learn Asian languages. We don't have a special relationship with Spain despite the fact that we have whole cities that are practically Spanish-speaking cities, like Miami and San Antonio. Frankly Americans do not take Spanish that seriously, which may be wrong, it may be a shame, but they don't. It all comes back to the English language. And that is our official language. It is how you get ahead.' Clive Barnes felt that in both England and America, 'We share a shocking inability to learn other languages. The American lack of command of French is only equalled by the Englishman's lack of command of French; ditto Italian. So thanks to the rules of the Common Market on the one hand and the artificial immigration barriers between England and America on the other, you have a situation where Englishmen can work anywhere in Europe where they can't work, but they can't work in America where they could work. And it's becoming increasingly difficult for Americans to work in Britain. I think if these barriers were removed and there was easier immigration then we would find that the Rich Tide would really flow much more than it does now.

'In the meantime, language does seem to me to be more vital as a link between people than any aspect of ethnic background. For example, if you take an American of Italian origin and he's in Europe – in Italy, say – and he loses his passport and he can't find an American Consulate, he will automatically go to a British Consulate. And what is more the British Consulate will not find that peculiar. Everybody's favourite aphorism, "Two nations separated by a common language," is in fact the absolute reverse of the truth.'

*   *   *

In the course of this book, we have encompassed a period from the very infancy of America when the child was totally dependent on the parent, through a most massive swing in the relative balance of power and on to the American predominance in the relationship today – though not to one, we hope, of parent and ageing grandparent! It is not so much that Britain's power has shrunk, though it has; it is that the power of the United States has grown with such unparalleled vigour. Which explains the occasional eruptions in the media and elsewhere in England of anti-Americanism. You only have outbursts like that against people who are bigger than you are. It therefore very rarely happens the other way round, except for the Noraid lobby with their anti-British feeling in a context – Northern Ireland – in which Britain appears to them, however inaccurately, to be "bigger" than the Catholics that they support. But even when a *Sunday Times* poll reveals (as it did in February 1986) that no less than one in three voters in Britain regard the United States and the Soviet Union as equal dangers to peace – and an additional one in five regard the Americans as the greater menace – the same poll also reveals massive support for the propositions "I like Americans" and "I would like to holiday in America". Commenting on the polls at the time Sir Peter Ramsbotham, Britain's Ambassador in Washington between 1974 and 1977, said, "We are all resentful of someone doing better than us. It's just surprising that we've done it with such good grace.'

There is similar underlying goodwill in the United States where, in a 1983 Census Bureau report, some 50 million Americans claimed British ancestry, in addition (to quote Senator Richard Lugar, who is of German origin) to those who are not of

British but of, say, Scandinavian or German extraction, who now claim a cultural empathy for Britain and its traditions as the very result of living in the United States of America. Summed up perhaps by the report of the American matron who declared, 'Goodness gracious, we wouldn't want to be descended from anyone else, would we?' Though even she would probably not go as far as Andrew Carnegie did when he once proclaimed, 'Let men say what they will, I say that as surely as the sun in the heavens once shone upon Britain and America united, so surely it is one morning to rise, shine upon, and greet again the Reunited States – the British–American union.' After statements like that, it was not necessary for George Bernard Shaw to have to invent too much when, in the play *The Apple Cart*, he has the American Ambassador to the Court of St James call on the British King Magnus with the interesting information that 'The Declaration of Independence is cancelled. The treaties that endorsed it are torn up. We have decided to re-join the British Empire.' He goes on, 'We Americans are at home here . . . We find here everything we're accustomed to: our industrial products, our books, our plays, our Christian Science churches, our osteopaths, our movies and talkies . . . A political union with us will be just the official recognition of already accomplished fact.'

That was fiction, but the ability to feel relaxed and at home with one another is fact. So are many of the other phrases and concepts that we heard: 'Ingrained', 'woven into the fabric', 'reverse lend-lease', 'subterranean flow', 'the sense of family', 'the bonds of shared traditions', and of course 'the language'. The difference between inputs and outputs is crucial too. Britain's outputs will never again match America's – but the British input into the American experience can remain disproportionately influential. When early in the twenty-first century the next generation writes about the Rich Tide, readers will still know what is being talked about. The Rich Tide will still be there with an ebb and flow that is sometimes unpredictable, often controversial, but still vigorous and still an indispensable ingredient of Western civilization. There may or may not be a Special Relationship, but the relationship will still be special.

SELECTED BIBLIOGRAPHY

Allen, H. C. *The Anglo-American Relationship since 1783*. London: Adam & Charles Black, 1959.

American Writers. A Collection of Literary Biographies. Volumes I and II. Leonard Unger, editor in chief. New York: Charles Scribner's Sons, 1974.

Armytage, W. H. G. *The American Influence on English Education*. London: Routledge & Kegan Paul, 1967.

Aspinwall, Bernard. *Portable Utopia*. Glasgow and the United States. Aberdeen: Aberdeen University Press, 1984.

Barbour, Philip Lamont. *Pocahontas and Her World*. London: Robert Hale & Company, 1971.

Baxter, John. *The Hollywood Exiles*. New York: Taplinger Publishing Company, 1976.

Berthoff, Rowland Tappan. *British Immigrants in Industrial America, 1790–1950*. Cambridge, Massachusetts: Harvard University Press, 1953.

Bigsby, C. W. E. (editor). *Superculture: American Popular Culture and Europe*. London: Paul Elek, 1975.

Brendon, Piers. *The Life and Death of the Press Barons*. London: Secker and Warburg, 1982.

Cobden, Richard. *American Diaries*. Edited with an introduction and notes by Elizabeth Hoon Cawley. Princeton: Princeton University Press, 1952.

Concise Dictionary of American Biography. New York: Charles Scribner's Sons, 1980.

Cowles, Virginia. *The Astors. The Story of a Transatlantic Family*. London: Weidenfeld and Nicholson, 1979.

Cremin, Lawrence A. *American Education*. 2 volumes. Volume 1: *The Colonial Experience, 1607–1783*. Volume II: *The National Experience, 1783–1876*. New York: Harper & Row, 1970–80.

Current Biography. New York: The H. W. Wilson Company.

Dickens, Charles. *American Notes for General Circulation*. Edited with an introduction by J. S. Whitley and A. Goldman. Harmondsworth: Penguin, 1972.

Dictionary of American Biography. New York: Charles Scribner's Sons, 1936 and 5 supplements, 1944–1977.

Dictionary of American History. 8 volumes. New York: Charles Scribner's Sons, 1976–1978.

Dictionary of Business Biography. London: Butterworths, 1985.

Dictionary of National Biography. London: Oxford University Press, 1882.

Durant, John and Bettmann, Otto. *Pictorial History of American Sport. From Colonial Times to the Present*. U.S.A.: A. S. Barnes and Company, 1952.

Eckhardt, Celia Morris. *Fanny Wright. Rebel in America*. Cambridge, Massachusetts and London: Harvard University Press, 1984.

Encyclopaedia Americana. International Edition. 30 volumes. New York: American Corporation, 1977.

Encyclopaedia Britannica. Macropaedia. 30 volumes. Chicago, London, etc: Helen Hemmingway Benton, Publisher.

Encyclopaedia of American Biography. Edited by John A. Garraty. New York: Harper and Row, Publishers, 1974.

Encyclopaedia of American History. Edited by Richard B. Morris. New York: Harper & Row, 1982.

Farnsworth, Edward Allen. *An Introduction to the Legal System of the United States*. New York: Oceana Publications, 1968.

Findlay Jr., James F. *Dwight L. Moody. American Evangelist 1837–1899.* Chicago and London: The University of Chicago Press, 1969.

Fleming, Kate. *The Churchills*. London: Weidenfeld and Nicholson, 1975.

Foner, Eric. *Tom Paine and Revolutionary America*. New York: Oxford University Press, 1976.

Fryer, Jonathan. *Isherwood*. London: New English Library, 1977.

Greene, John C. *American Science in the Age of Jefferson*. Ames: The Iowa State University Press, 1984.

Hamm, Charles. *Music in the New World*. New York and London: W. W. Norton and Company, 1983.

Harvard Encyclopaedia of American Ethnic Groups. Edited by Stephan Thernstrom. Cambridge, Massachusetts and London: the Belknap Press of Harvard University Press, 1980.

Hewitt, Barnard. *Theatre U.S.A. 1665–1957*. New York, Toronto and London: McGraw-Hill Brook Company, 1959.

Hidy, Ralph W. *The House of Baring in American Trade and Finance. English Merchant Bankers at Work, 1763–1861*. Cambridge, Massachusetts: Harvard University Press, 1949.

Hudson, Winthrop S. *Religion in America. An Historical Account of the Development of American Religious Life*. New York: Charles Scribner's Sons, 1981.

Hughes, Glenn. *A History of the American Theatre 1700–1950*. New York, Toronto and London: Samuel French, 1951.

International Encyclopaedia of Film. London: Michael Joseph, 1972.

Isherwood, Christopher. *Christopher and His Kind, 1929–1939.* London: Eyre Methuen, 1977.

Kenin, Richard. *Return to Albion. Americans in England 1760–1940.* New York: National Portrait Gallery, Smithsonian Institution and Holt, Rinehart and Winston, 1979.

Krout, John Allen. *Annals of American Sport.* Volume XV of the *Pageant of America.* New Haven: Yale University Press, 1929.

McCabe, John. *Charlie Chaplin.* London, Magnum, 1979.

Mahoney, Tom and Sloane, Leonard. *The Great Merchants.* New York, Evanston and London: Harper & Row Publishers, 1966.

Messerli, Jonathan. *Horace Mann. A Biography.* New York: Alfred A. Knopf, 1972.

Nevins, Allan and Hill, Frank Ernest. *Ford.* 3 volumes, 1954–1963. New York: Charles Scribner's Sons, 1963. 3rd volume reprinted by Arno Press, a New York Times company, 1976.

Norman, Bruce. *The Inventing of America.* London: British Broadcasting Corporation, 1976.

Notable American Women. 1607–1950. A Biographical Dictionary. 3 volumes. Cambridge, Massachusetts: The Belknap Press of Harvard University Press, 1971.

O'Connor, Richard. *The Scandalous Mr. Bennett.* Garden City, New York: Doubleday & Company Inc., 1962.

Oliver, J. W. *History of American Technology.* New York: The Ronald Press Co., 1956.

Oxford Companion to American History. Thomas H. Johnson. New York: Oxford University Press, 1966.

Oxford Companion to American Literature. James D. Hart. New York and Oxford: Oxford University Press, 1983.

Oxford Companion to American Theatre. Gerald Bordman. Oxford and New York: Oxford University Press, 1984.

Oxford Companion to Film. Edited by Liz-Anne Bawden. London: Oxford University Press, 1976.

Oxford Companion to Law. David M. Walker. Oxford: Clarendon Press, 1980.

Oxford Companion to Sports and Games. Edited by John Arlott. London: Oxford University Press, 1975.

Oxford Companion to the Theatre. Edited by Phyllis Hartnoll. Oxford: Oxford University Press, 1983.

Peach, Linden. *British Influence on the Birth of American Literature.* London: Macmillan, 1982.

Sharp, Cecil. *English Folk Songs From the Southern Appalachians.* Volume I. London: Oxford University Press and Humphrey Milford, 1932.

Sinclair, David. *Dynasty. The Astors and Their Times.* London and

Melbourne: J. M. Dent & Sons Ltd., 1983.

Spender, Stephen. *World Within World*. London: Hamish Hamilton, 1951.

Thistlethwaite, Frank. *The Anglo-American Connection in the Early Nineteenth Century*. Philadelphia: University of Pennsylvania Press, 1959.

Those Inventive Americans. Produced by the National Geographic Special Publications Division, 1971.

Trollope, Frances. *Domestic Manners of the Americans*. Edited by Donald Smalley. New York: Alfred A. Knopf, 1949.

Twombly, Wells. *200 Years of Sport in America*. New York: McGraw-Hill Books Co., 1976.

Vidal, Gore and others. *Great American Families*. London: Times Books, 1977.

Wall, Joseph Frazier. *Andrew Carnegie*. New York: Oxford University Press, 1970.

Waterhouse, Ellis. *Painting in Britain, 1530–1790*. London: Penguin Books, 1953.

Wilkins, Mira. *The Emergence of Multinational Enterprise: American Business Abroad from the Colonial Era to 1914*. Cambridge, Massachusetts: Harvard University Press, 1970.

Wilson, Mitchell. *American Science and Invention. A Pictorial History*. New York: Bonanza Books, 1960.

Wright, Esmond. 'Education in the American Colonies: The Impact of Scotland', in *Essays in Scotch-Irish History* edited by E. R. Green. London and New York: Routledge and Kegan Paul and Humanities Press, 1969.

Young, William C. *Famous Actors and Actresses on the American Stage*. 2 volumes. New York and London: R. R. Bowker Co., 1975.

PICTURE CREDITS

215 BBC Hulton Picture Library
216 Selfridges Archives
217–220 BBC Hulton Picture Library
221 Ann Ronan Picture Library
222,223 Wellcome Institute Library, London
225–229 Ford Motor Company Ltd
233 National Portrait Gallery, London
235 Courtesy of The New-York Historical Society, New York City
239 National Portrait Gallery, London
240T The Mansell Collection
240B By permission of the British Library (12295.e.5)
241 BBC Hulton Picture Library
242T By Courtesy of the Dean and Chapter of Westminster
242B Hamish Hamilton/Courtesy of Bell, Book & Ramall, London
242 Bodleian Library, Oxford (Arch K.c4.fol.57)
244 By permission of Sir Brian Batsford
245 Copyright reserved. Reproduced by gracious permission of Her Majesty The Queen
247 Reproduced by permission of the National Gallery of Victoria, Melbourne
248 From the collection of the Durban Art Museum, South Africa
249 BBC Hulton Picture Library
250,251 National Portrait Gallery, London
254 National Gallery of Art, Washington; Andrew W. Mellon Collection 1942
255 Reproduced by gracious permission of HM The Queen
256T The Metropolitan Museum of Art, Gift of Samuel P. Avery, 1897
6B Courtesy of the Royal Ontario Museum, Toronto, Canada
8 Courtesy, Museum of Fine Arts, Boston. Anonymous gift, 1978
9 National Gallery of Art, Washington; Ferdinand Lammot Belin Fund
0T National Academy of Design, New York
0B National Portrait Gallery, London
1T National Gallery of Art, Washington; Harris Whittemore Collection 1943
2 Courtesy of the Freer Collection of Art, Smithsonian Institution, Washington (Acc.no. 04.61)
4 The Bridgeman Art Library
6 Courtesy of The Pennsylvania Academy of the Fine Arts
9 National Portrait Gallery, Smithsonian Institution, Washington, DC
1 The Raymond Mander & Joe Mitchenson Theatre Collection
3 National Portrait Gallery, London
4 The Raymond Mander & Joe Mitchenson Theatre Collection
6T BBC Hulton Picture Library
6B,277L The Raymond Mander & Joe Mitchenson Theatre Collection
7R Museum of the City of New York, Theatre Collection
278 BBC Hulton Picture Library
279T National Portrait Gallery, London
279B,280,281 The Raymond Mander & Joe Mitchenson Theatre Collection
283–295 The Kobal Collection
296 National Portrait Gallery, London
297,298 The Raymond Mander & Joe Mitchenson Theatre Collection
299 Photo David Redfern, London
303 Independence National Historical Park Collection
304 Peter Newark's Western Americana
306 American Academy of Arts and Sciences, Boston, Massachusetts
308,309 The Mansell Collection
310 Peter Newark's Western Americana
311 BBC Hulton Picture Library/The Bettmann Archive
312 National Portrait Gallery, Smithsonian Institution, Washington, DC
313 The Mansell Collection
314 BBC Hulton Picture Library/The Bettmann Archive
315 The Illustrated London News Picture Library
316,319T Peter Newark's Western Americana
319B Popperfoto
320T Peter Newark's Western Americana
320B,321 The Illustrated London News Picture Library
322 The Mansell Collection
323 Churchill Downs Museum, Louisville, Kentucky
324 Peter Newark's Western Americana
326,327 The Illustrated London News Picture Library
329,330 BBC Hulton Picture Library
331 The Illustrated London News Picture Library
334–349 BBC Hulton Picture Library
350 Popperfoto
352 Popperfoto
354 Rex Features Ltd
355 Photo Lionel Cherruault/Camera Press, London
357–362 Popperfoto
363 The Photo Source
364 The New York Times
365 Popperfoto
373 Courtesy Hanson Trust
374 Courtesy of Zandra Rhodes
375 Camera Press, London
377 Photo Ron Wolfson/Rex Features, London
378 Photo David Graeme-Baker, Sipa Press/Rex Features, London
379 Punch Publications Ltd
382 Photo John Whitman/Camera Press, London

Colour

Facing

40 Reproduced by permission of the Trustees of the British Museum
41 BBC Hulton Picture Library
104 National Portrait Gallery, London
105 National Portrait Gallery, London (detail)
136 Courtesy of the Harvard University Portrait Collection
137 Massachusetts Historical Society
168 By permission of the British Library (460.b.8)
169 Historical Society of Pennsylvania
232 National Portrait Gallery, London
233 Royal Academy of Arts, London
264 The Tate Gallery, London
265 The Tate Gallery, London
329 Blenheim Palace, Woodstock, Oxford. Reproduced by kind permission of His Grace the Duke of Marlborough
361 Punch Publications Ltd